love WITH accountability

Digging Up the Roots of Child Sexual Abuse

love WITH accountability

Digging Up the Roots of Child Sexual Abuse

Edited by Aishah Shahidah Simmons

Foreword by Darnell L. Moore

Praise for *Love WITH Accountability*:

"To say that this anthology is long overdue doesn't even begin to cover it. For decades, and lifetimes, LGBTQIAA survivors of color have been the backbone of the anti-violence movement and frequently their voices have been pushed into the cracks of the mainstream. A fierce offering of complex, powerful, necessary narratives and critique, *Love WITH Accountability* dreams a new future into being: one where survivors are centered, and where we can dare to believe that accountability and true justice is possible. This is a gift of a book and the ripples of its impact will be with us for decades to come." —**Jennifer Patterson**, *Queering Sexual Violence: Radical Voices from Within the Anti-Violence Movement*

"Aishah Shahidah Simmons allows readers both to witness the community-building created through the sharing of the stories of deep harm to diasporic Black children, often caused by beloved family members, and to learn more about how all of us can—and must—do better to keep all of our children safe. Her reminders to breathe as we experience this sacred space, combined with the writers' collective calls to action, is guidance that will change our world." —**Sunu P. Chandy, Esq.**, Legal Director, National Women's Law Center

"Aishah Shahidah Simmons's *Love WITH Accountability* is a book that is wonderfully and sadly timeless. Simmons and the courageously skilled authors she's assembled write their bodies, memories, and imaginations into calcified cracks and bleeding silences. Each piece opens up the absolute terror and consequence of sexual abuse of children, but somehow the entire book is as interested in looking back as it is at looking forward. *Love WITH Accountability* reminds me that willful people make liberation happen and willful people and willful art can obliterate terror." —**Kiese Laymon**, author of *Heavy: An American Memoir*

"Not only have the contributors to this anthology found the bravery to share their survival stories, they have also developed practical and urgent solutions to one of the of most pervasive forms of violence impacting our communities at this time in history ... This is a book that should be taught in all classes that address gender, violence, family structure, parenting, race, sexuality, disability, and equality, and it should be read in organizations that address any of those issues as well. Thank you Aishah Shahidah Simmons for once again revealing an urgent paradigm of healing, a new and necessary definition of love." —**Alexis Pauline Gumbs, Ph.D.**, author of *M Archive: After the End of the World*

"I am still grappling with my childhood sexual abuse. *Love WITH Accountability* is an invitation for me and every survivor to take back our lives from the shame of this silent epidemic. The sacred collection of truths is a spiritual bath for every soul who's been impacted by loss, regret, and sorrow. I am changed forever by this anthology, and I am thankful to have a space to go to that looks and sounds like me regarding things I've never wanted to talk about with others." —**Elle Hearns**, Executive Director of the Marsha P. Johnson Institute

"Love is a claim about our most basic relationship to the outside world. And, too often, we are taught to love our world poorly, in destructive and dangerous ways, even and especially those parts of it closest to us and most in need of our cherished protection from predation. Aishah Shahidah Simmons has assembled an insightful group of truth-tellers, survivors, and advocates who challenge us to love more deeply and courageously, more protectively and purposefully. *Love WITH Accountability* is about articulating versions of love and caring with a radically inspired sense of personal and political possibility, of truly anti-racist and anti-sexist child advocacy. This is a book to read closely and to heed with an open and urgent heart." —**John L. Jackson, Jr., Ph.D.**, Walter H. Annenberg Dean of the Annenberg School for Communication, University of Pennsylvania

"With *Love WITH Accountability*, Aishah has done it yet again. And she brings an even greater team of radical powerhouses with her this time around. Let us rejoice in this gift. Let us rejoice. *Love WITH Accountability* is here." —**Heidi R. Lewis, Ph.D.**, Director and Associate Professor of Feminist & Gender Studies at Colorado College

"As a society, we've gravitated toward solutions to end sexual violence and child sexual abuse that are more about shortcuts and hiding and less about compassion and truth. Through their own suffering, healing, thriving, and deep wisdom, Aishah Shahidah Simmons and her contributors to the *Love WITH Accountability* anthology offer us a path forward that is real, compassionate, and true. This work fills me with hope!" —**Terri Poore**, Policy Director, Raliance and National Alliance to End Sexual Violence

"Aishah Shahidah Simmons has gathered a breathtaking set of perspectives that bring us closer to a world in which every child can be safe and free. *Love WITH Accountability* delivers a quantum leap forward in our insight into the complex trauma wrought by child sexual abuse and the visionary work underway to end it. Reading it is like taking a master class in the radical transformation offered by contemporary Black feminist thought and activism. It's a gift for all of us committed to social justice and liberation." —**Pamela Shifman**, Executive Director, NoVo Foundation

"*Love WITH Accountability* is an honoring of our ancestors who dared to struggle, a gift to our movements fighting to create thriving communities and a guide for future generations to continue this work. Through Simmons's self-work and community of activists, leaders, and scholars, they have produced a collection of writings to expose painful truths, while also providing a roadmap for accountability that is based on love, not more false solutions. This book is for anyone who is willing to do the difficult, yet necessary work to end the global epidemic of child sexual abuse." —**Charlene A. Carruthers**, author of *Unapologetic: A Black, Queer, and Feminist Mandate for Radical Movements*

"One of my first visceral memories of my own childhood sexual abuse occurred while I was being interviewed on a stage in front an audience of strangers. I gasped and immediately pushed the memory back into the dirt of my mind. Since then I've been turning and facing the truth that something terrifying happened, and it shaped me. I've been sifting through snapshots and sensations. I've been updating the landscape of my survival, adding new mountains to those I can mark as climbed and conquered. And here comes Aishah, standing next to me and taking my hand—I'm not alone. And on either side of us stand survivors, hands coated in black and red dirt, clay, gravel, mud. We are not alone, and we don't have to abandon love in order to live in justice. We have each other, and we are claiming our lives and our families, our transformation and our healing, together. Thank you for this sharp, tender, reshaping of a text." —**adrienne maree brown**, author of *Pleasure Activism: The Politics of Feeling Good*

"*Love WITH Accountability* is an interweaving of injustices and radical visions for change into a shawl of trauma and healing that cascades around the shoulders of the survivors, advocates, and witnesses. This important collection of writings drapes over the body enveloping the common threads of each story that pushes us to envision and work to create a world where accountability is the norm. *Love WITH Accountability*, and compassion, frees survivors from guilt, shame, and blame, places the onus for change on the harm-doers and the bystanders, and transforms the shawl into a cloak of liberation for us all." —**Quentin Walcott**, Co-Executive Director, CONNECT

"What Aishah Shahidah Simmons has created is not possible without a lifetime of intention. Simmons possesses a rare perseverance among activists and writers to produce a portfolio that holds lifelines and roadmaps for all of us to learn, heal, and evolve as human beings, survivors, listeners, and seekers. And because of that intention, there will be countless generations of pain that will find healing in these pages." —**Lisa Factora-Borchers**, editor of *Dear Sister: Letters From Survivors of Sexual Violence*

Love WITH Accountability: Digging Up the Roots of Child Sexual Abuse

© 2019 Aishah Shahidah Simmons
Foreword © 2019 Darnell L. Moore

ISBN: 9781849353526
E-ISBN: 9781849353533
Library of Congress Control Number: 2019933777

AK Press
370 Ryan Ave. #100
Chico, CA 95973
www.akpress.org
akpress@akpress.org

AK Press
33 Tower St.
Edinburgh EH6 7BN
Scotland
www.akuk.com
ak@akedin.demon.co.uk

The above addresses would be delighted to provide you with the latest AK Press distribution catalog, which features books, pamphlets, zines, and stylish apparel published and/or distributed by AK Press. Alternatively, visit our websites for the complete catalog, latest news, and secure ordering.

Cover illustration by Kathryn Bowser Graphic Design
Cover design by Morgan Buck
Printed in the USA

In memory of my maternal great-aunt, Jessie Neal Hudson. Born in the early twentieth century, Aunt Jessie was a child sexual abuse survivor who never received the "love with accountability" she desperately wanted and definitely deserved. She was also a pioneering, trailblazing, unapologetic race woman who loved her family and friends fiercely and dearly.

In honor of my paternal cousin and one of my closest confidantes, Marie R. Ali, who has journeyed with me in a way that *only* a family member who knows *all* of the secrets can. Marie has held me accountable, challenged me, cried with me, and loved me deeply. She has also charted her own healing and accountability journey as a daughter, a sister, an aunt, and a mother to Iyana Marie Ali-Green.

For my nieces and nephews who are a few of the many reasons that I dedicate my life to disrupt and end all forms of sexual violence: Zari Ciyani Thwaites-Simmons, Avye Dai Thwaites-Simmons, Kylin Nicole Simmons, Amaechi Amadeus Nze, Liam Brodie Clark, Chastity Leeann Edwards, and Joaquín Jose Bagua Allah Rivera.

If your house ain't in order, you ain't in order.
It is so much easier to be out there than right here.

—Toni Cade Bambara

What you do to children matters. And they might never forget.

—Toni Morrison

CONTENTS

Breathe

Breathe

Content Notice

Child sexual abuse is a global epidemic.[1]

The purpose of *Love WITH Accountability: Digging Up the Roots of Child Sexual Abuse*, both as a book and a project, is to prioritize child sexual abuse, healing, and justice in dialogues, writings, and work on racial justice and sexual violence. The majority of the chapters in this anthology give an in-depth and, at times, graphic description and examination of rape, molestation, human trafficking, other forms of sexual harm, racism, sexism, transphobia, homophobia, ableism, audism,[2] misogyny, misogynoir,[3] religious/spiritual abuse, and state violence committed against diasporic Black children through the lived experiences and work of diasporic Black adult survivors and advocates. Most of the chapters also offer ideas, visions, and strategies for how we can address, disrupt, and ultimately end child sexual abuse without solely relying upon systems that have continuously harmed diasporic Black people and other marginalized communities. All of the chapters offer insights about the healing journey and what justice can look like for survivors of child sexual abuse.

You may want to read this anthology by yourself, or in community with others. You may also want to consider reading this anthology in tandem with reading *Beyond Survival: Strategies and Stories from the Transformative Justice Movement*, co-edited by Ejeris Dixon and Leah Lakshmi Piepzna-Samarasinha (forthcoming, AK Press, 2020).

1. Joanne Stevelos, "Child Sexual Abuse Declared an Epidemic: World Health Organization Publishes CSA Guidelines," *Psychology Today*, November 29, 2017.

2. "Audism is a term used to describe a negative attitude toward deaf or hard of hearing people. It is typically thought of as a form of discrimination, prejudice, or a general lack of willingness to accommodate those who cannot hear. Those who hold these viewpoints are called audists and the oppressive attitudes can take on a variety of forms." Jamie Berke, "The Meaning and Practice of Audism," VeryWellHealth.com, June 18, 2018, https://www.verywellhealth.com/deaf-culture-audism-1046267.

3. Coined by queer Black feminist Moya Bailey, "misogynoir" is a word used to describe how racism and anti-Blackness alter the specific experience of misogyny for Black women. Trudy, "Explanation of Misogynoir," *The Gradiant Lair*, April 28, 2014, http://www.gradientlair.com/post/84107309247/define-misogynoir-anti-Black-misogyny-moya-bailey-coined.

The conscious breath can be a grounding anchor. It is in this context that I insert the word "Breathe" in between every five chapters to invite you to pause, take conscious breaths, and ground yourself while reading. Whatever you decide, please take your time, and please take compassionate care while reading.

Imagining and working for a world without violence,
Aishah Shahidah Simmons

Breathe

FOREWORD

Love Is a Reckoning

Darnell L. Moore

I thought that I was ready. I had access to the right type of language and popular theories. By the time we met, I had been a part of enough talks on rape culture and patriarchy to respond with the ease of an expert. I sat opposite her, however, staring back with a face wilted by shock after hearing what she wanted to share with me. She shared something I wished I hadn't heard. Shared something I wished could be undone. Shared something I wished she hadn't had to experience and feel and share at all.

Before we spoke, I felt a renewed faith in our human capacity to heal from the harms we've committed or experienced. Finally, I had come to believe in something other than punishment, prisons, and call-out culture to fix what has been bruised: so many hearts, so many spirits, so many bodies.

I believed that people, even those among us who have hurt others, could still grab hold of redemption, transformation, and justice. But a survivor had arrived at the bar carrying her coat and pain, testing my belief that people who harm can be set free from the worst parts of the self.

I had asked my cousin to meet me in Philly. It was the start of winter. She suggested a bar—we are, after all, the only obvious queers in the family. It was supposed to be a typical night out: get cheap drinks and catch up, talk shit and play matchmaker. So we ordered a round after we found a table.

"I've been depressed," she said before taking another sip of the Vodka Madras I ordered. I knew as much because she's brave enough to be vulnerable in ways that so many in my family are not, in ways I am not. She had shared as much on her social media pages. I did not know, however, that she barely slept at night. "Nightmares," she confessed. She couldn't sleep because she could not shake the presence of the person, the family member, our family member, who had sexually assaulted her. We didn't laugh anymore after this confession—only slow sips of our drinks and silence followed.

I didn't know what to say other than "sorry." I told her that I believed her even if our other family members did not. I listened as my stomach turned, as my heart broke, as she spoke heavy words. I could not fathom how many nights she had lost sleep as her stomach turned, as her heart broke, as she replayed in her head the words her assaulter had spoken to her signaling his indignation. I wasn't prepared. I knew only that I had to reassure my cousin that I would journey with her toward healing in whatever ways she desired.

That encounter in the bar with my cousin was the first time that a family member had confessed that they had been sexually assaulted by another person in our family. I thought I'd be prepared to journey with a loved one to the center of their nightmare. In that moment all that I thought I knew was not enough to manage all that surfaces when sexual violence, when long-held secrets, are brought to the fore. It was not enough to match the confusion, to exorcise the ghosted memories, to turn the forlorn encounter into one of happiness.

It became clear to me, as someone who knows a bit about the ramifications of sexual assault, that the tools so many people need to heal have yet to be imagined and created. Even now. Even in an unprecedented time when survivors' stories are centered in mass-mediated movements like #MeToo.

When I learned that my cousin's life had been forever altered by another family member whom I loved as much as I loved her, I needed something more to offer her. What she needed, which is what we all need, are documented practices that might move survivors in the direction of healing. We also need critical and radical tools that move beyond what we currently rely on—in a carceral state like the United States, a state whose prison system is already imploding with Black bodies—to transform harm-doers.

But the articulation of this need is far from new. Black feminists, Aishah Shahidah Simmons chief among them, have been at the center of this collective healing-justice work for decades.

Simmons has been doing the work—advocating and fighting to bring an end to child sexual abuse and adult rape—with the rigor and love of a Black feminist who believes that we can materialize our dreams of families and communities, where all people can be free of sexual violence. Simmons's critical anthology, *Love WITH Accountability: Digging Up the Roots of Child Sexual Abuse*, arrives at an urgent time and demands of the reader a practice and way of being that upsets the sexual violence that has emerged in the crossing that is, as Black feminist writer and theorist bell hooks has written, white supremacist capitalist cis-heteropatriarchy. Simmons has curated an anthology that includes testimonies and methods, questions and meditations, textured by and grounded in a Black feminist vision of a type of love that costs us something. Love that requires of us self-reflection, inner work, and accountability.

I didn't know what to do, to feel, to say when I sat opposite my cousin. I knew, however, that I needed to affirm her testimony and her view of what justice might mean for her. I didn't know what to do with the love I felt, which began to feel too expansive a sentiment in a moment when what was needed was a reckoning. I knew I needed to love her in that moment and after. And I am reminded after reading this work that if I loved the family member who harmed my cousin, then I have to be ready to be honest with him about the need for accountability.

Love WITH Accountability is a reminder that to reckon is, in fact, an act of love. Accountability is real love. It is radical love. And it is a just love that we need.

INTRODUCTION

Dig Up the Roots of Child Sexual Abuse

Aishah Shahidah Simmons

This is sacred space.

Libation . . . instead of pouring water on the ground, I pour words on the page.

I begin with this libation in honor of all of those unknown and known spirits who surround us. I acknowledge the origins of this land where I am seated while writing this introduction. This land was inhabited by Indigenous people, the very first people to inhabit this land, who lived here for thousands of years before the Europeans arrived and were unfortunately unable to cohabitate without dominating, enslaving, raping, terrorizing, stealing from, relocating, and murdering the millions of members of Indigenous nations throughout Turtle Island, which is now known as North America. I write libation to those millions of Indigenous women, men, and children; and those millions of kidnapped and enslaved African women, men, and children whose genocide, confiscated land, centuries of free labor, forced migration, traumatic memories of rape, and sweat, tears, and blood make up the very fiber and foundation of *all* of the Americas and the Caribbean.

To paraphrase the late award-winning Black feminist writer and cultural worker Toni Cade Bambara—who was also my teacher—"the mere fact that Indigenous, Black and other marginalized peoples are still breathing is a cause for celebration."[1]

This is sacred space.

When is the right time to talk about child sexual abuse? Even in our heightened contemporary awareness about sexual violence, we still

1. Kay Bonetti, "An Interview with Toni Cade Bambara," in *Conversations with Toni Cade Bambara*, ed. Thabiti Lewis (Jackson: University Press of Mississippi, 2012), 35.

do not talk about child sexual abuse, especially when it happens in families. How does one initiate in public spaces the often-silenced dialogues about any form of sexual violence, most especially child sexual abuse? How does one begin the conversation in the midst of the justifiable righteous outrage about the rampant and virulent racialized violence perpetrated against diasporic Black, Indigenous, Latinx, Arab, and South Asian people, undocumented immigrants, Muslims, transgender, intersex, gender non-binary, physically and mentally disabled people, deaf and hard of hearing people, and other marginalized people? How do we have these dialogues about sexual violence in the midst of the violence committed against our youth through our failing, underfunded, and militarized public schools, the school-to-prison pipeline, and the sexual abuse-to-prison pipeline, which is hoarding disproportionate numbers of Black and Latinx youth into the prison-industrial complex? How do we have these conversations where there are currently two members of the United States Supreme Court who are *known* and alleged to have committed gendered sexual harm? (I believe Anita Hill. I believe Dr. Christine Blasey Ford.) Or when the president of the United States, also a doer of sexual harm, harassment, and (alleged) sexual assault, mocks rape survivors, while his administration is doing almost everything it can to legally erase transgender people's existence (and, by extension, I add intersex and gender non-binary people's existence)?[2]

Everything that radical disabled, deaf and hard of hearing, able-bodied, cisgender, transgender, gender non-binary people of color, and anti-racist white people have fought and died for over decades is being dismantled before our very eyes. We are in the midst

2. I strive to use the word "harm-doer" instead of using the word "perpetrator." Harm-doers can commit one or multiple acts of violence. However, that is not their sole identity. I'm the first to admit that offering compassionate humanity is a tough pill to swallow when referring to people in power whose goal is to destroy humanity. However, this is the approach that I believe I must take if I'm committed to humane social change. See Aishah Shahidah Simmons, "Still So Much Work to Do to End Violence against Women," *New York Times*, October 13, 2016; Eric L. Green, Katie Benner, and Robert Pear, "'Transgender' Could Be Erased under Trump Administration," *New York Times*, October 21, 2018.

of an inferno of human rights violations in the United States, with global ramifications. Yet if we continue to keep child sexual abuse on the back burner, this pandemic will remain there, barely addressed, while millions more children suffer silently.

Sexual violence is pervasive and touches upon almost every single social justice issue including but not limited to race, gender, gender identity, disability, sexuality, education, housing, immigration, health care, mass incarceration, militarization, and politics.

This is sacred space.

I believe that child sexual abuse is a core factor in most forms of sexual violence that people commit. Therefore, in this time of heightened awareness about sexual violence among adults, all of us must prioritize the occurrence, treatment, and research about child sexual abuse.

I am a Black, feminist, lesbian, child sexual abuse and adult rape survivor who has dedicated the past twenty-five years—almost my entire adult life—to addressing these issues. My being out as a lesbian and as a survivor of child sexual abuse and rape is not solely political but is also deeply connected to my literal and metaphorical survival.[3]

Like too many children in the United States and across the globe, my introduction to my own sexuality did not include consent. My divorced parents are life-long radical activists who traveled frequently and extensively for their international human rights work. When my parents were on the road, I stayed with family or family friends and, while I was raised in a metaphorical village, it was my paternal grandparents who most often cared for me. But it was there, when I was ten years old, that my pop-pop, my step-grandfather (the only paternal grandfather I knew) fondled, touched, and kissed my Black-girl body for a period of two years (though the emotional, mental, and

3. A brief word on the homophobic myth that sexual violence makes someone lesbian, gay, bisexual, transgender, gender non-binary, queer: it is not true. I invite everyone to compare the statistics on gender violence with the statistics on LGTBQ identities. We must cease pathologizing LGBTQ identities and instead place our focus on ending all forms of sexual violence against *all* humans.

psychological terror of my not knowing if I would be molested again continued for many years after the abuse ended). I told my parents what Pop-Pop was doing to my body shortly after the abuse began, but tragically they never addressed, disrupted, or ended the sexual terrorism and subsequent trauma. Despite what I was told about my right to consent, my parents' complete inaction taught me that if a "trusted" family member was abusing me, I had no such rights.

My father never told Nana, his mother—my paternal grandmother and Pop-Pop's wife. My mother, who used to talk to Nana on a regular basis, never told her what happened to me. Nana was my closest confidante from when I was a little girl up until my first year in college, when she entered the initial stages of Alzheimer's disease. Despite all the things that I shared with Nana, I did not tell her about Pop-Pop. I want to believe she didn't have any idea that a grave harm was being committed in her home. However, the truth is that I do not know.

This is sacred space.

During Nana's demise, for ten years, Pop-Pop devoted all his time and energy to her care. If it weren't for him, Nana would've been living in a nursing home when she developed Alzheimer's disease. He was her literal savior and was celebrated as a hero, especially by my father, for being the dedicated and committed husband who carried the lion's share of his wife's care. Pop-Pop's celebrated hero status was also my father's way to assuage his shame and guilt for providing a minuscule fraction of her care. From my perspective, Pop-Pop was a flawed hero whose sexual terrorism against me was only acknowledged reluctantly and with tremendous shame in private, when I reminded my parents.

What if my parents had held him accountable? Would he have admitted to his sexually abusing me? Would Nana have believed me? I will never know those answers.

Despite the sexual trauma he enacted against me, I loved Pop-Pop. I enjoyed spending time with him, and I have many fond memories of our shared time together from my childhood until well into my adulthood. It was one big painful conundrum. When I became an adult, I was too aware of my sadness, anger, and fear to ever broach the topic with him of his having molested me for two years.

During the last three days of Nana's life in December 2001, I spent time with her alone in her hospital room. I rubbed her body, combed her hair, played African American spirituals and gospel music in rotation, and called upon our ancestors to welcome her. She wasn't conscious, yet she was present. I recognized that the end of her human form was imminent. I found my voice to share the one secret that I had kept from her for over twenty years out of a spoken loyalty to my parents and unspoken loyalty to my pop-pop. I laid my head in her lap and I sobbed almost uncontrollably while sharing what I always wanted to share with her for over two decades. I don't know what she absorbed, if anything, during my highly emotional disclosure. What I do know is that a shift occurred within me after my sharing with her. My incest burden was slightly lighter. At thirty-two years of age, I was no longer consistently afraid of the dark in the home where I was loved, nurtured, *and* repeatedly molested. It was as if Nana's spirit took that burden away from me when she joined the ancestral realm.

With Pop-Pop's encouragement and blessing, my father and I planned Nana's funeral. I wrote and delivered Nana's eulogy, from the pulpit, at Morris Brown A.M.E. Church in Philadelphia. Without any hesitation or encouragement from others, I celebrated Pop-Pop for all he did for his wife.

After Nana's burial, I continued to lovingly engage with Pop-Pop for another nine years. This also included my taking care of my father around the clock for over three weeks, at Pop-Pop's home and with his full support, when my dad had his first valiant bout with prostate cancer. Each night I was there, I slept in that same room where I was sexually molested. I would have to tell myself at night, "Aishah, Pop-Pop is not coming into the room in the middle of the night." Twenty-four years after the sexual terrorism ended, and I was still grappling with the trauma I had endured.

This is sacred space.

In February 2010, white, queer feminist Jennifer Patterson, a sibling survivor friend of mine, invited me to write an essay about my child sexual abuse for her anthology, *Queering Sexual Violence: Radical Voices from within the Anti-Violence Movement* (or, *QSV*).[4] At the time, I didn't know Jennifer very well, and she definitely didn't know the details of my incest herstory. She contacted me because of the impact of my film, *NO! The Rape Documentary*, on her life, and also because I publicly identified as an incest survivor. I was frightened by the invitation. I told her that I would consider it but very seriously doubted that I would be able to participate. This was the first time I had ever seriously considered writing about my child sexual abuse. Five years later, I eventually did contribute to the *QSV* anthology, which was right around the time that Jennifer was able to secure a publisher for the vital volume of writings.

Less than one month after Jennifer's invitation, Pop-Pop's life was in grave danger. I played a pivotal role in saving his life. I stayed by his hospital bed while standing my ground against doctors, who thought they were going to railroad me into doing whatever they thought was best without any input from me. I was Pop-Pop's staunch advocate with all medical personnel from the moment that he was rushed to the hospital, to until my father arrived in Philadelphia from his home in Europe, and Pop-Pop's daughter, my aunt, arrived from her home in another state. This is another example of the infinite complexities that many child sexual abuse survivors have to wrestle with—mentally, emotionally, and physically—every single day of our lives.

When I reflect upon my life, I'm stunned by the mental and emotional acrobatics that I performed for over three decades for the sake of maintaining family loyalty, a virtue that I was taught by my parents yet never fully received from either one of them. It was cognitive

4. Jennifer Patterson, *Queering Sexual Violence: Radical Voices from within the Anti-Violence Movement* (Riverdale, NY: Magnum Press, 2016); see also http://queeringsexualviolence.com.

dissonance at its best—or worst, depending on your perspective. These acrobatics that I have performed for most of my life help me to understand so much, including my compulsive overeating and the severe migraines that I've suffered since I was ten years old. I couldn't scream. So my body did, and the legacy haunts me to this day, forty years later. The body definitely keeps the score.[5]

Pop-Pop's illness and subsequent demise marked a major turning point in my life. I came to grips with the fact that the grave injustice done to me was not solely by Pop-Pop but also by my activist parents. I completely disappeared from all activity connected to Pop-Pop's care in spring 2010. He became an ancestor in February 2011. After much thought and very painful deliberation, I did not attend his funeral.[6]

This is sacred space.

I began taking the small steps, which over time became giant strides and leaps in honor of my own rebirthing process. I revisited my twelve-year journey when I made my film, *NO! The Rape Documentary* (2006). Through the first-person testimonies, scholarship, cultural work, and activism of Black women and men, the film examines the international atrocity of rape and other forms of sexual assault committed against women by men through the lived experiences of Black people. Throughout the entire process of making *NO!*, I was public about my status as a survivor of incest and rape. However, I rarely, if ever, shared the details about my child sexual abuse.[7] I always thought

5. Bessel van der Kolk, M.D., *The Body Keeps the Score: Brain, Mind, and Body in the Healing of Trauma* (New York: Penguin Books, 2015).

6. If you want to read more detailed writing about my experiences with Pop-Pop, Nana, and my parents from 1979 to 2015, I invite you to read my essay "Removing the Mask: AfroLez®femcentric Silence Breaker," in *Queering Sexual Violence: Radical Voices from within the Anti-Violence Movement*, Jennifer Patterson, ed. (Riverdale, NY: Magnum Press, 2016), 23–38.

7. *NO! The Rape Documentary*, directed by Aishah Shahidah Simmons (Philadelphia: AfroLez® Productions, 2006). For more information on *NO!*, visit http://notherapedocumentary.org. It is also available for streaming online on Vimeo On Demand: http://vimeo.com/ondemand/notherapedocumentary. See also Gayle Pollard-Terry, "For African American Rape Victims, a Culture of Silence," *Los Angeles Times*, July 20, 2004.

I was protecting Pop-Pop. Later, I realized that I was also protecting my parents, perhaps more than I was protecting Pop-Pop.

NO! probably wouldn't exist had I not been sexually abused as a child, nor would it exist without the steadfast support that I received from both of my parents while making the film, behind the screen as well as on it, as interview participants. My dad was also my confidante and an unwavering source of emotional support throughout the journey. I do not believe I could have made the film without my parents' love and support.

I didn't tackle the topic of child sexual abuse in *NO!* because I couldn't tackle it in my own family. Michael Simmons and Dr. Gwendolyn Zoharah Simmons are, without question, two undisputed heroes in the film. My father is the next-to-last person to speak in the film, and his words are truly profound:

> There was a period in my life when, like at least once a year, for almost four or five years, the place where I lived got robbed. The last time I lived in a place that I got robbed was maybe twenty years ago. I have just reached a point where every day that I come home I *don't* look to see if my door is open. That was twenty years ago. I wasn't at the house, there was nothing traumatic about me getting robbed. It was just that someone took my stuff and I felt violated. Now I can't imagine an emotional trauma like rape, how long it takes to get over that, if I'm coming home still nervous just about whether my television set is there.[8]

Thirteen years after the film's world premiere, my father's profound words in *NO!* break my heart on a personal level. *How long will it take for me to get over being sexually molested by his stepfather?* Throughout my life until early 2010, I was taught by my parents to love and care for my pop-pop, who was also my sexual terrorist. Despite this, in *NO!* I presented my parents without *any* flaws or contradictions in terms of

8. Michael Simmons quoted in *NO! The Rape Documentary*.

how they treated me. I wasn't even aware at the time of making the film that I was contradicting myself.

At times I have felt like I was digging concrete with my bare hands for years to reach the origins of my sexual trauma. Without question, it begins with what Pop-Pop repeatedly did to my prepubescent Black girl body from 1979 to 1981. It also includes how despite my telling what was occurring at the time, my parents never disrupted the child sexual abuse committed against me. Instead, they denied the truth for over three decades for their own selfishness and comfort.

I have done twenty-seven years of continuous work with Dr. Clara Whaley Perkins, a Black feminist and licensed clinical psychologist who specializes in sexual trauma. Her razor-sharp guidance and support have enabled me to pull back many layers and open bolted doors that were hiding festering wounds. My seventeen-year Vipassanā meditation practice taught by S. N. Goenka and twenty-five years of consistent involvement as a survivor-activist, filmmaker, and cultural worker in global anti-sexual violence and LGBTQIA movements are also core resources that, in addition to my work with Dr. Whaley Perkins, support my unending survivor healing journey.

This is sacred space.

In mid-January 2015, while pleading for and demanding a conversation with my parents about their failure to protect me, I signed "Love WITH Accountability" in virtually every email and text communiqué to them. In doing so I was emphasizing that my deep love for them would no longer shield their lack of accountability for the violence that I endured as a result of their inaction for two years and subsequent cover-up for thirty-one years.

I've been pruning in the anti–sexual violence forest since the early 1990s—yet it wasn't until January 2015 that I was able to cultivate the strength to finally and unapologetically dig up the roots of my child sexual abuse. As is the case with so many victim-survivors, this digging inevitably led me to questions of love, accountability, and family.

The overwhelming majority of us are taught from birth that regardless of any transgression we experience from a family member, we must protect our family at all costs. When child sexual abuse survivors break our silence about the sexual harm we experienced, we are often not believed. We are often accused of somehow inviting the sexual abuse, being mentally unstable, being evil or instruments of negative spiritual forces, and/or not caring about or loving those who "love us the most." These are just a few of the falsities that harm-doers and bystanders of child sexual abuse and other forms of sexual violence tell themselves and others to obfuscate the truth around sexual abuse. I know because some of these falsities were my lived experiences, as a child and, unfortunately, as a fully grown woman on the cusp of fifty years of living, with my parents who haven't been together since I was four years old. My father and I are still struggling, navigating, and loving, at times from a great distance. The struggle and love will coexist until we each take our last conscious breaths.

There's a painful, uncanny irony that, in the name of familial love and loyalty, child sexual abuse survivors are overtly and covertly encouraged to remain silent. Family members and other caregivers will go to great lengths to deny, discredit, muzzle, medicate, or institutionalize the silence breakers. This must change. We need models of "love with accountability."

Funded by the Just Beginnings Collaborative Fellowship, #LoveWITHAccountability is a project that I created in January 2016 to examine how accountability is a powerful and necessary form of love needed to address child sexual abuse. Its focus is on tackling the global epidemic of child sexual abuse through the experiences, insights, and perspectives of diasporic Black child sexual abuse survivors and advocates. I am interested in diasporic Black adult child sexual abuse survivors and advocates communicating across differences and in solidarity to share our testimonies and solutions for creating accountability for the sexual harm committed within families and communities.[9]

9. For more information on the #LoveWITHAccountability project, visit http://lovewithaccountability.com.

I believe the silence around child sexual abuse in the family plays a direct role in creating a culture of sexual violence in all other institutions—religious, academic, activist, political, and professional. We cannot and must not address rape (including campus rape) without also addressing child sexual abuse. For too many victim-survivors of adult rape, child sexual abuse is a precursor. Ending sexual violence starts with ending child sexual abuse, and ending child sexual abuse starts in the family, in religious institutions, schools, and other spaces in communities. For me, and for many survivors of child sexual abuse, the family is simultaneously a source of deep pain and love. I am committed to creating models of holding family members accountable without suppressing that love. And I am not alone.

Thirty-seven years after Pop-Pop first molested me, I invited an intergenerational group of twenty-nine diasporic Black cisgender women and men, transgender men, and gender non-binary people to join me in an online #LoveWITHAccountability forum that I curated and edited. The forum was published for ten days, from October 17, 2016, to October 28, 2016, in the online publication *The Feminist Wire.*[10] Each of the contributors to the forum explored what "love with accountability" could look and feel like in the context of child sexual abuse.

This is sacred space.

Violence does not happen in a vacuum. There are approximately forty-two million child sexual abuse survivors in the United States and millions of bystanders who look the other way as the abuse happens and cover for the harm-doers.

In her landmark text *Sister Outsider*, the late award-winning, self-defined Black, feminist, lesbian, mother, warrior-poet Audre Lorde wrote, "Without community there is no liberation, only the most vulnerable and temporary armistice between an individual and her oppression."[11]

10. For more information on *The Feminist Wire*, please visit, http://thefeministwire.com.
11. Audre Lorde, *Sister Outsider: Essays and Speeches* (Berkeley: Crossing Press, 1984), 112.

I am committed to co-creating communal responses to intraracial gender-based violence outside of the criminal injustice system. I believe people who commit harm in our communities must be held accountable.

Black feminist scholar, cultural critic, and prolific author Dr. bell hooks wrote, "For me, forgiveness and compassion are always linked: how do we hold people accountable for wrongdoing and yet at the same time remain in touch with their humanity enough to believe in their capacity to be transformed?"[12]

I do not believe incarceration is the answer. Prisons are not focused on rehabilitation but instead are a kind of modern-day enslavement as the incarcerated are disproportionately Black, Indigenous, and Latinx and are raped and degraded while in prison. Too often family and community bystanders ignore child sexual abuse, but the prison system does worse, facilitating its continuation. Equally as important, so many US laws that are in place to protect victim/survivors of child sexual abuse and other forms of sexual and domestic violence end up severely punishing and harming survivors more than helping. The national coalition Survived and Punished has not only documented this frightening reality, its members also "organize to de-criminalize efforts to survive domestic and sexual violence, support and free criminalized survivors, and abolish gender violence, policing, prisons, and deportations."[13]

I believe every victim/survivor must take the avenues that best support their full recovery and total healing. Strongly advocating for alternatives to the criminal (in)justice system helps to deeply interrogate how and why calling the police has been presented as the only solution to the violence that victim/survivors face, especially when so many of them are victimized again when the police or any representative of the criminal justice system becomes involved.

12. Quoted in Sean Parker Denison, "Mission Impossible Why Failure Is Not an Option," in *Assembled, 2015: Selected Sermons and Lectures from the General Assembly of the Unitarian Universalist Association* (Boston: Skinner House Books, 2015), 11.

13. For more information on Survived and Punished, visit http://www.survivedandpunished.org.

What are the ways in which we can hold harm-doers accountable without getting involved with the very state that brutalizes Black and other communities of color? How do we create accountability mechanisms that address the needs of the immediate survivors without discarding the harm-doers, including bystanders? What are the alternatives to prison that hold people who commit harm accountable by giving them consequences for the horrible atrocities that they commit? What do community accountability, transformative justice, and restorative justice look like in response to child sexual abuse and other forms of sexual violence?

My goals for this anthology are to provide multiple road maps that explore how we can disrupt, end, and prevent child sexual abuse. These writings have emerged from the lived experiences of a collective of diasporic Black child sexual abuse survivors, advocates, and one former bystander, my mother.[14] The anthology includes most of the texts that were originally published in *The Feminist Wire*, with some revisions. Additionally, there are fifteen new contributors. Although I was unable to cover all the perspectives that I had hoped for, I am grateful for my sibling-comrades who are a part of this anthologized journey. I am especially grateful for my mother's efforts to not only be accountable to me for what I endured, but also to be publicly accountable through her contribution to this volume, through which she underscores the detrimental impact of parents/caregivers not believing their children.

Many of the contributors in this anthology do not believe in police involvement in response to child sexual abuse. However, there are several who believe that we must make use of what few resources exist while we co-create something different for the future. Despite my core beliefs about the imperative need to completely dismantle the criminal (in)justice system and abolish the prison-industrial complex, I intentionally include diverse perspectives that aren't necessarily in agreement with each other in this anthology.[15] I believe it is important

14. I invited my father to contribute to the anthology. He shared that while he would be willing to try to write something, he was unable to do it within my timeframe.

15. Victoria Law, "How Can We Reconcile Prison Abolition with #MeToo?," *Filter*, September 25, 2018, http://filtermag.org/2018/09/25/how-can-we-reconcile-

to be in compassionate conversation with people who do not hold the same perspectives but share a goal of naming, disrupting, and ultimately ending child sexual abuse along with other forms of violence.

It is my affirmation that every single one of us will make the commitment to refrain from marginalizing or, worse, condoning child sexual abuse or any other form of gender-based violence in the name of any "greater issue," which in communities of color often means solely focusing on ending white supremacy. Having your body violated and invaded against your will as a child and also as an adult is a nonnegotiable atrocity that must be addressed. The eradication of racism and white supremacy alone will not make our families and communities safe. We should not have to be murdered by white vigilantes, the police, or any other apparatus of the state in order for our communities to believe that harm has been committed. For many survivors of child sexual abuse, physical death is not necessarily the worst thing that can happen to us, especially when we have to engage with our harm-doers over and over again without any form of accountability.

What I have learned so far through this work, and through my own personal journey, is that "love with accountability" is hard—perhaps nothing is harder—but it is worth the struggle. Child sexual abuse, by its nature, is complex, and together we must co-create accountability systems that honor that complexity. Until we do, we will not end this epidemic.

This anthology is a part of a very long continuum of individual and collective, known and unknown labor by diasporic Black child sexual abuse survivors and advocates. I especially lift up sister-survivors Melba Wilson and Robin D. Stone for their groundbreaking texts, *Crossing the Boundary: Black Women and Surviving Incest* and *No Secrets, No Lies: How Black Families Can Heal from Sexual Abuse.*[16] Their

prison-abolition-with-metoo.

16. Melba Wilson, *Crossing the Boundary: Black Women Surviving Incest* (London: Virago Press, 1997); Robin D. Stone, *No Secrets, No Lies: How Black Families Can Heal from Sexual Abuse* (New York: Broadway Books, 2004). Robin interviewed my parents and me for her book. She used the pseudonyms, Maya, Irma, and Allan, to tell our story in three distinct voices on pages 60–74.

work, along with other work, broke ground in Black communities and without question paved the way for this anthology.

I bow deep in honor of the vision, labor, and courage of Wilson, Stone, and each contributor to this anthology, especially my mother.

In honor of the ancestors, and for the current and future generations of children.

This is sacred space.

[Versions of this essay were first published as "Digging Up the Roots of Child Sexual Abuse" in the #LoveWITHAccountability online forum in *The Feminist Wire* on October 17, 2016, and as "Accountability Is a Radical Form of Love," in the Spring 2017 edition of *The Resource*, the National Sexual Violence Resource Center's magazine.]

CHAPTER 1

Love WITH Accountability

A Mother's Lament

Dr. Gwendolyn Zoharah Simmons

My name is Gwendolyn Zoharah Simmons, and I am the mother of my only child/daughter, Aishah Shahidah Simmons, who was sexually molested by her (step)grandfather from when she was ten until she was twelve years old. When Aishah first told me that her grandfather was sexually molesting her, *I did not believe her*. I told her that she was having a bad dream and that her beloved Pop-Pop would never do anything like that. He presented as an upstanding family man, hard worker, proud provider for his wife, Aishah's grandmother, whom he loved dearly and tenderly cared for. My daughter's grandmother had a lingering illness and did not work outside the home. She doted on Aishah, her "Pie" as she called her. For her, the sun rose and shined on Aishah. The feeling was mutual between the two of them; my daughter loved her grandmother dearly. I thought she loved her more than she loved me, and I was a bit jealous of their relationship at times.

But I also felt so fortunate that my daughter had grandparents who cherished her, and I felt that she was *safe* staying with them when I had to be out of town for long stretches due to my job, which had me traveling across the country and sometimes internationally. I *needed* my daughter's grandparents' home to be *safe* so that I could travel and work without worrying about her well-being, knowing that she was loved and *protected* by both grandparents (or so I thought).

For my daughter to tell me that her grandfather was sneaking into her bedroom, late at night, and was touching and feeling her vagina and forcing her to kiss him in the basement—these were monstrous acts beyond my imagination. It could not possibly be true, I thought. It was he who drove me, Aishah, and her father home from the hospital after her birth. He carried her in his arms as her father wheeled me to the car in a wheelchair. I did not believe it! I told her so. If it were true, massive changes had to occur; changes that would disrupt my life. I hoped that it was just a bad dream and that the matter would go away. Oh, how I wanted and needed it to go away!

It did not go away! My daughter insisted that this was happening. When I would question her about the facts, she would be perplexed about why I didn't believe her and cry hysterically. I finally began to believe her, but I did not know what to do. While I was becoming outraged at the possibility that my daughter was being sexually violated by her grandfather, I was, disgracefully, also concerned about what would happen to my job if she could not stay with her grandparents when I had to be on the road. Her father and I were separated at that time, and I had serious doubts about leaving Aishah in his care for extended periods of time because of our ideological differences about child rearing. The issue of how to raise Aishah was the one big source of contention between her dad and me, and unfortunately this probably played a role in my inaction during Aishah's ordeal at the hands of her grandfather.

I told her dad that Aishah's grandfather, his stepfather, was coming into her bedroom late at night and sexually molesting her. He did not believe it, saying that there was no way his stepdad would do anything like that. I shared that I too had not believed it initially but that Aishah was so insistent that it was not a dream, that she was not making it up, that I now believed it was true. I said that we had to do something to stop it, but what? As I noted earlier, Aishah's father and I had been separated for several years. He was also dependent on his parents providing childcare for our daughter when either one of us was on the road. As a busy international human rights activist and labor organizer, he also traveled a lot. Also, as I mentioned, his mother had a serious illness and was totally dependent on her husband for her comfortable lifestyle and the excellent health insurance (via his job) that provided the doctors who, we all believed, were keeping her alive. Aishah's dad kept saying it would kill his mother to tell her that her husband was sexually molesting her granddaughter, and that we had to keep it a secret from her *at all costs*.

What is so outrageous about Aishah's dad's behavior and mine was that, it seems in retrospect, we were equally—if not more—concerned about his mother's well-being, my job, his job, our movement work, and our reliance on them for childcare than we were about the tremendous harm being done to our daughter!

After much hand-wringing and discussion, Aishah's father said he would speak to his stepfather, warn him that we knew, and tell him that he had better never touch her again. I agreed to this plan. Later, I was told that this conversation had occurred. What I find shocking and shameful about my behavior is that I made myself content with this and never spoke to her grandfather myself. I am dismayed that I did not confront him myself, me the activist referred to as an "Amazon" by some of my male SNCC (Student Nonviolent Coordinating Committee) comrades. I had earned this title because I instituted one of the only sexual harassment policies on a project in Laurel, Mississippi, that I directed during the Mississippi Freedom Summer Project in 1964, when I was barely twenty. As I said in an interview in *NO! The Rape Documentary*:

> Everyone on my project had to go through an orientation that included a segment on sexual abuse and were told that they would be exposed and dismissed if they committed such crimes. As a result of that I became known as an Amazon and many of my SNCC male comrades refused to work on the project.[1]

I have been the victim of sexual assault on several occasions and risked life and limb to stop these attempted rapes—in the first incident, the attack came from my Morehouse "brothers" while I was a student at Spelman College. I had also fought off a high Nigerian official who was on a State Department tour of the country, which I helped to host as a Spelman student. The most terrifying attempted

1. Gwendolyn Zoharah Simmons, quoted in *NO! The Rape Documentary*.

sexual assault and battering was by a Houston Oiler, one of the first African American football players for a major AFL-NFL team—also during my years at Spelman. He also tried to run me down with his car after I escaped from his clutches. The most painful of all sexual assault attempts I endured was from a fellow SNCC "comrade," who I had to fight off at the 1964 Mississippi Freedom Summer Project Orientation in Oxford, Ohio. This was at the hand of someone I admired and trusted, as Aishah had admired and trusted her grandfather. But what was even more painful than the actual attempted rape by a SNCC comrade was that, when I reported him to a SNCC official, I was told that they (the SNCC leadership) did not have time to deal with a *trivial* matter such as this. Adding insult to injury, I was told: "Why are you making such a fuss? We don't have time for this. You should have given him some!" I cried myself to sleep that night and a few nights after, as I now had to add worry about being raped by a comrade in addition to dodging bullets from Klansmen and other white supremacists who had vowed to kill all of us who were going to Mississippi that summer.

In spite of having endured these sexual assaults, I, in reality, did nothing to save my daughter from being sexually molested in her grandparents' home by a family member, someone I trusted with her safety. Why? I have no answer, and it troubles me deeply that I still cannot explain my inaction. It makes no sense other than me prioritizing my need to keep my job and our somewhat middle-class lifestyle! Somehow, I rationalized that this was the best I could do.

Additionally, Aishah's father and I agreed that he was supposed to spend nights at her grandparents' home when our daughter stayed overnight, which happened often, to act as a deterrent to any additional molestation. I'm not sure that he adhered to this plan. Yet, I continued traveling for my job, leaving Aishah there while deluding myself into believing that the situation was taken care of.

This was a lie. It was not taken care of. Yes, my life went on as usual, as did Aishah's dad's. The only person left to suffer in fear and anguish year after year was Aishah. What happened to her, and her dad's and my inaction, has haunted her—and our relationship—for thirty-seven years. Aishah has had to struggle, without my understanding and support for what happened to her beyond the molestation, for almost four decades. This is because, what is even more outrageous than my not intervening directly with Pop-Pop, for three decades after the sexual violation her father and I expected her to continue to go to her grandparents' home, sleep in that same bedroom where she was molested, and help out with her grandmother's care after she developed Alzheimer's disease, spending days and nights with the man who molested her for two years!

Oh, yes, I apologized after she began to lash out at me for leaving her there all those years and tacitly expecting her to function with her grandfather as if nothing had happened, long after he stopped sexually molesting her. As far as Aishah knew, neither her dad nor I had done anything. On the surface, nothing had changed between us and him. As far as she knew we had done nothing to end the nightmare, nor was he publicly or privately censured by me in *any* way for his crime.

For these three decades, I could not understand why Aishah could not "just get over it." I was in denial about the great harm that had been done during and long after the actual molestations took place. There was the great harm of Aishah's father and me acting normal around this man. Never letting on to other family members that he was not as he appeared but was someone who caused our daughter great harm, who we were protecting for our own selfish reasons. Worse, we had expected our daughter to keep it a secret; to *never tell her grandmother* ("it would kill her," we kept repeating over and over) or all of the other family members who regularly gathered to celebrate birthdays and holidays over these three decades. *We acted as if all was normal!* I never understood the tremendous harm I was inflicting on my daughter. What is worse, I never thought about what she must have been going through at all those parties, dinners, and gatherings held in that house. We wanted her to put it behind her; to forget about it; to not upset the happy family. I did not understand until August

2018 why Aishah was still angry with me, and why our relationship was so troubled. I was oblivious to the fact that the harm continued way beyond the two years she was being actively molested.

As a civil rights, women's rights, and human rights activist, I am shocked and ashamed of myself. I am ashamed that I let my only child, a woman child, suffer all these years in silence. I am ashamed that I did *nothing*, really, to take her out of the horrible situation she endured during and long after the molestations occurred by wanting her to keep quiet, to keep it secret. To go there regularly and act as if nothing had happened. *I don't know how I did this!* I am just now admitting and coming to terms with my inaction with this great evil that I covered up and expected Aishah to cover up. I am just now—thirty-seven years later—coming to terms with the terrible spiritual, psychic, emotional, and physical toll that this has taken on Aishah for almost four decades. I am just now becoming *accountable* to her for the love I have always proclaimed that I have for her, my daughter.

I am so sad about the overt and covert harm that I caused my only child. I am grateful that in spite of this great harm I have caused, Aishah has persevered, risen like a Phoenix from the ashes, and held me accountable for my silence and for covering up a monstrous evil. She has broken silences with her film *NO! The Rape Documentary*, with her numerous writings in print and online, her national and international lectures, workshops, and now her project #LoveWITHAccountability. I can only pray that she forgives me and that I continue to learn from her example, her writings, and the personal experiences she shares with me on how a parent should act when one's child is sexually abused:

- **First and foremost:** Believe the child! Check it out. Confront the perpetrator.
- **Second:** Remove her/him/them from the site of the molestation and do not make the child continue to go there and act as if everything is normal.
- **Third:** Report the crime to family members and possibly the

authorities—unless he or she makes amends, especially within the family unit.

- **Fourth:** Get professional help for your child, other family members, and yourself.

I am proud of and salute Aishah's work to stop this horrible scourge of sexual violence against girls and women that is at pandemic levels in this country and around the world. Thank goddesses and gods, *Aishah is silent no more.*

[This essay was originally published in the #LoveWITHAccountability online forum in *The Feminist Wire* on October 28, 2016.]

CHAPTER 2

Paying It Forward Instead of Looking Backward

Loretta J. Ross

There is an intense dialectic between being a professional feminist who works to end all forms of violence against women, and being a survivor of childhood sexual abuse. My life experiences propelled me into the anti-rape movement, and the movement made sense of my life experiences. I've survived stranger rape at age eleven, family incest at age fourteen, forced pregnancy at age fifteen, college gang rape at age sixteen, and medical sterilization abuse at age twenty-three, but I would not forego any of those experiences. They contoured my glorious emergence as a proud, self-aware, and self-determining Black woman who unflinchingly looks life in the eye and struts proudly against all adversities. I had to decide that my trauma did not define me, although it grooved deep crevices in my mind, into which it can be too easy to slip into depression. I fight these patterns daily and grow stronger with each victory. My spirit's soul is the boss of me, not my mind or my body or the men who left their dirty fingerprints on my life story.

In my twenties, my service at the DC Rape Crisis Center in the 1970s taught me how invaluable professional therapy is in helping me stay present in my life and not seek to escape my lived experiences, as I used to do through drugs and sex work as a teenager. Instead, I learned in the company of other anti-rape sisters that fighting the numbing violence of sexual and reproductive oppression could become fuel for my passion and deepen my love of activism. Activism is the art of making my life matter. When, over the past four decades, I've told my story in small gatherings and national media outlets, other women have appreciated my example and found the courage to speak their own truths and be awed by the results.

All this self-confidence in the knowledge I've gained through lived experiences and years as a Black woman working in the Black nationalist, feminist, and human rights movements came crashing to a halt a few years ago at a family reunion. A forty-year-old niece secretly revealed to me that her father—one of my brothers—had committed incest against her when she was twelve. Burdened with this knowledge, I urged her to confront her father and let him know the secret was out—at least to her and me. She courageously did, and her story was confirmed when my beloved brother spent the rest of the reunion studiously avoiding me. Every time I entered a room, he caromed away as if we were two billiard balls struck by the same cue.

I wondered what next to do, besides continuing to talk to my niece. I'm from a family of elderly women; my fondest fantasy is to finally be old enough to sit at the big girls' table in the kitchen while other younger family members wait on us, bringing food and drinks and tenderly seeing to our needs. Since I am still mobile in my sixties, I'm not quite old enough yet, and I'm still the step-and-fetch-it kid to my aunts, great-aunts, and older cousins. But that day I needed to sit at that kitchen table and ask my elders for advice.

How could I be there for my niece in a way people had been there for me nearly five decades before? I believe with all my soul that this continuing cycle of childhood sexual abuse needs to end in my family, but I don't know how to do it. My siblings are all grandparents, sometimes babysitting our grandchildren or even great-grandchildren. How can we protect the vulnerable children of whom we are so proud?

I wanted my brother to be held accountable, but I had no idea what that meant. He's battling prostate cancer, and we fear every reunion will be his last, as his seventy-seven-year-old-body shrinks inexorably inward, seeking relief from his chronic agony. I wanted to shout out my new knowledge, but feared what it would do to my niece, my elders, and me.

My late mother was an incest survivor from age eight to sixteen, until she married to escape an abusive uncle who lived with her in a multigenerational farmhouse during the Great Depression. She was a passionate reader and a frustrated itinerant scholar. She refused to go to a local college when she had the opportunity in the 1930s because that would have meant continuing to live in the same house as her abuser. I wondered if my great-uncle also abused the surviving sisters and cousins sitting at this kitchen table with me. Did I have the courage or even the right to pull the scabs off their wounds when these women were in their eighties and nineties?

If I don't speak up, do I join a conspiracy of silence in which the men we deeply love continue to have sexual access to inexperienced girls in my family? They may be good men who do bad things. I can't stop loving my brother after sixty-five years because I've recently learned about his abuse. I can't turn love on and off like a light switch. Does that make them bad men or complex people predictably acting out distorted masculinities? As a victim/survivor, I have very complicated feelings about how to hold the people we love accountable, and, in my heart, I don't believe anger is the answer. What does accountability look like when it moves from theory to reality?

What is our responsibility now as elders? Do other nonviolent men in the family get a pass, and, if not, what is their responsibility in breaking the silence and maintaining our love for each other? Our excessive sheltering of our girls and fierce insistence on the respectability politics of Christianity did not shield any of our generations—my mother's, mine, or my niece's.

I thought I knew the answers to these questions. Mom used to say, "Tell the truth and shame the devil!" This advice seemed sacrosanct until I became the one caught in the hinge of accountability. Fighting childhood sexual abuse no longer seemed so black and white, as my feminist principles demanded that it be. The nuances of family love, family healing, and family unity compromised my determination to excise this festering canker in the hidden center of our relationships. Before I found the courage to speak up, my niece asked me to stay silent because she was not ready for her story to be more public. This was, at best, a temporary reprieve, because her father babysits his granddaughters. It was a postponement of the truth that begs the question of whether the truth is even capable of providing healing as a pathway to justice and accountability.

Another of my five brothers noticed something was amiss at the reunion and asked me afterward why my joy had abruptly disappeared. I shared the story with him. He doubted its truth because it painted an elder brother neither of us recognized. Another brother became extremely mad at me and barely speaks to me to this day because he thinks I'm using my feminist voice to "shame" the family by airing our dirty laundry. He accused me of "profiting" from my family's pain. Whatever. After nearly fifty years, I'm used to my radical politics embarrassing my respectable, hyper-Christian family. While they are often perplexed, they have never tried to silence me—until now. My niece's story is now threatening to blow open many secrets hidden for too long.

I think my niece chose to tell me her story because of my history. My cousin from my extended family, Melvin, was a married twenty-seven-year-old father of three who chose to rape me when I was fourteen. By getting me drunk, he was able to force sex on me, underneath the radar of my family's close attention. They feared strangers, not relatives. I became pregnant, and the truth came out. Melvin fled the country by joining the merchant marine, escaping my father's wrath. He abandoned his families while I raised his son, Howard Michael Ross. Abortion was not an accessible option for me in 1968, so my only choice was whether to keep my child or give him up for adoption.

I never heard from Melvin again. My family had news of him but understandably did not share it with me. I didn't hear any news about him until my son went on a father hunt when he turned twenty-one, wanting desperately to understand his history and connect with his sperm donor. Melvin wasn't hard to find. Family, you know. Predictably, the much-anticipated meeting did not go well. My son discovered that his father cared nothing about him and made promises he did not keep.

A few years later, Melvin died of a heart attack. My son asked if he should attend the funeral. I tried to answer as thoughtfully and honestly as I could. I had no desire to even see Melvin's corpse. But I asked my son to consider his choices: how would he feel about himself if he didn't go to his father's funeral?

Howard attended the funeral and, incredibly, met his half-brothers and -sisters who were apparently united in their disgust for their father. He bonded with that part of the family, staying in frequent contact for over twenty years, but he kept this news from me, not wanting to trigger painful memories. It turned out that Melvin was a serial abuser: I was one of several teenagers he had impregnated over the years.

This account of multigenerational childhood sexual abuse in my family is probably not that unique. The secrets of female childhood sexual abuse in Black families can be attributed as a legacy of slavery or the emasculation of Black men by white supremacy, or even dismissed as the politics of gender entitlement in society. We exist in a pervasive rape culture that normalizes and sometimes even celebrates violence against women. We live with and love many Black men who are themselves failed patriarchs who overcompensate through exaggerated sexuality, just as white men fetishize guns to express their insecure masculinity. They believe violence is power.

***

Today is August 25, 2016. There will be a long pause in the middle of writing this essay (for the 2016 #LoveWITHAccountability online forum in The Feminist Wire*), because I received the terrible news that my son died earlier today of a heart attack. He was only forty-seven years old and his name is Howard Michael Ross, and without him much of my life would not have been possible. I can't finish this now or maybe ever. I have to go to Texas to be accountable to this child. My rapist is dead. My son is dead. Now I have to see that I don't die too soon to ensure that his brief life matters too. Peace, my sisters . . .*

***

Postscript: I now know the stark difference between sadness and depression, because my depression comes and goes. The sadness of immense grief never totally dissipates but gets easier to bear each day. The support from my Black sisterhood helps in ways I can never express: the pinochle-sister Edith who came in her walker despite her physical pain to be with me that night. The best friend Dazon who slept with me so I would not be alone. The SisterSong leader Monica who helped elicit donations to pay for expenses. My older blood sister Carol, who helped raise Howard alongside her son Mickey. She talked to me every day but couldn't attend the funeral because of her own disabilities. I am grateful for all of them and thankful that I was not alone in my grief, unlike how I was isolated during my childhood traumas before I could tell anyone what happened. I can now share my story because of the anti-rape movement, and each telling helps the healing.

I was anguished when Howard died of an enlarged heart, a hereditary condition that made all of Melvin's children vulnerable to early death. Aishah asked me if I wanted to revise this first draft a few weeks after the funeral. At first I declined, but then I thought about it some more. I had the joy of raising my son Howard when he was a child and a teenager. At his funeral, I learned about my son's life as a man in ways I didn't know before. His life was a lesson in love with accountability.

I wrote the following Facebook post thanking everyone for their love and support:

> I witnessed at Howard's wake and funeral how more than [two hundred] people loved and appreciated him as a man. He was a son, a father, a husband, an engineer, a math tutor, a college professor, a chapter president of Omega Psi Phi, a Christian, a mentor, an organizer of food for the homeless, our family nexus, a barbecue expert, a champion pool and domino player, and a proud Black man! From the students who talked about how he helped them through difficult classes, to his frat brothers who laughingly complained that he got them out of bed early many mornings to deliver food to the homeless, he was a man who touched many lives. This feminist mom was gifted with such

> a thoughtful and caring child who grew into a fabulous man. Although he was born of rape and incest, he made me love him immediately when they put him in my arms at the hospital, and I could not go through with the adoption. I saw how he helped others love him throughout his life of service to his family, community, Q brothers, and people. One example of how exceptional he became was demonstrated by the six siblings he sought out to bring his father's children together to be brothers and sisters in unity, despite his father's dubious history of violating young women. What other child of rape would do that?

Our family ties are strong, so these brave children managed to love each other as siblings. That's when I learned about how much my son regretted being an only child and how much energy he spent in bonding with Melvin's other children, including those born of rape as he was.

Another strange thing happened at Howard's funeral. I met Melvin's sister for the first time. She offered condolences, but I was too distraught to really understand anything she said. Two years later, she contacted me again, wanting to talk, but we missed each other and only exchanged voicemail messages. At first, I was angry at her for attempting to talk to me. My son was forty-seven years old when he passed. Why hadn't I heard from her in all those years?

Where was she when I was a fourteen-year-old trying to raise her nephew and could have used some support then? I'd never had a word from Melvin's family, not an apology or a check-in, much less the offer of assistance to a child trying to raise a baby. What does it mean that the sister of the man who committed incest against me keeps reaching out?

What if Melvin's first victims were even closer to home than I was? Did he practice incest on his sister before he met the other teenage girls he violated? Was she now calling to ask me to become her confidante and witness to her story as well? Were her decades of silence evidence of her own trauma, and did she lack the words to share her experiences with me? What is driving her urgency to connect with me now?

I don't know what to do. I lack my son's bravery, so I'm hesitant to try to call her again. I don't know if I am strong enough to hold memories of her abuse without triggering my own. She's in her eighties now and from a generation who generally keep silent about these types of family horrors until death. In reaching out to me, she may be seeking an emotional lifeline for a Black woman who has kept her silence for so long. What is my responsibility to her, and how do I honor my son's memory while protecting myself from feeling like Melvin is raping me all over again?

I named Melvin in this story because I wanted to name the man who violated my innocence yet inadvertently gave me the gift of my beloved son. Howard's death closed a circle of life for me, but Melvin's sister wants to reopen that circle. Howard honored this other family, and I want to be worthy of the boundless love he had. But I'm afraid, so I'm writing this down to partially expatiate my guilt born of fear.

Howard's son knows some of this story about his grandfather, and we've talked about masculinity, violence, love, and family. My grandson is the reason I don't feel reproductively terminated, and we've grown measurably closer since his father's passing. Perhaps I should ask him for advice, because he may want to eventually connect with his grandfather's family. Accountability must include him as well, as this is also his family's history.

For now, I'll just sit on this until I can make peace with trying to be a better and stronger person than I feel I am. I celebrate my son because he taught me what accountability actually looks like. I had to be accountable to him and my decision to keep him. He was accountable to me and his siblings. Maybe love with accountability is paying it forward instead of looking backward.

[A version of this essay was first published in the #LoveWITHAccountability online forum in *The Feminist Wire*, October 25, 2016.]

CHAPTER 3

Soul Survivor

Reimagining Legacy

Chevara Orrin

Suffocating silence became my survival. I soon discovered that there was no safety in the dark recesses of my mind where I wandered to escape. Wrestling with a burden that became too heavy to bear, not yet discovering my strength. The secret had nowhere to hide, and I began to define myself and the world around me through the complex language of childhood sexual abuse.

I know well the weight of secrecy, the intricacy of family, and the difficulty of speaking truth.

I am a survivor of incest. I am a survivor of incest at the hands of my father: hands that crafted the 1963 Birmingham Children's Crusade; hands raised in fiery indignation at Brown Chapel in Selma, Alabama, on the night my father urged a crowd of six hundred to march and demand that segregationist Governor George Wallace stop "disenfranchising Negro people"; hands that lay still across his chest after he succumbed to stage IV pancreatic cancer.

I am a survivor of sexual and domestic violence, brutality perpetrated by the hands of Black men I loved. I am the mother of Black sons, raised by my hands with intention to resist patriarchy. Intimately, I understand the complexity and challenge of simultaneously protecting our community and holding ourselves accountable. For much of my life, I struggled with reconciling my father's abuse of my body while also honoring his legacy and healing my soul.

Somewhere between becoming a mother of Black sons and discovering that the most radical form of love involved diving into the depths of self-forgiveness, I began to heal. Forgiveness has been at the core of the personal work I have navigated for several decades to rid myself of shame and reclaim agency.

I once believed, as I told a reporter, "He altered my life. Whoever I was to become: I am someone else."

Several years later, I held a new truth. I was exactly who I was meant to be—because of, not in spite of, my father. That revelation is startling yet powerful.

One of my sisters would remind us often during our father's 2008 incest trial, "We are all better than the worst things we've ever done."[1]

Cycles of sexual violence, hidden and unspoken, do not shield future generations from abuse. In our silence, we stand complicit. Forgiveness and reconciliation are challenging to navigate, and survivor scars run jagged and deep. Remembered pain holds hostage dreams and possibilities. My journey has morphed throughout the years as I sought understanding, love, and truth, and it has become important for me to use my voice to build a world in which women and girls are free from violence in all its forms.

***
***

This is how my healing journey began: the silence was stifling. I couldn't stop the roaring in my head, fierce pounding of my heart, and angry tears streaming down my cheeks. The silence was unbearable. I couldn't breathe. I'd waited for this moment most of my life, and now he'd robbed me with just three words.

"It. Didn't. Happen."

But it did, I remember. His warm breath against my neck, I was terrified when he climbed into my twin bed. His tongue sliding in my ear, whispering that I was a woman now. His coarse hands touching my breast-less chest. His semen sticky on my thigh. He slipped out from beneath my sunflower-covered sheets as silently as he crept in. In a panic, I darted across our bedroom and shook my younger sister until she awakened. We locked ourselves in the bathroom, twisting the old-fashioned key in the latch until it clicked. My tiny body trembled

1. Les Carpenter, "A Father's Shadow," *Washington Post Magazine*, May 25, 2008.

while she ran warm bathwater. We climbed in together and huddled close. Salty tears smeared my cheeks as she tried to wash away the stain of childhood sexual abuse. I was ten. She was seven.

***

My father, Rev. James Luther Bevel, described in his *Washington Post* obituary as a "fiery top lieutenant of the Rev. Dr. Martin Luther King Jr. and a force behind civil rights campaigns of the 1960s."[2] My father, a brilliant strategist who initiated some of the most important moments in our modern-day history. My father, who fought for my freedom before I was even born . . . before he violently molested me.

Early on, I refused my mother's gentle suggestion that I speak with a therapist. Sitting silently as the psychologist impatiently checked her watch until the hour elapsed, I buried the dark pain deep in a place that protected and shielded me. For years, I shared with no one. Then only a few trusted friends. Struggling internally, overwhelmed with isolation, insecurity, and feelings of inadequacy. Oftentimes destructive and causing harm to those I loved most, including myself. I, like so many others, cloaked and veiled my childhood sexual abuse in secrecy and shame.

When I first confronted my father about the incest, I was in my mid-twenties, a young single mother of two sons, dedicated to thoughtful and intentional parenting. I was angry and filled with so much hatred toward him then. The abuse informed how I raised my sons in so many ways. When they were little boys, I was determined that they would be mindful of their male privilege and understand the agency of their own bodies. As they entered puberty, I shared sexual violence statistics, teaching them that many of the girls and women they would encounter throughout their lives would be victims and survivors. We delved deep in our "safe sex" talk. We explored the concept and importance of thoughtful partner intimacy. I shared my own

2. Alexander King, "King Adviser James Bevel, 72; Incest Sentence Clouded Legacy," *Washington Post*, December 20, 2008.

experience with my father in an effort to build understanding and better contextualize for them how I came to be.

I received word my father would be in Memphis for a speaking engagement and called to ask him to meet with me on my terms, in a space that felt safe. When he said yes without hesitation, I imagined he must have known this day would eventually come. Consumed with hate, my heart heavy, I practiced what I'd been rehearsing in my head for years. I had even thought about the many excuses he'd make. And how I'd destroy his feeble attempts to absolve himself.

My mother and younger brother came as support. My father sat stoically, legs crossed, on the living room floor, draped in Black ministerial garb, wearing a colorful yarmulke. My sons were upstairs, occasionally letting out shrieks of laughter as they played, oblivious in their room.

My voice quivered with anger as fifteen years of pain poured forth.

His abandonment as a parent, never providing even the basics—food, clothing, shelter. I grew up in abject poverty. Food stamp lines, government-issued powdered milk that never quite dissolved in lukewarm water, welfare worker visits, roaches in the refrigerator. My mom worked multiple low-wage jobs to keep a roof over our heads.

I yelled as I accused him of destroying my life. I stared into an all too familiar face. We share the same rounded nose, full lips, caramel-colored skin, and rapid pace of speech. We share the same eyes, including the crease that begins at our inner corner and disappears into high cheekbones. *We were not the same.* I felt overwhelmed.

"You know nothing about me! Do you know the day I was born? Do you know my birth date? Do you?"

I'm unsure why that was suddenly so important.

"You never bandaged a knee, read a book, prepared a meal, sailed a kite, or listened to a piano recital! You weren't there when I graduated high school or college or when your grandsons were born!"

My father peered at me with deep intensity, sat silent for a moment, then leaned close, and in a calm, steady voice that I've not forgotten, said,

"I got you the right to vote."

His words pierced with an indifferent injustice.

Filled with fury, I finally unleashed what I had shared only with a trusted few . . .

"You climbed into my bed. Your semen was on my thigh. I was a little girl. I am your daughter."

Ready for anything he might say, I took a deep breath and stared into his eyes. He simply looked at me with a calm defiance for which I was unprepared and said,

"*It. Didn't. Happen.*"

I'm mindful that the U.S. Civil Rights Movement looms much larger than my father or his pivotal work, yet I'm unable to dismiss the fact that there were men in the movement who created a culture that marginalized women and set the stage for various types of abuses. Oftentimes, not upholding the very principles upon which they stood, some of these same men viewed the accountability we demanded of our father as an assault against the movement.

When my father died three months after final sentencing, I was confronted with reconciling closure and quickly discovered that far from being a destination, it is a continuum. Lingering questions hindered resolution.

A few years ago, I saw the film *Mighty Times: The Children's March*, which tells the story of my father initiating and executing the Birmingham Children's Crusade, and I could barely get through the award-winning documentary without crying. When I was a little girl, I often wondered how a human being so filled with brilliance and love for humankind, so gifted, could be so tragically flawed. During his trial, he adamantly denied all abuse against my sister, and he never publicly confessed to any of our allegations.

As though the universe knew I required answers, we discovered a single undated page from his journal:

> Though I had the power to heal and bring others into the kingdom, I instead chose to use the power to illicit sex from

> ignorant, immature girls. And as a result, God withdrew himself away from me. And since that day, I have not experienced his love nor the joy of my salvation. And I have not confessed this sin and error because of shame and pride. And thus, I am a liar and an enemy of God.

Truth is complex. My father secured my liberation and he betrayed that freedom. Perhaps we both paid too high a price.

After my father's funeral, a journalist asked if I loved my father. Speechless because I had never pondered the question, I responded a few days later:

> I do love my father. I love him for the sacrifices he made that have enabled me to enjoy political freedom. I love him for his role in the passage of the 1965 Voting Rights Act and the vote I was able to cast in November 2008 that helped put a Black man in the White House. It is also that love that gave me the strength to sit in a courtroom and hold him accountable.

I sometimes imagine the conversations we will never have, the intersection of our justice work on which we might have collaborated had he been willing to hold himself to truth and own the harm he caused. Vengeance was never the catalyst for the incest trial. Restorative justice was always my intention—a desire for my father to be held accountable through the prism of love, the protection of a community safe from sexual predators, and healing for my little-girl-self and my sisters.

My father is perhaps not the monster I once believed him to be but more simply a man with human frailty, sexually abused as a child himself, ensnared in a past from which he never healed, incapable of facing himself in the end.

My life is forever shaped in immeasurable ways by the fiery, principled parts of him—remnants of love, resilience, and brilliance that helped him shape a movement. My life was altered by his violation and strengthened by my resolve to reimagine love and legacy and use the horror of my abuse in ways that are healing and empowering.

My legacy is mine to create—the hope and promise of an emergence that I dared not dream before. Each brave voice that names abuse and abuser gives strength to us all. I have discovered that the complexity and constant evolution is worth exploring despite the pain. I have learned to honor my experience, hold space, and release.

I have chosen to use my ongoing healing journey to amplify the voices of those who have yet found strength to share their truth. This is #LoveWITHAccountability.

[A version of this essay was first published in the #LoveWITHAccountability online forum in *The Feminist Wire*, October 17, 2016.]

CHAPTER 4

Fast

Dr. Kai M. Green

There was once a little Black girl who liked digging holes in the mud. She liked to feel the slime of worms. She reveled in the feel of the damp grit beneath her fingertips. Dirt did not bother her. It was only that she knew if she got too dirty, she'd probably get in trouble for messing up her school clothes. This little Black girl liked to play with the boys. She liked to take off her shirt and run around the yard like the boys. She did not think that she was a boy, but she had never been told that there were certain things that she would eventually have to become. Black girl. The becoming was a lesson. The becoming required a disciplining of the body. The becoming required a naming of the body, a naming that made what was hers both sacred and a burden, a naming that made what was hers not hers at all. The becoming made her mother afraid. Black mother wanted baby to play, but Black girls' play is often interrupted by other things. Black mother never wanted those other things for her little girl, so she tried her best to protect her baby's body.

Black mother took Black girl to the doctor because she baby be growin' and bubblin' over.

Her chest be becomin' breasts. Black mother frets over not having more time. Too fast. Training bra becomes a necessary armor for her kindergartener. Her baby's body was becomin' the ground upon which many battles would be fought. Black mother had already been a battleground body, she too had once become a Black girl and then woman. Black mother's body had already been made to bend and break and hold and birth somethings that she would have rather not birthed. She wanted to protect her Black girl baby. She wanted to keep her whole and clean, but she knew the world did not care about the sacred text that was her baby's body. The world was too big and too cruel. That world was also too small and too close, like family.

Black mother decided that the only way to keep Black girl safe was to wrap her up in chains, chains like Jesus, Bible, silence, secrets, and ancestral scars. She longed to keep Black girl from unsolicited touch, those who might harm her, some of the same people who had harmed Black mother. But chains failed at slowin' Black girl's body growin'. The chains did create a distance, though, between Black girl and herself, her own body, which she could no longer touch without fear or shame. Black girl's battleground body become burden, become this thing that she didn't ask for, inherited. Her body grew fast, and as much as Black mother tried to keep her, she could not.

When it came out, what had happened that summer, three years after her Black girl body first started to show signs of becomin', when Black girl came to Black mother and told her all of the things that had happened to her Black girl body, Black mother responded with a question: "Did you like it?" Black girl was confused by the question, but responded, "No." She knew that the question was used to evaluate if she had become *fast* like her cousin, who was five years older. Black girl wanted more than anything to *be good*, so she learned to love being good but never learned to love what she liked. What she liked, she didn't know how to name after that moment. Healing for Black girl came in the form of learning how to name what she liked, learning how to ask for what she liked and believing that she deserved to have what she asked for.

Black girl is a childhood survivor of incest and sexual abuse. When Black girl told Black mother what was happening, there was nothing done to remove her from the situation, so she learned to live with it. She learned to appreciate the moments when her abuser was nice to her. Black girl basked in those sweet moments, knowing that they would always come with a side of cruelty. She still remembers what it felt like to be slapped hard across her face. There were never any bruises because Black girl's skin was dark, and she could take just about anything, she believed. There were no visible traces, the traces were all much deeper than skin could ever reveal.

Black girl would go on to remember that summer every day for the rest of her life. After that moment migraines, depression, and shame become hers. She tried her best to reverse the stain of being *fast*. She became good. But good is not free. And protection is not the same as discipline. Black girl and Black mother's body had been disciplined, but it was rare that they were ever protected. Black girl had to reeducate herself. Every day when she remembers that summer, she also affirms her own right and power to protect her body and spirit. Black girl carried shame and guilt as she grew and moved through many emotionally abusive adult relationships. She learned to seek out partners that affirmed her insecurities. They kept her in her place, kept her unhealthy and unhealing. They kept her feeling ugly, as if she didn't deserve care. Abuse felt a lot like love to her, because of its familiarity; it kept her. Black mother wanted to keep Black girl safe, but the body can't be disciplined into safety. The worlds around Black girl bodies must be reshaped to be able to hold her, *fast* as she may be. So quit slowing her down, she was made to fly!

Coda

But the question that we were all to respond to in this book is: what does accountability look like after Black girl done become?

After recounting Black girl's tale (which is not just her own but, of course, also her mother's shame, her auntie's denial, her cousins' tears, her play-cousins' confusion—there are too many Black girl battleground body stories), the question we are left with is: What does accountability look like when you are the only one who *remembers* what happened? What does accountability look like when you remind your loved ones of that thing that happened, that was not love, and they say, "I don't know what you're talking about" and walk away? How does silence fill your mouth after that? Your body remembers. Your Black girl spirit remembers. You know what happened, and you want to heal, but there are no apologies to be had. You are forced to swallow an inherited silence that your Black family has built as a wall of protection.

So what does accountability look like in the face of deep forgetfulness? It might look like walking away. It might look like a refusal to stop asking for those who were there to bear witness—*tell the truth!*

In the end, I don't know what an accountability process for Black girl would look like. I know some things, though. I know accountability requires responsibility. Those who have harmed must learn how to say, "I have harmed, but I am not harm," "I have acted like a monster, but *I am not* a monster." Those who have harmed must commit to becoming better. Our Black families and communities need our people, and we need them to be well. Currently, we do not have enough tools or even language to articulate an effective model of accountability that does not replicate a carceral imaginary. Accountability requires an abolitionist ethic. We must ask ourselves: do we seek healing or punishment? The answer, of course, for most survivors fluctuates—respect that.

We must ask: what is the relationship between accountability and transformative justice?

Justice that transforms harm into something else, like Black love, is hard work. This kind of justice changes both individuals and systems of oppression. In order to envision and create this new world we sometimes have to suspend our notion of reality, which is always steeped in history. What we have experienced can sometimes confine our imaginations, so we have to work against that non-creative force. This work requires intentionality. What is accountability for Black girls whose bodies re-remember family secrets that were supposed to be kept buried—forgotten? But like ghosts, they rise. You must remember and affirm your truth in spite of forgetfulness.

Accountability looks like even more struggle after the harm has been done, after the PTSD, after the nightmares, after all that. Accountability looks like an investment in the healing of the harm-doer. We desire for harm-doers to cease harm, but accountability asks something else of those who have been harmed. It asks us to believe that the harm-doer can be different and do better. Accountability initiates transformation in the lives of those who were harmed and those who have harmed (sometimes one person can be both). Accountability moves us toward a world where Black girl won't have to inherit Black mother's trauma. Black girl and Black mother no longer lean into the false protection of respectability politics, body policing, religion, and covering up—they can't (be) fly all bogged down like that!

So I'll repeat it for re-memory's sake: The worlds around Black girl bodies must be reshaped to be able to hold her, *fast* as she may be. So quit slowing her down, she was made to fly!

[This essay was first published in the #LoveWITHAccountability online forum in *The Feminist Wire*, October 18, 2016.]

CHAPTER 5

On Moving Forward

Ferentz Lafargue, Ph.D

One of the many conversations with my editor prior to the publication of my 2007 memoir, *Songs in the Key of My Life*, that sticks out is an exchange about what the book's publication might mean for the person who sexually assaulted me when I was a child. Although I had not yet shared what I was thinking, as the public disclosure of my status as a survivor of childhood sexual assault neared, I had begun visualizing how my memoir's debut might facilitate getting justice against my assailant.

Visions of court deliberations and depositions with lawyers began persistently loitering in my mind. In these dreams, the assailant and I were on equal footing, and I was forced to consider whether I was prepared to go forward with facing him for the first time in two decades. Then, just as swiftly as this possibility had overtaken my life, it disappeared when my editor reminded me that fewer than 3 percent of sexual abusers are ever imprisoned.

While I had long been aware of this statistic, for some reason I thought that at this point in my life, the outcome might be different—after all, I was no longer a child hoping someone would believe me; I was now an adult, a well-educated professional. I thought my word would be as good as his.

Years later, I still think back to that moment, not just the conversation with my editor but rather that moment in time when I had steeled myself for the inevitable pivot toward justice and my assailant being held accountable for his abuse.

The questions conjured by my recollections of this period are essentially the same ones that I was asked when approached about contributing to #LoveWITHAccountability:

- What does accountability look like when tackling child sexual abuse (CSA)?
- Can we have accountability around CSA without punitive justice?
- What does restorative and transformative justice look like to you?

Accountability looks like healthy families and communities. Accountability does not begin after any abuse has been perpetrated but rather before anything happens. For example, I remember looking on in awe a few years ago as a friend spoke to her toddler daughter about not letting people touch her unwillingly. More to the point, I was taken aback by how deliberate she was using the word "vagina." Later, when I asked her about this exchange with her daughter, she told me that being frank in reference to her child's body was one of steps she was taking toward stemming the long history of child sexual abuse that had long infested her family.

My partner and I are similarly direct with our children, making sure to refer to their body parts by their correct names. We refrain from indirect or infantilizing references to their bodies. For example, we do not tell the boys to clean their "wee wees" in the shower. Instead, it is "wash your penis." By modeling for them that we are not afraid of discussing their bodies, we are empowering them with templates to do the same. Therefore, in treating them as sole proprietors of their bodies, we are helping frame their interactions with others around their bodies so that they may be better equipped to fend off would-be abusers.

That said, parenting strategies aren't foolproof, nor does the existence of sexual abusers indicate familial failings. The intersection of personal and social responsibility in this matter is particularly fraught in large part because there is a greater struggle to effectively articulate and acknowledge that sexual predators are in our midst and, in some cases, in our own homes. And not unlike other areas of the criminal justice system, what constitutes a transgression worthy of being included in a sex offenders registry is wildly inconsistent.

As a staunch opponent of mass incarceration, I loathe advocating for imprisonment in most instances, and sex crimes are no different. Therefore, a multifaceted counseling strategy is, in my view, the strongest resource to curbing child sexual abuse. As part of that strategy, I would include quality education about sex and general health because schools and curricula shape individual and communal behavior. Again, it is important for young people to learn as early as possible that sex is not something to be ashamed of or to be kept secret. Moreover, incorporating teaching about mental and emotional health in schools will help every student for life beyond school, preparing them for how to process and articulate what is happening in their lives and, more specifically, what is happening to them. Expanding knowledge about healthy practices will not only lessen the likelihood that individuals might commit crimes; it may also increase awareness about unacceptable behavior for young people.

Additionally, removing the threat of prison is also likely to bolster the odds that victims and their families come forward and challenge abusers. The prospect of losing a relative to incarceration, especially when that person is possibly a breadwinner or contributes to the household in another significant capacity, is daunting for many victims and their families.

Lastly, as presently constituted, most prisons and jails in this country do not have the staff and other resources to effectively rehabilitate criminals. American prisons, for the most part, are devoid of counseling services capable of providing ongoing support for inmates. Reentry programs also lack the necessary staffing to facilitate mediation between assailants and their victims, a service that is vitally needed, given that many victims were likely abused by either a relative or another person close to their family.

In order for this to work, restorative and transformative justice systems must be created with the priority of protecting victims, helping make them whole after they have been abused, and creating safeguards that will diminish the likelihood that assailants can continue abusing others. If restorative and transformative justice processes can ensure that victims feel comfortable coming forward, they will in turn increase the likelihood that assailants receive necessary counseling, enabling them to see and acknowledge the harm they have caused by their actions and helping to prevent them from recommitting these forms of violence.

A decade after that conversation with my editor, I still occasionally reflect on whether I should be doing more to bring the person who abused me to justice. It has been well over twenty years since he and I last saw each other, and I have no idea as to his whereabouts. Years ago, when a person from the neighborhood where I grew up would friend me on Facebook, I would cull through their friends list in search for clues about what might have become of my abuser. Nothing ever materialized. These days I find myself less engaged in trying to track him down and more focused on ensuring that my own children have the necessary tools to avoid the kind of harm I suffered. I do not believe that justice has been served, but I do believe that I am using the pain and anguish I suffered to transform the prospects for future generations of my family.

[This essay was first published in the #LoveWITHAccountability online forum in *The Feminist Wire*, October 27, 2016.]

Breathe

CHAPTER 6

Social Silence and Sexual Violence

Cyrée Jarelle Johnson

I didn't start talking until I was approaching five years old. This is not uncommon for some people with autism and its associated disorders, but it is relatively uncommon for people diagnosed with Asperger syndrome. In fact, a criterion of being diagnosed is that there are no significant delays in language. It's one of the myths of Asperger's (and what does "significant" even mean?). Others myths paint autistic children as cold and unloving, violent and defiant, and less intelligent than their peers. Like many children with Asperger's, I was a creature of obsession: blue whales, the sea in general, and, as I grew older, Greek mythology—particularly that material myth Socrates.

Sometimes obsession leads me to reread Plato's *Symposium* and cry; more often, it looks like me quoting Socrates and visiting his bust at the Met. I was recounting my interest in Socrates recently, during a meet and greet for incoming MFA students at Columbia, when my classmate looked over at me, with a grin on his face. Half asking, half accusing, he said, "Didn't Socrates diddle little boys?" Of course, the answer is yes. The ancient Greeks were invested in a cultural pederasty that, in their society, defined romantic norms. Pederasty was a social phenomenon, embedded in their myths, their men, and their gods.

Yet I take issue with my classmate's question, one meant to cast history as a tragedy that has ended. Questions like that ignore that Americans also have a culture of child predation—we just prefer to look away. As a Black person, I know that child molestation and child sexual abuse are embedded within our culture. It's in the silence around Michael Jackson's terrible personal boundaries and numerous accounts of child molestation.[1] It's with the people still willing to

1. The People of the State of California vs. Michael Joseph Jackson, case no. 1133603: http://www.sbscpublicaccess.org/docs/ctdocs/032205mjmemospprtobj.pdf.

defend him against these still-mounting claims in the present day. It reappears when we can still dance to new music by R. Kelly, a man known to prowl high schools and shopping malls for teenage girls, offering them gifts in exchange for sex, the same man miraculously acquitted of raping his own teenage goddaughter not so long ago.[2]

Even if there weren't any famous examples, we could look to our family reunions, cultural events, places of worship, and homes to find evidence of this culture. We can look to our neighbors and friends for proof. Sexual violence is part and parcel of the emotional and social violence that occurs within our communities. My initial inability to tell anyone about the sexual abuse I was experiencing at the hands of an elderly female neighbor created the perfect environment for it to continue. My family didn't run to check on me because they were simply relieved to be rid of me for a while.

Autistic children are accused of being burdens to our parents and families. We are asked to be thankful when we are not murdered by their hands. We are asked to keep still when we stim, calm down during a meltdown, be quiet when we are echolalic, and stop any ticks or repetitive movements that adults find objectionable. These messages are violent and justify violence against autistic people. They express beliefs that allow child sexual abuse to continue. When we ask children to be things that they are not, and to express themselves only in ways that we deem appropriate, we communicate the message that what we want for their bodies is more important than their self-determination. If we truly want to end child sexual abuse, we need to recognize the autonomy children have over their own bodies. That doesn't mean that they can do whatever they want; it simply recognizes that they have the final say over their bodies when safety is not a concern. It insists that a child who flaps their hands, doesn't speak at all, won't make eye contact, or never stops talking doesn't need to be "fixed" just because adults don't like the behavior. My family and

2. Jessica Hopper, "Read the 'Stomach-Churning' Sexual Assault Accusations against R. Kelly in Full," *Village Voice*, December 16, 2013, https://www.villagevoice.com/2013/12/16/read-the-stomach-churning-sexual-assault-accusations-against-r-kelly-in-full.

community would have needed to revise the way they thought of me to make space for my agency before they could effectively demand accountability from the woman who molested me.

Personally, I believe that the accountability model is a conservative and confessional one. It stops at the level of admitting to the violence—an important step but only the first one. When I hear about "community accountability," what I think people mean is that the whole community will work to hold a single person "accountable" to a harmful action or series of actions. This model forgets that abuse thrives in silence and isolation, and that can only occur when a community turns away from great injustice. Thus, whole communities are implicated in all instances of child sexual abuse. I don't need anyone to confess their guilt publicly—I already know who harmed me, and in many cases, so does everyone else. I need a community where everyone recognizes the role they played in that violation.

Child sexual abuse flourishes under the hot lights of the church because of the "mind your own business" culture it creates. We can no longer afford to mind our own business and say that we act in solidarity with one another and with the most marginalized parts of our families. To stop child sexual abuse, the way that parents treat their children must be considered a matter of public concern. Most importantly, abuse can no longer be treated as something unknowable. When a child speaks of having been violated, the response should never be disbelief and interrogation. Being a child is confusing enough without exploitation. Negative responses make it more difficult for victims of sexual abuse, particularly victims of molestation, where the perpetrator is more likely to be a trusted part of that child's life than a scowling outsider.

One reason why communities—a word I use here to mean some amorphous combination of families, neighbors, congregations of faith or worship, and institutions such as school or local government—choose to ignore child sexual abuse is because the response is assumed to be necessarily punitive and to require an overwhelming amount of evidence to prove. Nobody wants Uncle Jerome to do jail time. How can you *prove* the pastor touched you? Aren't you too young to even *know* what rape is? The victim is punished because the perpetrator is unavailable to receive punishment or too important to punish. Victim are of no importance because they are sullied by the crime and are suspect just for telling someone. Instead of radical communities constantly asking for ways to make child sexual abuse accountability less punitive for those who perpetuate it, I would like to first see it become less punitive for the children who have endured it.

It would take reparations to restore communities after child sexual abuse has occurred. I don't think that these must be monetary, but it is important to recognize that in such acts of great violence, something material is taken. If communities provide CSA survivors with somatics or therapy, people may be less likely to continue the cycle of abuse and could heal from the addictions and harmful coping mechanisms that often come with having experienced violence. If communities paid for training or education for CSA survivors, we could gain a new dream in exchange for all the ones that were squashed and snuffed out. I don't think it is realistic to try to restore the relationship between abused and abuser after CSA, but I believe that we can restore the relationship between children and their community by offering services and benefits after such a violation.

Please, give us our reparations if you knew that someone was hurting us and we couldn't cry out for ourselves. Please check on us, make sure we don't hang ourselves, don't hurt ourselves. It is a Sisyphean burden to carry each day. All we can do is try to be accountable to ourselves, to our healing. All we can do is teach children that they own their bodies and that adults who ask them to keep secrets want to harm them. All we can do is be the vanguard of the movement to end child sexual abuse.

[A version of this essay was first published in the #LoveWITHAccountability online forum in *The Feminist Wire*, October 21, 2016.]

CHAPTER 7

Embracing Our Humanity in the Accountability Process

An Interview with Tracy Ivy

How can we transform societal understanding that accountability is a radical form of love, most especially around CSA?

We first and foremost need to acknowledge that the person is human. Acknowledge their beauty. Acknowledge their ability to breathe as their right to life. This, in and of itself, is us practicing accountability on some levels. This is a necessary first step: to recognize and honor the humanity of the person(s) involved.

It is important that we recognize the person who caused harm is also a victim of their own violence. We need to examine our own fears and try to reach an understanding of how our own behaviors are reinforcing the behaviors that allowed the violence to happen in the first place. It is only then that we can, with care and concern, approach the person(s) who caused harm and tell them that we see them. It is important that they know we see them, and it is also important that they know we are working diligently to hold them accountable. If they continue to repeatedly cause harm, we have to work within our larger community resources to work together and figure out other ways to hold them accountable. By doing so, we are showing them that we love them enough and care for them enough to do this.

What can compassionate accountability look like when tackling CSA?

Compassionate accountability is—as hard as this is for me to say [*deep breath*]—recognizing that they are human first before they become rapists.

[*Deep breath. Pause. Puts hand on chest and closes eyes.*] They have a heart. We just need to understand what happened—something happened that steered them toward causing harm to someone else—and we need to help them through that.

Compassionate accountability involves us not judging but working to understand. Help me not to be afraid of you. [*Bows head down, closes eyes, places hand on forehead. Shakes head.*] Help me to not be afraid of you. Wow. That's powerful.

Can we have accountability around CSA without punitive justice?

I'm going to go back to my original point of us needing to remember that those who commit acts of child sexual abuse are human. They were not born thinking they would rape another person. They are human and have lost their way in this world. It's not to say that what they did is okay—it's not! But punishment doesn't get us healing. Humanity and love get us healing. This is not easy; it is, however, necessary.

Now let's talk about what nonpunitive accountability looks like. I'm thinking that these individuals, who sexually abuse a child should be required to give presentations or workshops to different audiences. This will not only help us community members and advocates understand better why they did what they did but will also open the door for them to go within and start to learn more about their own behaviors and how they can work toward being authentically accountable and help themselves heal in the process.

How we, as community members, can help ensure accountability transpires without punitive justice is to recognize that we have an obligation—a duty—to spread more awareness and to discuss what we learn from these experiences and processes. To go back to our families and children, to love our children enough to have a deep and meaningful dialogue on what sexual violence looks like and how we can respond to it in a collective manner which promotes healing and non-punitive justice.

What does restorative justice and/or transformative justice look like to you?

With regards to transformative justice, it is my job to keep an open mind in an effort to understand what happened. My job is to understand what it means to me—what does the violence or harm that happened mean to me and my Black community, my deaf community? And what can I do to change the conditions around the very systematic things that allowed for this violence to happen in the first place?

Restorative justice is, to me, trying to figure out: How can we earn back the trust again? What can we do to repair the harm that was done on an interpersonal level? What is my part in that process?

CHAPTER 8

Peacock Feathers and Love

An Interview with Najma Johnson

How can we transform societal understanding that accountability is a radical form of love, most especially around CSA?

First, we need to shift the way we think about violence, because all people experience violence on some level, and all people contribute to violence in some way. Hurt people hurt people. When someone hurts a child, my first thought is: "Who hurt you as a child?" And, truthfully, I grieve for the little child inside the adult survivor who causes harm to others because they don't know what love looks like. We need to show them what love looks like and help people understand that accountability is love and love is accountability; you can't have one without the other.

It is imperative that we have these conversations around accountability. We need to reframe the concept and practice of accountability as an authentic act of love where our conversations look like this:

"I see you and I'm talking to you because I love you."

"I'm holding you accountable because I love you and I know you can do better, be better."

If we, as a community, can practice showing more love, then we are actively working to reduce people's pain because most of them don't know what love looks like. When we work together to take away the pain of those whom we care about by showing love, then we are modeling what love looks like and the many different forms it takes.

Honesty is also a crucial component of this accountability process. You have to love yourself enough to be brutally honest, because this is very important to the process. Without this, accountability is superficial at best, and healing hollow.

What can compassionate accountability look like when tackling CSA?

Compassionate accountability must be selective when tackling CSA. The "deafer" or "darker" a person is—regardless if they are the survivor or the person who caused harm—the more one requires full solidarity from our community members. The compassion cannot be the same for all because the oppression faced, from a system perspective, is extremely different than for those who are "less deaf" or are lighter-skinned. The fact remains, Black and Brown lives are in danger. As such, the level of compassion must be deeper. This is not to say the accountability is lighter, but rather that the approach to the accountability must come from a place of complete solidarity.

Compassionate accountability is also recognizing that apologies may have never happened. If nobody apologizes to you, I apologize that that happened to you. Even if I am not the one who caused harm, I am still accountable on some level, and thus it is important that an apology is acknowledged.

Can we have accountability around CSA without punitive justice?

It is possible. But not now, because the legal system is what we deaf community members know. The legal system is what most people know. Regardless, those who are Black or Brown know the system is not our friend. Therein lies our eternal struggle for authentic accountability, justice, and healing. Someday . . . we can only hope, someday there will be accountability around CSA without punitive measures.

What does restorative justice and/or transformative justice look like to you?

In the most real and raw manner, if I am a person who experienced harm, I feel like people need to back the shit off and sit your damn ass down. I need to figure my shit out. Don't come to me with an "at least I tried" attitude by telling me what all my options are and that I can do this or that. If I want restorative justice, I will ask for restorative justice. But mainly, I just want to address the harm in my own ways. If I am unsuccessful in getting the person who caused harm to talk with me, then fine—at least I tried, and I am more than content with that because it still beats working through the criminal legal system. Going through the criminal legal system is something we as Black people never recover from. At least I can recover from an attempt to tell the person who caused me harm that they fucking hurt me. I can recover from them having dissed me.

Restorative justice feels very individualized, whereas transformative justice is collective. Deaf people embrace the collective model more than the individualized one. Even if people don't want restorative justice, we still *need* transformative justice; especially if we want to see less Brown and Black bodies dead, we *must* utilize transformative justice.

When I think of transformative justice, I think of a peacock—a very collective approach with each feather representing a different colorful contribution to the whole. Transformative justice is, indeed, beautiful. We all need to embrace this approach to ending violence if we want to survive this world.

CHAPTER 9

"An Outro to LILACS | Syringa vulgaris"

Thea Matthews

Take your filthy hands off me.

I SAID—Take your scarred wounded
hands off me.

Your weight has no
power over
my wobbly toddler knees.

Your old construction hands callused
with generations of incest
beatings children screaming pulverized
my amethyst flowers. How could *YOU?*

I remember choking on the size
of your retired labor-union
tongue when my gums were getting ready
to release their first set of baby
teeth.

I remember you stretching my legs
after kindergarten graduation
I stopped liking school then my tights stained
a rite of passage to the first grade.

I remember you spreading my legs
at night when Grandma went to take a
l o n g

bath. Your oldest son pulled the same move
like father like son two years later
    His gallant badge radiated from
        extinguishing fires still your son
            this firefighter used his hands to
    to burn the lips between my thighs.   Yet I

survived. A field of lilacs who
runs with the four directions.
Great Spirit oversees this Field. I

clear-out my throat
each time I taste your mucoid saliva. I

lose my appetite   when I feel
your fingers circling my soft areolas. I

smudge my body   with sage sweetgrass rose petals
    transmuting your residual sweat
        into tears leading me to the Ocean.

I scream into waves

Yemaya holds me   the shore-
line's salty foam releases my prayers.

I dive deep soar high
I unwind on the spine of a humpback whale.

Her oscillating muffled words travel miles.
Her cryptic tones swirl violet within my aura.

I DECLARE—
you

have NO
power over me!
You have NO POWER
over
me!
YOU
HAVE
NO
POWER
OVER
ME!

When dawn breaks I rise
in the direction
of the East I pick
up shovel & seeds
I sow I weep
I sow I weep I sow I weep
For many moons I renew
an ethereal field of lilacs!

Swallowtail butterflies rest
on petals pulsating purpureal shades of violet.
Leaves dance while oak trees wave their arms
in celebration. At last

I return to where I first saw her
where I first see me as a little girl
& where I tell her
I love you.

I've always loved you
& I never left you

I never will leave you.
She roams in this field.

She Rests In Power.

Thea's Rendition of Love with Accountability

Love—an undeniable enigmatic force of expression—reverberates from within and is experienced from without. Love has the power to remind people of their humanity, humble the suffering self. In my adolescence, I remember the absolute disdain for myself, because I blamed myself for what I was forced to endure early in life. I physically harmed myself as a teenager because the silence after my grandfather molested me and my uncle sexually assaulted me was unbearable. My rites of passage were incest. The bullying at school only poured salt on infected familial wounds.

The foundation of my existence had a gaping hole devoid of healthy love, let alone accountability. After disclosing to my mother that my grandfather molested me, I still found myself at my grandparent's house, seated next to him at the family's Thanksgiving dinner. The silence was excruciating. More painful than the incest itself. My grandfather died when I was in high school, and my uncle disappeared from my life. Last time I saw him was at my grandfather's funeral; he looked scared—avoided eye contact with me and barely acknowledged my presence. He is the one who has to live with himself knowing that he, an ex-firefighter, molested a young child. I don't know if my grandfather and uncle molested anyone else, but I do know my grandmother was abused, my mother was abused, and I was abused. My grandmother and mother live with untreated trauma. And my grandmother, who is ninety years old, will die with the silence of never knowing that her husband and at least one of her sons were child molesters.

Where is the accountability in that? Well, I have come to realize that, in my healing, alcoholism, addiction, and child abuse—specifically incest—run through my bloodline. If I want to live free from these diseases, I must be willing to learn how to each day genuinely love and be accountable to myself first and foremost.

Initially, I was introduced to accountability through activism. Negligence propelled me to action. I was learning how to demand through political action that state authorities and local police forces take responsibility for racial disparities and other injustices, in public education and especially in regard to the killings of unarmed Black and Indigenous people. However, I soon realized that if I want others to be accountable, I must also ensure that I am held accountable for my actions. What have I done to wrong others, including myself? And what do I have to do to keep my side of the street clean?

Growing up, I was very much a victim of my circumstances. The abuse started when I was preverbal and ended by the time I was roughly nine; the school bullying continued for many years afterward. My fundamental years of emotional and brain development were robbed. My childhood was robbed; consequently, I live with complex post-traumatic stress disorder. In spite of what I endured, I have no excuse for treating myself and others poorly. It is so easy for the hurt to hurt people. Love with accountability stops the cycle. I know.

Today my reverence for life distinguishes responsibility from control. I am responsible for my actions, but I cannot control anyone else's decision-making. I strive to cultivate conscious acts of love with accountability to continue serving myself and others. As I indicate in "LILACS," I pray, meditate, and utilize ritual as well as ceremony to continue deepening my healing. Ritual is highly important to me, because I get to ground myself in the spirituality I have, which reminds me I am not the almighty. I can't dictate how people choose to live. I can only assist in their own process of realization, I cannot force it.

Hence, I don't need an "apology" to actually heal. I don't need an external recognition to liberate myself. Amends are actually for the harm-doer, not for the one harmed. One must be willing, not forced, to amend one's past in order to welcome one's future, because coercive accountability, if you will, is very temporary and also inauthentic.

To be authentic, I am willing to engage in the lifetime practices of self-love and love with accountability. No one can will themselves into transformation. It simply comes when it comes. And the absolute truth is: I cannot force anyone else's transformation. My revolution began when I nearly jumped off the Golden Gate Bridge in 2011. Surviving that, and recognizing for the first time that I played a part in getting myself to that point, was the beginning of a long journey ahead.

Accountability must first and foremost come from within. And practicing the acts of love with accountability ultimately ensures the personal as well sociocultural transformation many of us seek in this world.

[A version of this poem and essay were first published as "*activist, poet, prison abolitionist, human rights advocate, incest and rape survivor*," in the #LoveWITH-Accountability online forum in *The Feminist Wire*, October 26, 2016.]

CHAPTER 10
Whose Child Is This? She Is Mine

e nina jay

Prologue

When I received the email from Aishah asking me to be part of the #LoveWITHAccountability online forum, my immediate answer was yes. It was unquestionable for me. I believe in Aishah's work and her intentions. I read the word "incest." I read the words "child sexual abuse." Or I believed I had. It took me days, maybe even a couple of weeks, to realize that I may not have truly heard her.

Having worked in rape crisis centers for over a decade, having written hundreds of poems about rape and incest, having performed at endless Take Back the Night marches, I thought perhaps it was possible that those words had become just words to me. Perhaps in order to do the work effectively, I'd distanced myself from them in ways I'm not aware of. Perhaps I've become numb. I thought this, at first, as I could not feel anything as I sat to write. That's what I told myself. I didn't feel anything. This wasn't true.

As the 2016 deadline approached, I felt anger. Why did I agree to do this? I didn't have time. I told myself I didn't have the patience. I told myself I had no idea what "love with accountability" means. I told myself Aishah was making me angry. She wanted too much. She's never satisfied. She's always pushing me. I told myself a lot of things, except this truth.

I was afraid to intimately engage this process because the person I felt the least accountable to had been myself. To the parts of myself that needed healing. For me it's easier to focus, fight, and love another *womon*, a community, a society. It's not difficult for me to contextualize childhood rape trauma when I'm reaching to love somebody else. I deeply understand that I still live in a myriad of silences. I still knowingly live in shame.

So, with the 2016 forum, I'd done what I've always done when dealing with childhood traumas. I'd just attach them to all the traumas and feel them together. At a point, it became clear to me that I was going to have to dig deeper. I was going to have to talk about it at the same time that I was loving and being accountable to myself. I wasn't sure I knew how to do that. I found this a stunning revelation.

I told myself it would be easy. I'd simply walk into the room where I stored all the files related to my incest and grab something quickly. That's how I talk about it in my mind. It's easier that way. Sounds like business. Almost clinical. Controllable. Contained. I expected that I would be able to just walk into the room and open a drawer, pull an old file out to send to Aishah, and simply walk back out of the room and close the door. Tightly.

As the third deadline extension approached, I awakened in the mornings telling myself I was irritated with Aishah. The truth is I wasn't irritated with Aishah. I was afraid. I was angry at her, though, perhaps, for knowing me deeply enough to know I wasn't present. Even if she didn't have the words for it, I could hear her doing her work by the tone of her voice and her emails. She was struggling, perhaps hurting. It didn't sound like she was just walking into rooms and pulling files out of drawers. If my sister isn't doing that, how could I?

I understood I was going to have to write, which, for me, meant jumping into a volcano and praying I would be able to climb back out without getting burned alive. I wasn't certain if it would be possible. I had to decide it was worth the risk. And I have decided that it *is* worth the risk. Whatever fears I have about the kind of nudity this forum demands of me, it is an opportunity for me to face them and to reach toward the possibility of my dreams, for survivors like me.

I believe that we are our most powerful when we are able to embrace every inch of ourselves. I believe our collective loving and healing lies in our ability to acknowledge who we dreamed to be, what has interrupted that dream, and who it is that we are now, as individuals and as a community. I believe it is possible to turn pain into power, and this is not a metaphor. I believe pain unspoken can never be transformed into power, and true power cannot be held inside the same hands as secrets.

Two Years Later

In late spring 2018 Aishah invited me to contribute to this anthology. I realized that what I submitted for the online forum in 2016 was not my most honest work. I felt unsettled by it. I couldn't look at it or read it once it hit the internet. I pretended it was not my story. It was not my voice. I felt like a liar because I had denied myself transparency. I knew I would have to revise or rewrite what I had previously offered.

In a way that was similar yet different from my process in 2016, there were delays on my end, followed up by multiple email, text, and phone reminders from Aishah. It took me what seemed like forever to find the words I needed to release. I had to dig through layers of pain, rage, and erasure to find them and, in some cases, breathe life back into them. You can read this as breathing *worth* back into me. I offer this work while still in the midst of this painstaking and complicated process of healing.

So now the question becomes "Who will do this writing/speaking?" As I have begun to move intentionally through my healing journey, it has become obvious to me that there is not just one entity living this life. There is the little *gurl* who was raped by her uncle and banished into the silent parts of my body, mind, and world for the last thirty-nine years. There is also the *womon* who has already survived. She is outspoken, powerful, and, out of survival, tends to ignore and silence the little *gurl*.

Each of them has very different things to say.

When I think about being accountable, I know which of us I must allow this freedom. It has to be the little *gurl*. Any other reckoning would feel hypocritical. I can't attempt to speak openly or strongly about practicing loving accountability while knowing that I'm ignoring being accountable to the child survivor within myself.

She wants to assert herself and demand some accountability—for what she suffered then and what she suffers now.

Every other person who needs to be held accountable for the blood in the *gurl*'s story is dead. I am the only one left alive. The grown *womon* who is the strong one and outspoken one. She is the one who, even now, keeps the *gurl* locked in a closet of some room inside this body.

***

A Poetic Offering

first time i notice her, she is laughing. first time i notice her, she is bleeding. first time i notice her, i don't recognize her.
there she was, in the park alone, pushing a swing that held no other child.

i ask softly, "who are you here with? where are your parents?"

she runs away from me, without answering.
the only sound she makes is laughter. the only footprints she leaves are bloody.
i do not want to follow them. i feel i have no choice.
the entire inside of my body moans. and groans. i run after her.
she is just laughing and running. this bleeding child.

blood flings itself from her body as she runs. she wants me to chase her. something in her laugh.
i can hear her laughter falling backward through the air. winding itself around her neck. through her ponytails. down her backbone. into my pain.

"whose child is this?!?"

i'm chasing and screaming questions . . .

"where is your momma?"
"where do you live?"
"why are you bleeding?
"PLEASE STOP RUNNING!"

she turns a corner i didn't see. suddenly i am standing on a city block. and night has come calling us. it is dark. i see a house.
there is only one house on this block. i approach it, terrified. it's just an old house. just a regular house. the closer i get, the darker it gets.
i walk up the stairs. the door is heavy and thick wood. there are 4 padlocks to keep me out.

i reach to knock. the door just falls. and there i stand. i'm standing in the doorway.
under my feet is glass. i notice the floor is covered with crushed glass.
i look at the windows, expecting broken. but they are not.

who lives here, i wondered. it doesn't look or smell or feel like anybody is living in here.
i have entered the house of mirrors, i think to myself.
a house with locked doors that are not locked.
a house with broken windows that are not broken.
this house isn't safe for anyone.
i have got to find this child.

"little gurl . . ." i call out. sweet but urgent.
i follow bloody footprints up a staircase. i don't know where i'm going.
i know exactly where i'm going.
i can hear her laughing, i think. or is she crying now?
i walk faster to the top of the stairs. the hallway is long with too many doors.
i can hear her laughing, i think. or is she crying now?
"LITTLE GURL! WHERE ARE YOU?"
my fingers touch each door as i pass. tiny, bloody footprints down the

hall. i know exactly where i'm going. where am i going?
i know where she is. i stop before a door where the footprints disappear. my hand rests on the doorknob. i am terrified to turn it.
i have got to get to this child. she needs help. i am the adult. i have to help her.
perhaps some other adult has hurt her. perhaps some other adult has seen her blood. perhaps some other adult left her. bleeding.
but i am who is left. i now have seen this child. i now have seen this blood. i now know who this child is.
i enter the room. the room is empty. just a closet door.
i know who this child is.
i hear giggling. or is it moaning? or is she laughing? something in her laugh. is she crying?
"little gurllll" i sing it this time. tears run down my face but i am not crying. i am slowly walking backwards, but running to the closet.
i am in agony but i have not been hurt. this house of mirrors.

i need her to come out. i silently beg her to come out. i don't want to have to open the door. i know i don't want to open the closet door.
somehow, i know, i don't wanna have to find her. i don't wanna find her. what will i see?

"little gurlllll" i sing it.

something in me knows.
she is not gonna walk out of that closet. on her own. she needs me to find her. there.
she wants me. she wants me to open. she needs me to open the door.
see where she lives. she needs me to open that door.
i am terrified to open that door. i somehow know what's behind that door.
i don't wanna see it. the mess he is making of her.
i am terrified to see it. i don't wanna see it. will never un-see it.
i have lived my whole life

trying to un-see it.
trying to un-know it.
trying to un-feel it.
this bloody life.

she wants me to know. to see. just how he hurt her. and where.
she wants to show me
perhaps
what i pretend to want to know

just where the blood is coming from

she needs me
to stop the bleeding.
wrap my hands around the open wound.
hold it tight.
look in her eyes.
make sure she knows
i am here
i won't leave her
again

promise

i will let her speak
i will let her cry
i will let her laugh, if she needs to
i will let her scream
i will dress her in clean clothes
i will slay the dragon for her
i will do what nobody ever did
i will love her more
than any dragon
i will wipe the blood from her mouth

i will let her use my throat
until i help her find her voice
i will let her tell her story
in her words

i will hold her
and rock her
and kiss her
and believe her
i will let her live
i will let her heal

[A version of the essay portion of this piece was first published as "a place to live" in the #LoveWITHAccountability online forum in *The Feminist Wire*, October 19, 2016.]

Breathe

CHAPTER 11

Becoming Each Other's Harvest

Lynn Roberts, Ph.D

Throughout my writing of this essay, I have grappled with what it means to break the silences surrounding childhood sexual abuse. My own silence began when I was around six years young and, while I have broken my silence several times since, I have retreated back into various forms of silence over the course of my fifty-eight years in this world as I know it. I am not certain if my initial silence was a response to being coerced by my brother (who is four years older) to engage in sexual acts without my consent, to the violence I witnessed almost nightly between my parents, or some combination of these events. Or maybe it was the case of child sexual abuse that shook our entire community when an eight-years-young Black girl was abducted, brutally raped, and murdered, allegedly by a Black man who was a friend of her family. She was the little sister of my first crush, the first boy I ever kissed. At the time, I was terrified that what happened to her could happen to me, to any of us Black girls. My voice became one of the few things I could control in my childhood. No one could make me speak if I did not want to. When I did finally choose to speak in public—around the age of thirteen—I spoke clearly and confidently of many things, and my parents were so pleased to hear my voice that I was not reprimanded for the occasional sprinkling of curse words (many of which I learned from them). But I still did not speak about the coerced sexual interactions between my brother and me. While I don't recall my brother ever telling me not to tell anyone, it was clear in my own mind that if I dared to tell anyone, chances were, I would not be heard or worse.

And so it goes with the power of silence to betray us. While I can now wholeheartedly embrace and endorse Audre Lorde's admonition, "Your silence will not protect you," there were times in my life when

I thought silence did protect me.[1] After I had been harmed and *did* choose to talk about it, my silence protected me from the feelings that result from not being heard. It protected me when I endured being raped while I was a college student and afraid—first for my life, and then of being blamed by my mother for being raped. Such feelings can be just as deep and soul-taking as the ones that result from not being protected from harm in the first place. To quote one of Lorde's poems: "[A]nd when we speak we are afraid our words will not be heard nor welcomed / but when we are silent we are still afraid / So, it is better to speak remembering we were never meant to survive."[2]

It took me forty-something years to share my childhood sexual abuse with my mother (I never shared about my college rape), and, just as I could have predicted, she did not hear, let alone comfort me. Instead, she expressed her anger at me for not telling her then—when I was a young child—at a time when she could have done something about it. My waiting all those years to speak about it, she reasoned, had led my brother to withdraw from the family (and specifically her) out of his supposed shame and guilt. My mother might have been right. After all, my brother did not have any contact with any of us for several years, but the only conclusion I could draw from her reaction was that my mother valued my brother more than she valued me. It was very painful and all too familiar. In my family, and in my observations of the world, Black women and girls have often been expected to put the needs of our husbands, sons, and brothers before our own. What right did I have to bring up my harm when my brother was already broken from the blatant abuse and disregard of living as a Black cis man in a white supremacist society? Of course, I knew that as a Black woman living in that same society, I had every right to bring it up, but how could I expect my mother to acknowledge my right to do so if she had not fully recognized her own?

1. Audre Lorde, "The Transformation of Silence into Language and Action" (paper delivered at the Modern Language Association's "Lesbian and Literature" panel), Chicago, Illinois, December 28, 1977; reprinted in *Sister Outsider*, 41.

2. Audre Lorde, "A Litany for Survival," *The Black Unicorn: Poems* (New York: W.W. Norton, 1995), 31–32.

With this in mind, I recently asked my mother, then eighty-six, about her own experience with child sexual abuse. I had only vague snippets of my own memory of what she told me many times during my childhood—if only to strike fear in me when going outside the house to play. She recounted for me what it felt like to be nine years old, alone and frightened as a Black girl growing up in racially segregated Los Angeles in the 1940s. I already knew that her child sexual abuse involved a White man and a stranger, not a family member. I did not know that, like me, she had never told her mother. This time, my mother and I were able to imagine together what it would be like if she *had* told someone, specifically if she had told her mother. With my urging, she practiced aloud with me what she would have wanted her mother to say to her as a child to make her feel heard, or do to assure her protection if she had broken her silence. I silently wished that my mother would ask me to do the same, but I was not prepared to break my own silence and ask for what I needed.

Accountability without Further Harm

I believe that "love with accountability" should lead us to healing and is necessary not because we wish punishment or harm to the person who has violated us, but because we seek to live in a world without child sexual abuse and other violence. In a world with "love" and "accountability," we can envision our own child self—that child who existed before the harm—or the adult we would have become if the harm had never happened to us in the first place. When we have love with accountability we can ask for what we need, even many years and decades after the harm. Through love with accountability we can envision the person who sexually abused us (or a loved one) as a child, still dwelling with us in this world (or family or community) and not burning in hell or locked up for life in a prison cell. We can see them as also capable of healing and less likely or no longer capable of causing further harm to us or anyone else.

Healing Happens in Relationship and Community

I have not felt a need to claim or to shape my own identity out of what has happened to me, or to label others based on the harm they have done to me. I do not refer to my brother as a perpetrator any more than I consider myself to be a victim or even a survivor of child sexual abuse. This does not mean that I deny his actions had a significant impact on me. Up until the child sexual abuse I experienced, I was developing what I now consider was a very healthy sense of my sexuality. I can remember masturbating without shame in private. When I was five and was caught "playing doctor" with my same-age playmates, our mothers did not shame or punish us. All that changed, and I was later shamed into silence after being told that incest was wrong—something only backwoods "PWT"[3] did (yes, back then my parents used such racialized, disparaging language), not educated Black folks like us. It did not occur to me then that because he was four years older than me, my brother was exercising power over me, and that was also wrong. I now realize that this early sexual contact without my consent might have shaped not only my intimate relationships but also most, if not all, of my subsequent personal and professional relationships. Maybe it contributed to my always being the one pursued rather than the one to initiate a relationship with someone I liked. Maybe it made me question then (and even now) whether I was sexually attracted to boys or girls, both, or neither. Surely it has contributed to my heightened ability and propensity to anticipate, empathize with, and respond to the needs of others long before my own, whether those others are family, friends, colleagues, or even strangers. Even now, I am more concerned about how my writing this *peace* will help or harm others rather than my own need to speak about this.

Twenty years before I told my mother, my brother and I talked about his abuse of me. Neither of us had the tools or the wisdom necessary to hold him accountable for his actions. With the silence finally

3. This is an acronym for the ethnic slur "poor white trash," once commonly used to refer to lower-class whites living in rural enclaves in the United States.

broken, I felt some relief, but I was not healed. I figured we would always be family and that his harmful actions, however unreconciled, would not change that. Indeed, for the second time during our adulthood, my brother has come to live with me. Had I seen him only as the perpetrator of my childhood, I am certain I would have felt unsafe welcoming him into my home, especially with my daughters, and now also my young granddaughter, living with me. Instead, I have viewed this as an ongoing opportunity for my brother and me to continue our journey toward healing from all the harm caused, witnessed, and experienced during our childhood.

That said, my practice of love with accountability requires that my granddaughters and grandsons must be given the tools they need to tell someone should their sexual and bodily autonomy ever be threatened. This should happen without stifling their natural sexual curiosity and explorations. Just as important, the adults who care for them must also be given the tools they need to hear them, to protect them, and to hold other adults accountable.

As my mother and I talked that afternoon, and on numerous occasions with my brother, I have discovered it is in these moments that all our strengths and weaknesses as individuals and as a family are revealed and healing becomes possible. When we categorize and label the members of our family and community on the sole basis of their transgressions against us, it removes the historical, familial, and social contexts in which all our human interactions occur, freezes our most horrendous actions in time, stymies our opportunities for growth, and offers little hope that we can stop or prevent future harm. The pursuit and practice of love with accountability that I continually strive for as a parent is different than what I have experienced and strive for with my brother or an elder parent. I have learned that there can be different pathways to love with accountability that are unique to each individual, each family, each community, and each set of circumstances regarding the harm. The man convicted of raping and killing the baby sister of my childhood friends was sentenced to life in prison, and he continued to claim his innocence. Six years ago, he appealed to the Supreme Court of Pennsylvania to review the case with support of DNA evidence obtained by The Innocence Project.[4] The original verdict was upheld and, unless he has since died, he is now seventy-three years old—having spent the past forty-five years in a state maximum-security prison. I wish more than anything that this beautiful Black child would have been better protected and free to walk to a friend's house in her own neighborhood without harm, as much as I certainly wish the person who sexually abused and killed her could be held accountable for his actions while also being treated for his own afflictions. He too was a child once, perhaps also sexually abused, and with a family in need of healing.

Crafting New Tools to Dismantle, Envision, and Rebuild

While we must continually strive to dismantle the patriarchy, white supremacy, misogyny, homophobia, and xenophobia that undergird childhood sexual abuse, we must simultaneously build a new foundation of families and communities strong enough to ensure the safety and well-being of all our children. Every child is not as fortunate as young Zuri to have a parent like spoken word artist and activist Staceyann Chin teaching her that "No means NO!"[5] That is what makes this anthology so critical and is why we must use every organizing, educational, cultural, artistic, and social media tool at our disposal to counter the hegemony of rape culture that pervades American society from the cradle to the grave. Let us envision a society that does not empower the carceral state to intervene in the affairs of our families and communities but instead builds Black feminist magical spaces for multigenerational families to gather and be healed from the multiple harms of systemic oppression, especially child sexual abuse. Inspired

4. Sarah Cassi, "Some Evidence Missing from Rape and Murder Case of Bethlehem Girl," *Lehigh Valley Live*, February 20, 2009, https://www.lehighvalleylive.com/northampton-county/index.ssf/2009/02/some_evidence_missing_from_rap.html.

5. "Living Room Protest III- No Means NO!," YouTube video, posted by Staceyann Chin, January 10, 2015, https://www.youtube.com/watch?v=YsaPukypOU4.

by the writings of Toni Cade Bambara and Audre Lorde and quoting one of her students, bell hooks describes this magic in her book, *Sisters of the Yam*: "healing occurs through testimony, through gathering together everything available to you and reconciling."[6]

The beauty and promise of approaching child sexual abuse as preventable, and as a family and community crisis rather than as a secret or a crime when it does happen, is that it allows us to see and embrace each person involved as wounded and in need of our support and guidance rather than our judgment and punishment. When this support is provided with love and accountability, then we are each also more capable of healing from our hurt, reconciling our anger, and further evolving as human beings. I am reminded of and take to heart the words of the poet Gwendolyn Brooks, pulled from her powerful ode to freedom fighter Paul Robeson:

> that we are each other's
> harvest:
> we are each other's
> business:
> we are each other's
> magnitude and bond.[7]

[A version of this essay was first published in the #LoveWITHAccountability online forum in *The Feminist Wire*, October 28, 2016.]

6. bell hooks *Sisters of the Yam: Black Women and Self-Recovery* (Boston: South End Press, 1993), 17.
7. Gwendolyn Brooks. *Family Pictures* (Detroit: Broadside Press, 1971), 19.

CHAPTER 12

Pops'nAde

A Courageous Daughter and Her Non-Abusive Father on Loving Lessons, Living Legacies (L)earned after Sexual Abuse

Adenike A. Harris and Peter J. Harris

I am looking . . . to a new and different future in which fathers are whole enough to love their sons and their daughters, to anchor them in trust and security, and to affirm them in the dreams and identities they claim in the free space of independence and wholeness.

—Gloria Wade-Gayles, *Father Songs: Testimonies by African-American Sons and Daughters*

And if there ain't no beauty / you gotta make some beauty.

—Earth, Wind & Fire, "All About Love"

Our Healing Questions

What could a father and daughter write, which dialogue could a biological father have with his youngest daughter, that would adequately confront the root shock of her rape by a stepfather? How could we ethically convert our rage into a story that wouldn't be ruined by a subsonic rant against whatever god or devil could allow a child's safety to be destroyed in her own home? How could our deep communion with such painful emotional wounds open the door to an even richer revelation between us so that we can actually control the impact of evil on our futures?

A Healing Call-and-Response

Ade [Adenike Harris]: The only way to heal through things is to communicate and to talk. Without words, there is no real connection. This relationship has been built on communication. It was always there, but it got deeper when I shared my experience, my trauma. Also, it shifted, and got deeper, when I was able to tell you what I need and what I wanted. That I didn't want you to lead with your reaction.

Pops [Peter J. Harris]: You gotta figure out a way to find words and, as an adult, to integrate even challenging stuff, even ugly stuff, dangerous stuff, that could suck you down, you know, into a hole. And I mean an h-o-l-e, not a w-h-o-l-e.

Ade: But our relationship is fun, it's friendly; it's also real. I mean we definitely have had an argument. There are moments where, like, I still find myself as "the daughter." I still find myself as the child. I sometimes find that I remind myself, *Oh, you are an adult.* You can say what you want to say but still have the respect, still have, as I've learned, the *home training*—like I know what *not* to say. I ain't crazy. That is the difference of us as adults, Pop'nAde, versus like me being younger and getting my hair braided.

Pops: On a simple level, I am my daughter's father. I really love her. I want to see her succeed as a grown, successful adult. That's important for me to say. So "Pops'nAde" is not some brand! She calls me Pops. That's how I sign my emails to her or when I've written her letters. Or when I leave long-winded voicemails, I tell her, "Hey, it's Pops, what's happening?" So I think what I contribute is a loving, male power. A tender masculinity.

Ade: I love his conversation, his compassion. What I keep with me all the time is knowing that no matter what, I know that I can call him. I know that he will answer. And even if he doesn't, he'll always call me back. But the thing I love most, and the thing that I keep with me always, is literally that he's just Pops. That he is unwavering. That he is there, he doesn't shift. He's consistent. He's my dude. He's my dude!

Interlude

We tell folks that after experiencing sexual violence, you don't get to where we've gotten without confronting everything that scares you. You've got to engage with each other way beyond your comfort levels. We tell folks that only doing the real work—through tears, candor, imagination, even hard-won laughter—rewards you with Loving Lessons and Living Legacies. Learning and earning go hand in hand! After Adenike revealed her criminal ex-stepfather had sexually abused her from ages fourteen to twenty-two, every step we've taken since then has been in the spirit of "Lift Every Voice and Sing." Our goal is to be twenty-first century conversation starters and healing partners. We want to be living examples whose powerful service offers a roadmap to rich, loving, and inspiring non-abusive relationships. We want to embody our motto: "We're all worth healing, and no silence is good that keeps you from talking to people who can help you."

Pops: I was devastated. The guy who I had met, and who I thought was a good man, whose hand I shook, that guy had violated my child? I was insane. And I felt violated in a different way. Black man to Black man, I shook this guy's hand. I was back in DC. We were at a baseball game for my son. This guy came up to me. He shook my hand. He said, "Peter, I just want you to know, I'm not trying—" I remember this like it was yesterday: "Peter, I'm not trying to replace you with your children." You know, *blah, blah, blah*. Then I learned what Ade had experienced, and the havoc that he had wreaked in their household! I had visited their home. I had a meal in their home. I felt like I had been disrespected. You know, my daughter was criminally assaulted, but I felt like, as a fellow brother, I was treated with total disrespect. He was masquerading and fooled all us.

Ade: Speaking up finally was scary. It was not something that I wanted to do, but it was a need inside of me; I needed to tell. I needed to change my life. I couldn't live with pretending, and it was scary. I mean, that's the only word that I have for it. You always have doubts that your family won't believe you. You have doubts that other people won't believe you. You have doubts that you'll be judged, but I just trusted what was placed inside of me. I just trusted that my mom would believe me, my dad would believe me, and a change would be made.

I went through blaming myself, feeling guilty, feeling like I did something to deserve this. Or maybe I was a bad kid—especially fourteen to eighteen, it was like, *Well, what am I doing that makes this man think this is okay?* But then not feeling strong enough, because, well, my mom trusts him, and he's not like everybody else. He's not hitting me. He's not beating me. I'm living in the middle-class . . . in this upper-middle-class family in Prince George's County. People look at us like, "Oh, we're the Black Brady Bunch!" We were this blended family, and I just went through a lot of, like, caring about everyone else but myself.

Pops: My daughter asked me not to do anything. When she testified about what had happened to her, she made me understand that was her most profound wish. She said, "Dad, I want you to be my father, again, in a deeper way." And so that was the easiest decision at that point. As I say, I'm not a gangster, so, my first reaction to trauma was not to suddenly become a dude who can wreak trauma on somebody else. Furthermore, and in a deeper way, as I began to really, really engage with you, it just became that much more important to see the work I had to do with you was a part of my journey to be a whole, healthy human being, a whole healthy Black man who is all about survival with grace, and joy, and happiness.

Interlude

Pops'nAde, father and daughter, Black father, Black daughter—our work to answer our healing questions will take the rest of our lives. But our lives will not be defined by our work to answer these healing questions. We've chosen to devote most of our work to living and loving and dedicating ourselves to futures of joy and inspiration, and loving lessons we've learned and living legacies we've earned.

We started by confronting the acts of a criminal predator, prosecuting and convicting him, swearing off revenge at Adenike's insistence and direction, then igniting a transcendent conversation that has excavated all our fears, explored and confronted the history of our nuclear and extended families, while simultaneously tapping the energy we needed to make—and be available to—beauty in our lives.

In all honesty, we do not want to talk about sexual trauma in our family—neither what Adenike had to confront from ages fourteen to twenty-two, nor the grand and intimate reverberations that we confront in real time every day. We wish that we were an anonymous daughter and her father living quiet lives of satisfaction and simplicity. We wish our lives hadn't been tainted, if not cursed, by the manipulations of a criminal masquerading as a doting suburban father and husband.

But in the words of our elders: what don't kill you makes you stronger! So we lift our voices to sing; we speak because we must, and we speak without shame, trepidation, or doubt that we have a right to express ourselves.

Ade: It's God. It's a purpose that I know was placed in me, because I always thought, just like I believe all survivors do, "Why *me*? What did *I* do?" And it was really brought clear to me, and God was like, "You didn't do anything. I need you to be an advocate, to be a voice, to show strength, to speak for those who have no voice." I knew that there were children who were experiencing abuse and sexual assault and rape. But I also never connected to them, so my motivation, or what forced me, or pushed me to bring my story forward, outside of just my family, was that there was also someone else who doesn't have the family that I have. Who doesn't have the support system that I had. And that person may need a voice. That person may need to know that they're not alone.

I wanted to make myself as unattractive as possible, so I was super tomboyish—big clothes, baggy jeans. I mean I went through so much. My feelings of self-worth, not feeling worthy. It was hell! It was an experience that I think a lot of survivors experience. You internalize it. I compartmentalized my life. I disassociated during the abuse. I'd literally leave my body. I would think about other things. "Ah, let's get it over with, so then I could go back to living regular life."

Like, to me, the abuse wasn't real. As I got older, maybe like from eighteen to twenty-two, I was full of anger—I would fight more. I would demand space. I would yell at my stepfather more. It would always just become volatile. It became more like a protection of my body. Like there was still a lot of shame, a lot of guilt, a lot of feeling like I prompted this. I was the cause of all of this. Until that pivotal moment at twenty-two, when I was like "No!" I was shown things, and given strength internally, from a place that I can't pinpoint. I can't say one thing did it. So I attribute it to my spiritual self. God was like: "Now is the time! Now is the time to step forward. Start with your mom. Start with yourself. Rebuild relationships." And I just know without a shadow of a doubt that it was just God's way of redirecting to get me to where I needed to be.

Interlude

Our dialogue helped Ade discern that her development should include more profound service to others. In 2015, Adenike was certified as an Integral Coach by New Ventures West, School of Professional Coaches, in San Francisco, California. She is a Whole Living Coach, helping clients heal core issues and negative patterns while empowering them with effective "integrative" tools, techniques, and specific action plans to make effective changes in order to cultivate mental, emotional, spiritual, and physical wellness.

As a father, fully engaged in a necessary, risky, dialogue where nothing is taboo, Peter has insisted on cultivating his own mental, emotional, spiritual, and physical wellness. Part of keeping his own balance was creating the Black Man of Happiness Project (www.Blackmanofhappiness.com) and writing his book *The Black Man of Happiness: In*

Pursuit of My "Unalienable Right," an unprecedented meditation on Black men and joy, which was awarded the American Book Award in 2015. His poetic personal essays range in scope from Thomas Jefferson's era to the Digital Age, seeking to answer the simple, provocative question: what is a happy Black man? Peter devotes a chapter titled "Learning the Language of My Daughter's Hair" to sharing how he "learned that happiness pulses even within the seams of what's unthinkable."

Frankly, we have recognized that our healing style represents the temperaments of two folks who are fighters, who refuse to allow a criminal any kind of victory in our lives. Our way may not work for others grappling with the legacies of sexual trauma in their lives. For us, however, for Pops'nAde, we are exhilarated by the most amazing lesson we've learned from our tears, candor, and imagination: no silence is good that keeps us from talking to people who can help us.

And *we*, it turns out, have become our most inspiring conversation partners. We are living examples of a father embracing ethical, dynamic parenting and a daughter claiming her daddy, her father, her Pops. We are living, breathing examples of how one family is living out—day by day, with stops and starts, without a single request for interpersonal refund—an actual, non-abusive relationship, even though our DNA includes the pain of sexual trauma that was imposed on us.

It's our hope that we can offer a rich, loving road map for others on their journeys to nourishing, non-abusive relationships.

Ade: Working with you, Pops—it's just real. It is the realist of the real. It is conversation, and it is grounded in honesty, truth, and trust. I trust you, you trust me. I can tell you whatever I want. I don't tell you everything. But I can—that's the point, that I really know I can.

Pops: Look, if you can tell me what you told me about your fake stepfather, criminal stepfather, then you can tell me anything.

You know, I'm a literary man. I'm a storyteller. I'm a myth-maker. And I understand that human lives, you know, are made through how you handle your obstacles in life. I'm from the old school. You know, "keep on pushin'," that's what Curtis Mayfield said. You come up to the big wall, you either go through it or you go around it or you help each other climb it. Learn from the overlap. Because life is lived in overlap. It's lived at the same time. Live your whole life. As you know, I'm an ex-shortstop, so I love saying, "Play to the end of the game."

Ade: Or as a track athlete, you run to the tape. You never stop before the line. You run all the way. You don't ever stop before the line.

Pops: That's right. You play the whole game and you play to win.

Ade: Right.

[In 2011, Adenike completed her master's thesis in women's studies at Georgia State University. *Restorative Notions: Regaining My Voice, Regaining My Father: A Creative Womanist Approach to Healing from Sexual Abuse* is available at https://scholarworks.gsu.edu/cgi/viewcontent.cgi?referer=&httpsredir=1&article=1023&context=wsi_theses. Adenike and Peter's 2018 TEDx Pasadena Talk, *Healing vs. Retaliation: Surviving Trauma and Sexual Abuse,* is available at https://www.youtube.com/watch?v=Gpt7b_KfIZU.]

CHAPTER 13

Love-Centered Accountability

Dr. Danielle R. Moss

Childhood sexual abuse. The words sit still, dank and sickening in my throat. Childhood sexual abuse. It is the violation that breaks, upends, and cripples those of us who are survivors. Barely old enough to name our hands and feet and arms and toes. Barely old enough to spell our names and write our names in print. However, for some, we were just old enough . . . When I see it abbreviated to "CSA," my quivering stomach quiets a bit; the acronym gives me the distance I need to speak life into a new world order—where children are safe and free and thriving. Like many survivors, I learned early on not to talk about this pain out loud to anyone, not to name the offender, because it was a pang of guilt, a sick kind of unholy covenant, that we now shared together. I learned early on what it means to be silent, tight-lipped, isolated, and broken.

CSA is the dirty secret we gift to our children through our silence, our rage, our shame—over generations. Whether the abusers are family members, family friends, or authority figures with access to our children, we teach our young ones that sex and feelings and bodies don't make for polite conversation. We give their genitalia nicknames. And, though we have created a sexualized world—a world that has few spaces where children can live free from gender roles, our fraught notions of sexuality, and our mixed cultural signals about sex—we struggle to speak its existence and create healthy pathways to sexual identity.

The reality is that despite our contrived sexual conservatism, sometimes—and for the worst reasons—childhood and sex come together. Moreover, the resulting wounds live on as permanent scars because we teach our children that the things that cut into them the most must not be named, spoken of, or confronted. In fact, most of the cultural lexicon on American childhood pivots around the notion that children are powerless, and the social arrangement relies on children's ability to submit to and recognize authority. In many communities of color, the mantra that "children should be seen and not heard" is not just a funny quip we overheard our grandmothers say—we live by a code that promotes the invisibility of our kids, and that devalues their voices and experiences even when their lives depend on their views being heard.

So what does this mean with regard to loved-centered accountability? Most of us don't understand what "love-centered accountability" means, because, when it comes to accountability, the themes of punishment and pain and discipline are central to our culture. How many of us when we were growing up heard parents say they beat us out of love? We condition our kids to a love/pain connection early on that leads to the acceptance of all kinds of emotional and physical violence because they don't know the difference. Our propensity for using embarrassment and humiliation to solicit compliance and cooperation from our children is another reason we are challenged by love-centered accountability. At home, in school, and even through social media, part of the way we solicit children's cooperation and obedience is by the fear of public shame. The social contract we've created with our children makes it incredibly difficult to initiate conversations and communication that could actually keep our children safe. Ironically, the shame that even parents and other protectors experience about childhood sexual abuse undermines people's ability to protect children adequately.

Our concepts of healthy sexuality and how to hold people accountable in a way that doesn't leave us owning their sins make some children's brave disclosures fall on deaf ears. Many survivors talk about the added isolation and rejection they experienced as their brave disclosures went unrecognized. Did my mother, grandmother, father really not believe me, or did they see my violation as a commentary on their ability to adequately protect me? The denial and rejection of brave disclosure are rooted in the same concepts of shame and fear that make it so difficult for victims to come forward in the first place. Beyond our failure as a society to adequately address CSA as a problem that cuts across race and class, the reality is that even what goes unnoticed, unacknowledged, and unrecognized grows roots that sprout and expand and incapacitate our children as they climb toward adulthood.

A few years ago, I heard a comedian call out childhood sexual abuse in an arena full of thousands of people. He was talking about a well-known rape case that had dominated the coverage of several news outlets, and he said, "Some of you defending this dude are still scared to go to the family cookout because you know you're going to see that molester relative there." The crowd swayed, laughing/not laughing, in palpable discomfort. The joke suggests that accountability is entirely out of the question, that the spiritual imbalance of secrecy and shame are members of the tribe and wedded to our identities. The social contract for CSA survivors and perpetrators—even when they embody the same beings—is silence and distance. What do you do when the people who hurt you the most are part of the very fabric and foundation of your life, or at the very least people whose power and authority you may have to negotiate again? What do you do when their stories, joys, tears, faith, misery are all entwined in the heartbeat of your life?

We don't understand accountability and love as the same, because we are a crime-and-punishment society. We define and confine people by their worst actions without a road map leading back to restoration and redemption. Thus, we make the process of accepting accountability an unimaginable risk because repentance can never interrupt the abuser identity. This is the dilemma we are facing on the public stage of sexual assault accountability. Is shunning and punishment at the beginning or the end of the story?

Living in a punitive, crime-and-punishment society makes the idea of "love with accountability" almost unimaginable. What on earth would be unearthed if we began to explore this notion in the context of child sexual abuse? However, everything we live through, we have created. Moreover, we are always more than capable of creating something different, something courageous. We can tackle our private spaces on this issue in ways that lead to healing and restoration when restoration is possible. This requires brave disclosure, confession, a commitment to acknowledge hurts and to right wrongs, tangible restitution, and a release from shame. We also have the opportunity to engage in broader, public conversations that allow survivors and abusers and those indirectly affected by CSA to engage in dialogue without the fear, exposure, and judgment that can come with brave disclosure. Creating a shame-free discourse on childhood and power, sexuality and sexual identity, and bodies and consent is central to clearing the way for love with accountability.

Accountability is a way of loving ourselves and being in meaningful relationship and connection with others after the storm. Love makes space for truth, and the truth is the only way toward restorative reconciliation. This is particularly important in cases when abusers and survivors continue to be in a relationship. Restorative reconciliation says, "You did this to me, you are sorry, and neither of us has to be defined by the worst thing you ever did." Truth makes forgiveness, even when it is not requested, possible. Love knows that truth is sometimes a one-sided conversation. It means that survivors must love themselves unconditionally, courageously, and entirely because of who they are, and not because of or in spite of what they've endured.

[A version of this essay was first published in the #LoveWITHAccountability online forum in *The Feminist Wire*, October 17, 2016.]

CHAPTER 14

Self-Love with Accountability

CeCelia Falls

I have been accused of living in the past when I disclose my being a survivor of childhood sexual abuse. The ease with which I now disclose having been raped as a child by an adult male family member is uncomfortable for many people to hear, even when we are actually talking about incidents of childhood rape. Sometimes there is an audible gasp, accompanied by a physical pulling back. Often there is simply silence or a cliché offered to pack up the disclosure. Something like: "You have to stop living in the past," or, "It's time you got over that and moved on."

Our personal histories, like our collective histories, are living things. They shape our present and, if left unexamined and untended, lay the foundation for our future. As people of African descent in the United States, we are all too familiar with the results of erasing uncomfortable history. How is it then that we can't see that these outcomes show up in our own families when we attempt to do the same things with our personal histories? Like the white supremacist resistance to toppling Confederate statues, we too resist toppling the illusions of our community and our family lives.

These illusions allow childhood sexual abuse to continue in our homes, churches, schools, and other community spaces. We suffer from a societal disconnect from the reality of childhood sexual abuse—its nature, prevalence, and impact on the survivor, families, and community at large. I find this response both common and odd. Common because childhood sexual abuse is an uncomfortable, ugly, and painful reality. Why would we want to delve into this horror? Odd because, though it is all of those things, it is an incredibly common occurrence, across cultures and socioeconomic groups. So why are we still so silent?

Some will point to the books, movies, talk shows, and so on that have addressed childhood sexual abuse as indicators that we aren't as silent as we were in previous years. There are also a number of celebrities who have disclosed about the sexual abuse they experienced as children. Yet there is still an air of secrecy and shame that pushes many survivors back into the silence they bravely escaped. There is very little room for dealing with the ongoing consequences of abuse for the survivor in real life.

Part of the problem is the centering of the perpetrator in the response. It's understandable—to a degree. We can all agree that raping children is horrific. Something should be done about it, and children should be safe from this type of soul-killing abuse. Punishing the perpetrator becomes the immediate goal to address the issue. While this is important, it does little to address the long-term impact of the abuse on the survivor—another one of those things that is odd to me, given how we admit that there are long-term effects, but so little is done to address them.

My work is centered on survivors and what happens after disclosure, when there is a trial—or no trial at all, which is more often the case. How do we heal? How do we actually negotiate those "long-term effects?" How do we "move on"? Like many survivors of childhood sexual abuse, I continue to discover what healing means, looks like, and feels like on a day-to-day basis. Though I have an advanced degree in counseling, I don't come to this work with all of the answers of an expert. I come as a sister-survivor seeking to create a life I love and that works for me. Surviving, healing, and thriving is at the core.

On my healing journey, being in community with other survivors and expressing myself artistically has been critical. Having a community helps to end the stigma and shame that often comes with identifying as a survivor. I started the volunteer group Harlem SUN (Souls United to Nurture), to support survivors of African descent and to raise awareness about the nature, prevalence, and impact of childhood sexual abuse in Black communities. We use the arts to give voice, exposure, and momentum to our experiences as survivors. We are also committed to nurturing ourselves, our families, and communities to create a world free from sexual violence. Clearly, this is a lofty goal, but it can't be done in silence or without a loving accountability to ourselves as survivors.

I am reminded of an initial session I had with a new therapist. After that introductory question, "So what brings you in today?," I quickly laid out my history, including being a survivor. I recounted all the incidents to "prove it," crossed my arms, and waited for her response. I could read the discomfort in her face and body, but it was different than what I had previously experienced.

She began with her concern for *me*, noting my lack of emotion as I recounted the horrors inflicted upon my ten-year-old self. Her discomfort was in the acknowledgment of how disconnected I was from the impact of my own history of abuse. That discomfort came from knowing the costs of disconnection from the self, from the body. And I was paying for it. Up until that point, I had not allowed myself to feel anything—especially not anger. I was so out of touch with myself that it was difficult for me to meet my own needs. I've since learned that this is not uncommon behavior.

So when asked to address "love with accountability," I begin with the love of self, which is something denied to, and also denied by, many survivors. For me, self-love and self-care is more than pampering. It is connecting with the self on every level—mind, body, and soul—and with meeting the needs of the self. When we disclose the abuse we experience as children, and the abuse is allowed to continue or we must continue to interact with our abusers, we receive the message that our safety and our needs are not important. It is a message that occurs so early in life that, tragically, for many of us it becomes a core truth, even if we can't articulate it. Our healing begins with the awareness that we are valuable, mind, body, and soul.

Our wounded parts are owed acknowledgment as well as healing. We deserve it, and we can't wait for the rest of the world to catch up to us. Yes, we need to hold perpetrators accountable for their acts, but it doesn't end there. That is just a first step. From my survivor perspective, it's not even the most important step. "Love with accountability" is giving survivors permission to love ourselves to health and the full good lives we deserve. "Love with accountability" is supporting the work of survivors to heal and end abuse. "Love with accountability" is every member of the community committing to the safety of our children and the healing of all survivors, regardless of our age or stage of life.

[A version of this essay was first published in the #LoveWITHAccountability online forum in *The Feminist Wire*, October 25, 2016.]

CHAPTER 15

In My Mother's Name

Restorative Justice for Survivors of Incest

Liz S. Alexander, MA, MSW

> *"____________: I, Marla request that you no longer appear at my home due to past crime committed to self—lasting several years, non-provoked; Crime consisting of both physical and sexual abuse. When in your presence you are not to put your hands on me in any shape or form. Because of you, I have suffered detrimental effects, which have intruded constantly into my life, affecting me as a woman and human being."*[1]

I am the daughter of a survivor of physical and sexual abuse.

During my mother's childhood and all throughout her adolescence, she was repeatedly abused physically and sexually by her older brothers. All of whom have never been held accountable for their actions. All of whom have been and continue to be protected by the pervasive silence, secrecy, avoidance, and denial that seem to be entrenched in my Black family.

As early as eight years old, I can recall my mother, Marla, telling my brother and me about her experiences of sexual and physical abuse during her childhood at the hands of her brothers. Coming from a home of parental absenteeism and neglect, my mother figured her only form of escape from the abuse was becoming pregnant at age sixteen by a boy from whom she "sought emotional comfort." In my mother's attempt to tell me of her abuse, I was unable to fully grasp the depth of what had happened to her. At the time, I couldn't even begin to conceptualize the abhorrent act of sexual violence. However, I was acutely aware that her experience shaped how she chose to mother me, her only daughter. I can recall that, regardless of my mother's financial status as a single parent raising four children, at

1. Correspondence from Liz Alexander's family archives.

each place we lived, I always had my own room. Even if it meant that my brothers went without one. Additionally, my mother was attentive to what I wore, and she was extremely sensitive to how boys and men reacted to me in public—especially since I always presented older than what I was because of my Amazonian physique. In one case, I can vividly remember my mother confronting a man in public who had attempted to engage with me inappropriately.

Unfortunately, my mother's experience of physical and sexual abuse is not unique. According to statistics on sexual abuse gathered by the Department of Justice, an estimated one in four girls and one in six boys are sexually abused before the age of eighteen.[2] And, according to RAINN (Rape, Abuse, & Incest National Network), in 93 percent of sexual abuse cases, the perpetrators of the abuse are a family member or someone the victim knows.[3] For Black women and girls, 60 percent of Black girls experience sexual assault by the time they reach eighteen, and for every Black woman who reports her sexual assault, there are at least fifteen who do not, according to the preliminary findings by Black Women's Blueprint.[4] Additionally, given the legacy of historical trauma in the Black experience in the United States, coupled with the incessant subjection to violence and victimization under a white supremacist, capitalist, and patriarchal regime, Black women and girls are often shamed into silence out of the need to sacrifice themselves, in order to protect the "Black race."

In her book *No Secrets, No Lies: How Black Families Can Heal from Sexual Abuse*, Robin D. Stone identifies the following as the cultural taboos and social dynamics that Black women and girls have to navigate, in addition to the sexual abuse they endure, when confronted with incest and other forms of child sexual abuse in a familial context:

2. "Facts and Statistics: Raising Awareness about Sexual Abuse," U.S. Department of Justice, National Sex Offender Public Website, https://www.nsopw.gov/(X(1)S(vmi4f5n2fxkhdqbyk2bvvvxz))/en/Education/FactsStatistics.

3. RAINN, "Children and Teens: Statistics," https://www.rainn.org/statistics/children-and-teens.

4. Black Women's Blueprint is a transnational Black feminist organization. For more information, see http://Blackwomensblueprint.org; see also Black Women's Blueprint's "The Truth Commission on Black Women and Sexual Violence," 2012.

- Fear of betraying family by turning offenders in to "the system"
- Distrust of institutions and authority figures, such as police officers
- Reluctance to seek counseling or therapy
- A legacy of enslavement and stereotypes about Black sexuality[5]

Given this, to appropriately support Black women and girls who are survivors of incest and other forms of child sexual abuse within the familial context, in my experience, it is imperative that a restorative justice healing framework be realized and implemented, where the needs of women and girl survivors are centered.

In my personal experience, despite the physical and sexual abuse my mother endured at the hands of her brothers, in her adulthood she maintained contact with them. In fact, during my childhood she allowed my siblings and me to spend the night in their homes unmonitored. Granted, by this time, her brothers had families of their own. And when I went to their homes, I was neither harmed, nor did I ever fear for my safety. I say this to point out that in my Black family, where abuse was and still may be present, the survivors and perpetrators are in contact with each other. And if contact is inevitable, it should be done so in a restorative justice context.

Restorative justice (RJ) is an Indigenous practice that has been used to mediate conflict for centuries. However, as a Westernized theoretical concept it was introduced in the 1990s by John Braithwaite, Howard Zehr, and Mark Umbreit, among others. RJ is a nonpunitive process that seeks to mediate conflict between victims, offenders, and the community at large. The purpose of RJ is to heal the harm and foster rehabilitation for all parties involved. Moreover, for families, RJ involves "acknowledgment of fault by the offender (and family); restitution of some sort to the victim, including both affective apologies

5. Robin D. Stone, *No Secrets, No Lies: How Black Families Can Heal from Sexual Abuse* (New York: Broadway Books, 2004).

and material exchanges or payments; new mutual understandings; forgiveness; and an agreement for new undertakings for improved behaviors."[6] Rather than isolating offenders, RJ reconnects them back to the family while also holding them accountable.

Additionally, if RJ is to become an effective framework for Black families to heal survivors, offenders, and the entire family from sexual violence, as well as to dismantle familial sexual violence, the healing needs of Black women and girls must be centered. When Black women and girls are centered in this process, RJ creates the space where they are empowered to decide what justice is. They also have the power to choose to forgive and accept restitution or reconciliation (or not), as well as to choose what they think is the proper balance between reconciliation and family peace. And the first step to centering the needs of Black women and girls is to believe them.

Unfortunately, my mother will never have the opportunity to experience the process of RJ because she died prematurely as a result of negative life outcomes that were a direct result of her childhood experiences of physical and sexual violence. However, she devoted the latter part of her life to healing herself, reclaiming her power, confronting her abusers, and raising a daughter who would one day call out and disrupt the pervasive silence, secrecy, avoidance, and denial regarding physical and sexual abuse that seem to be entrenched in her Black family.

I am the daughter of a survivor of physical and sexual abuse,
And
I claim healing in my mother's name.

[This essay was first published in the #LoveWITHAccountability online forum in *The Feminist Wire*, October 24, 2016.]

6. Katherine von Wormer, "Restorative Justice: A Model for Social Work Practice with Families," *Families in Society* 84, no. 3 (2003), https://sites.uni.edu/vanworme/articles/restorativefamilies.pdf.

Breathe

CHAPTER 16

The Coiled-Spring First Grader Deep Inside

Sexual Violence and Restorative Justice

Dr. Sikivu Hutchinson

Why should we believe her? She's not a white girl. Hers is not the life story that the media makes visible as gospel, tragedy, and redemption story. If she comes forward, she could jeopardize her family, its livelihood, and its standing in the community. Besides, the real issues that we should be most concerned about are racism, deadly force, and the military presence of police in our neighborhoods. Rape and sexual assault are white preoccupations that distract, because "if you loved your community, you would be silent."

In the toxic litany of messages that Black female victims and survivors receive about sexual assault, this last is one of the most soul-killing and the most deadly. I have written often about how, when I was sexually assaulted as an elementary school student, there was no language, program, or messaging that existed to make my experience visible. I have written less frequently about the shame and disassociation I still feel toward the child who it happened to, the coiled-spring first grader nestled deep inside, the one who loved handball, the swings, *Electric Company*, and *Golden Legacy* comic books.

On the block, in our neighborhood, silence was required for daily survival. Silence meant allegiance to Black men and boys splayed in the white man's radar scope; it meant tacit recognition of their greater suffering, their greater historical sacrifice. Even now, as the political landscape has shifted with the white feminist mainstreaming of the #MeToo Movement, originally created by Black feminist activist Tarana Burke for Black and Latinx girls—and as critiques of campus rape, rape culture, and victim-blaming inform mainstream discussions about sexual assault—the specific context of Black girls' experiences is absent from national policy discourse.

The discrediting of Black girls' experiences starts in preschool and kindergarten, where they are taught to endlessly check, police, and second-guess themselves. It is symbolized by the hand games that are deemed too aggressive, the dancing that is too "sexual," the "signifying" that is too loud and disrespectful, and the outfits that the white and Latina girls can wear without getting sent to the dean's office. It is due in part to this context that, although Black women have some of the highest rates of intimate partner violence and sexual assault, we are the least likely to report having been victimized.[1] Even considering the ways in which fear of policing and criminalization in white-supremacist capitalist patriarchy hinders us, there is the trauma of constant vilification from within.

The Black church has always played a key role in enforcing this regime of silence. Because this institution is one of the most devoutly religious communities in the United States, heterosexist and homophobic attitudes among Black folk often perpetuate stigmas against the sexuality of Black women and LGBTQ folk.[2] Biblical references to women as property, rape objects, seducers, and subordinates who should remain "silent" are still deeply ingrained among folk who attend churches where the public face of leadership and authority is straight, cis, and male.

When the Women's Leadership Project does sexual violence prevention work with high school students, we begin by talking about the destructive power of misogynoir within the context of their everyday teen lives.[3] It seems as though new terms are coined every month to

1. Gail Wyatt, "The Sociocultural Context of African American and White American Women's Rape," *Journal of Social Issues* 48, no. 1 (1992): 77–91; Robin D. Stone, *No Secrets, No Lies: How Black Families Can Heal from Sexual Abuse* (New York: Broadway Books, 2004), 1–10; *NO! The Rape Documentary.*

2. Theola Labbé-DeBose, "Black Women Are among Country's Most Religious Groups," *Washington Post*, July 6, 2012; Pew Religion Research Forum, "A Religious Portrait of African-Americans," January 23, 2009, http://pewforum.org/2009/01/30/a-religious-portrait-of-african-americans.

3. Founded by Sikivu Hutchinson, the Women's Leadership Project is a feminist mentoring, civic engagement, and service learning advocacy program designed to educate and train young middle- and high school–age women in South Los Angeles to take ownership of their school communities. For more information, see https://www.womensleadershipla.org/. The term "misogynoir" originated with Black feminist Moya

smear Black girls' sexuality. Over the past few weeks, the term "gerb" has become popular, joining "ho," "thot," "ratchet," and umpteen other epithets designed to check the "hypersexual," "unfeminine" behavior of Black girls. Of course, mainstream vocabulary has always been boundlessly creative when it comes to demonizing women's sexuality. Walking students through the historical context of these terms (e.g., the way "wench," and "Jezebel" were used to justify the rape of Black women under slavery by branding them as hypersexual breeders) is critical to providing youth with context about the relationship between racist, misogynist representations of Black women in the past and that of the present. Here rape culture has foundations in the white supremacist imagination, which are then reinforced by obstructionist policies regarding prosecution, law enforcement investigations, and inadequate rape kit testing, all of which make it more difficult for sexual assault survivors to come forward.[4]

Moreover, the connection between the sexualization of Black girls and criminalization cannot be overstated. A 2017 Georgetown University study entitled *Girlhood, Interrupted* examines the ways in which Black girls are widely perceived as more mature, less innocent, and in less need of protection than white girls.[5] According to the report, Black girls are routinely "adultified," potentially leading to harsher punishment by adults in the education system and "more punitive exercise of discretion . . . greater use of force, and harsher penalties" by authorities in the juvenile justice system. The Georgetown findings are hardly revelatory for Black girls and women who have lived this experience for centuries. That said, they powerfully illustrate

Bailey. It "describes the particular brand of hatred directed at Black women in American visual and popular culture." Moya Bailey, "They Aren't Talking about Me," *Crunk Feminist Collective*, March 14, 2010, http://www.crunkfeministcollective.com/2010/03/14/they-arent-talking-about-me.

4. Human Rights Watch, *Capitol Offense: Police Mishandling of Sexual Assault Cases in the District of Columbia*, January 24, 2013, https://www.hrw.org/report/2013/01/24/capitol-offense/police-mishandling-sexual-assault-cases-district-columbia.

5. Rebecca Epstein, Jamilia J. Blake, and Thalia González, *Girl Interrupted: The Erasure of Black Girls' Childhood*, Georgetown Law Center on Poverty and Inequality, August 2017, https://www.law.georgetown.edu/poverty-inequality-center/wp-content/uploads/sites/14/2017/08/girlhood-interrupted.pdf.

how these negative perceptions contribute to higher rates of suspension, expulsion, pushout, and incarceration among Black girls.[6] The perception of Black girls as more adult-like and mature also influences the way they are perceived as sexually available, "fast," and promiscuous—the antithesis of "feminine," "innocent" white girls.

During a recent Women's Leadership Project and Young Male Scholars' peer education training with members of the football team at a South LA high school, it was clear that the demonization of Black girls' sexuality played a key role in boys' inability to empathize with sexual assault victims. In a survey we conducted at three South LA high schools, a majority of girls of color felt unsafe on campus and had experienced some form of sexual harassment. Some felt victimized by a jock culture that encourages cis boys to openly rate girls' bodies, sex partners, and desirability, spilling over into social media attacks. The explosion of social media platforms has made it easier for young people to participate in sexual harassment and assault through sexually explicit posts that often cause their victims to leave school and/or harm themselves. As the young people in our training talked about the dissing that happens on popular social media sites, virtually everyone in the room admitted to knowing a girl who'd been targeted. According to the Pew Research Center, African American teens access social media at greater rates than do non-Black teens.[7] For Black girls, online predation—whether it's through Facebook, Instagram, or Snapchat—is also one of the most prevalent sources of sex trafficking. Poverty, joblessness, low access to educational opportunities, and high rates of foster care representation all contribute to African American girls having disproportionate rates of being victimized through domestic sex trafficking.[8]

6. Ibid., 1.

7. Amanda Lenhart, "Teens, Social Media and Technology Overview 2015," Pew Research Center, April 9, 2015, http://www.pewinternet.org/2015/04/09/teens-social-media-technology-2015; Aaron Morrison, "Black Teens Have More Smartphone Access, Social Media Use than Hispanics, Whites," *International Business Times*, April 9, 2015, https://www.ibtimes.com/Black-teens-have-more-smartphone-access-social-media-use-hispanics-whites-study-1875696.

8. Rights4Girls, "Domestic Sex Trafficking and Black Girls," August 2016, http://rights4girls.org/wp-content/uploads/r4g/2016/08/Af-Am-Girls-Trafficking-March-2017.docx.pdf; Malika Saada Saar, Rebecca Epstein, Lindsay Rosenthal, and

Further, the onslaught of films memorializing and contextualizing victimized white women (be it in portrayals as seemingly disparate as those involving Nicole Brown Simpson, the women killers of the Manson Family, or Amanda Knox) continues to convey the message that white women's pain should always have priority. Pervasive #MeToo Movement images of white women who are the victims of sexual harassment and violence in corporate America and the entertainment industry further marginalize Black female survivors. When young people of color see these portrayals ad nauseam, they are socialized to believe that these are the most authentic narratives vis-à-vis women's experiences with abuse and sexual and intimate partner violence.

Restorative justice with accountability means actively engaging and training boys and men to challenge rape culture, sexism, and misogyny against Black women and girls.[9] It means educating boys and men that when they demean us they are ultimately demeaning their lives, communities, and families. It requires a transformative vision of Black masculinity, one that confronts the way sexual violence is often framed as a "natural" part of Black men's heteronormative sense of identity. It demands that community and government resources be shifted to prevention programs as well as therapeutic initiatives that provide critical healing space for victims and survivors—away from the prisons, police, and weaponry that lock down Black communities. And it also demands bringing forward marginalized histories of the modern Civil Rights Movement with its origins in Black women's resistance to sexual terrorism and rape.[10] Finally, it asks us as Black feminists/womanists/survivors who love and work with Black

Yasmin Vafa, *The Sexual Abuse Prison Pipeline: The Girls' Story*, Human Rights Project for Girls, Georgetown Law Center on Poverty and Inequality, and the Ms. Foundation for Women, February 2015, http://rights4girls.org/wp-content/uploads/r4g/2015/02/2015_COP_sexual-abuse_layout_web-1.pdf.

9. Sikivu Hutchinson, "Woke Feminist Men: Engaging Black Men and Boys on Sexual Violence," *The Feminist Wire*, May 26, 2016, http://www.thefeministwire.com/2016/05/woke-feminist-men-engaging-Black-men-boys-sexual-violence-activism.

10. Danielle L. McGuire, *At the Dark End of the Street: Black Women, Rape, and Resistance—A New History of the Civil Rights Movement from Rosa Parks to the Rise of Black Power* (New York: Vintage Press, 2011).

children to continue to be on the front lines as culturally responsive adults bringing the elimination of sexual violence into the narrative of liberation struggle. It is the legacy that our Black women ancestors, clashing against the code of violent silence and invisibility in their own homes, families, and communities, left for us.

[A version of this essay was first published in the #LoveWITHAccountability online forum in *The Feminist Wire*, October 25, 2016.]

CHAPTER 17

Our Silence Will Not Save Us

Considering Survivors and Abusers

Dr. Thema Bryant-Davis

As a womanist psychologist, minister, and sacred artist, my reflections on effective response to child sexual abuse necessitate an examination of the journey of survivors and offenders within their cultural context. I invite you to join me in considering these pathways to safety, love, and accountability through poetry and essay, art and science, heart and mind. After wading in these waters for many years, it is clear to me that any effective solution will need to be holistic and interdisciplinary. In other words, all that each of us has to bring to the table is needed for the co-creation of transformative care, healing, and justice.

Molestation gets buried
In the rib cages of children
The pelvic bones of children
The hearts, lungs, and memories of children
These children, we children, grow up
And from the vantage point of strangers
We may look like sturdy oak trees
But those who dare to look closely
See the sores on our bark
Experience the tangled roots of our emotions
Witness the disconnected gaps in our branches
But most don't look
Retreating habitually to the averted gaze of eyes shut
. . . refusing to bear witness
Willing our children to stand under the weight
Celebrating those who manage to soar despite the weight on our wings

We, directly and indirectly, give our children the script of silence
No one, after all, wants to hear about ghosts that came in the night
Often sharing our same last name
No one wants to think about the intrusions on toddlers, the fingers or the hellish hot breath whispers
The violation of bodies still young enough to carry lunch boxes and backpacks
No one wants to sit with the whole truth of the dismantling of adolescents
Those left sobbing in the fetal position
Limping back to homeroom
Shallow breath as intruders descend upon us
It's easier to talk about God or report cards or television shows or what's for dinner or even problems facing
the Black community
Anything really is more palatable than shh . . .
Our silence does not save us, and it definitely does not heal us
But even with the demand for silence, the violation speaks
Often in riddles
The violation discovers the code of nonverbal communication
The abuse screams in the muffled voice of depression, anxiety, PTSD, eating disorders, anger, panic attacks, addiction, dissociation, suicidality, ADHD, oppositional defiant disorder
Translated in our communities with other labels like bad attitude, too sensitive, drama queen, troubled, zapping out, spacing out, irritating, troublemaker, bad hygiene, forgetful, too grown for her good, shy, secretive, quiet, weird, emotional, cold, moody, off
Forgetting they told us with words and deeds to hush
But we need space to think, feel, speak, connect, process, restore
We need seeing eyes, listening ears, open hearts
The silence strangles us again
Again and again
Yet often those who encourage silence would in most cases say they love us

It's the kind of love that walks on eggshells around sexual violence
The type of love that would defend us against the sting of racism or the mistreatment by a teacher, stranger, or in some cases a bully
But when a vagina, penis, anus, breasts are involved our loved ones run out of words
Cloaking themselves in silence or uncomfortable laughter
After all most grew up in houses where those words were neither uttered or alluded to
Especially in relationship to children
They were not given the vocabulary for this test
So they leave their paper blank
Putting roof overhead, food on the table, God in your heart, goals in your mind
And this my sisters and brothers is love
But this silenced love does not save us when the vultures have come to eat up our flesh
Desecrating our temples
Leaving 4-year-olds, 10-year-olds, 15-year-olds to gather the sharp edges of shattered pieces of themselves . . . alone
Loved ones can think silence is a gift
Hoping children will forget, not dwell on it, and not focus on it
If we don't speak it, we can falsely believe that we have erased it
But it remains busting out of the seams of our souls

***

Not only is silenced love insufficient for survivors, it is also a disservice to abusers. Abuse thrives in silence and secrecy. Abusers grow in power with the more eyes that are closed. The denial of family, community members, teachers, social workers, and judges are the wind beneath the wings of predators. While children are often silent because of shock, fear, confusion, and shame, what keeps non-abusing adults silent? The reality is, most abusers are not strangers. There are abusers we know whom we consider monsters, and these abusers we often fear, even as adults. We do not believe most known abusers are monsters. They often are loved ones. They are our partners, spouses, siblings, children, aunts, uncles, neighbors, teachers, coaches, principals, troop leaders, and ministers. We often believe that the godly response is to love them unconditionally. We want to believe it was just a mistake, a case of bad judgment, a response to stress, a regretful act that only occurred because of substance abuse, or an error brought on by the child who was too grown, too developed, or too fast. In some cases, we are silent because of our distrust of the criminal injustice system. We have seen too many Black bodies dehumanized behind bars, so instead of adding to the numbers, we exchange our children's Black bodies for the freedom of our kindred who are perpetrators.

To be honest, our silent love is not just a gift we give our loved ones who are abusers. It is also a gift we give ourselves. We do not want to think about it and do not want to talk about it. We wish it had not happened, so we act as if it never happened. Our silence intensifies the suffering of survivors and gives free license to molesters to continue to violate our children or someone else's children.

Our silence, intentionally or unintentionally, supports the abuser. It does not support their transformation or growth but instead gives them license to continue acting out their quest for power and control on the bodies of children. If we love someone who has abused, we must accept that true love requires honesty and accountability. If we love them, we have to want better for them and of them. We often retreat into silence in the presence of those who have abused children because we do not know what to say and we are afraid to hear their answers. Love with accountability means that I have to speak truth to the person who abused a child or adolescent and dare to discuss the impact of their actions. In the context of our silence about these ongoing consequences, the abusive person embraces the myth that moments of violation are simply insignificant flashes of the past unworthy of confrontation. Abused children, as well as adult survivors of child abuse, continue to live with the physical, psychological, social, and even spiritual consequences. If I love someone who has abused a child, I have to love them enough to have an honest conversation and authentic dialogue about those whom they have violated, the consequences of that abuse, and their current thoughts about abusing again. To love someone who has been abusive is to actively engage in conversation and take concrete steps to reduce the risk of future abuse. We must take risk reduction off the shoulders of children. Risk reduction is not simply telling children to "stay away from them" or "tell me if they do it again." Not only must I be willing to wade into the water of truth-telling with loved ones who have been abusive, but I also have to step beyond my comfort and actually require accountability that includes reporting the abuse. Sexual abuse is a violent crime, and to treat it as if it is not gives abusive persons the message that violating children is acceptable and excusable. If I love someone who has abused a child, I have to tell him or her the truth, and the fact is, the abuse of children is a major violation that requires major intervention.

Our current prison-industrial complex does not have a praiseworthy record for transformation or rehabilitation.[1] However, it is problematic for us to send the message that stealing televisions and physically assaulting strangers should result in a punitive action, but sexually violating children does not warrant a punitive response. If we are going to transform the entire prison-industrial complex, it should not be a piecemeal approach that we construct on a foundation of silent support of sexual predators. If incarceration is part of the response, the incarceration of offenders should be humane. Incarceration should not include mandatory unpaid labor, solitary confinement, overpopulated prisons, routine rapes, torture, and unsanitary conditions and unsafe conditions.

A punitive response, however, is not the only possible response to child sexual abuse. Punitive responses alone are not effective in transforming the hearts, minds, and behaviors of offenders. It should not

1. Cynthia Golembeski and Robert Fullilove, "Criminal (In)justice in the City and Its Associated Health Consequences," *American Journal of Public Health*, no. 98 (2008): S185–S190.

take psychological research funded by a multimillion-dollar psychology grant to surmise that locking human beings behind bars, where there is a high likelihood of them being the victim of sexual assault, does not lead to improvements. Transformative justice, on the other hand, can include mandated long-term counseling, monitoring, and registration. Restorative justice models should prioritize the experience and needs of the survivor, instead of primarily functioning to serve the needs of offenders.[2] Restorative justice can provide a survivor with a safe space to tell their stories if they so choose, statements of support from both persons in their intimate circle and from authority figures, and resources for counseling and to assist in other areas of the survivor's life that may have been affected by the abuse (e.g., housing, education, and medical health). According to the research findings of psychiatrist Judith Herman on adult survivors' perceptions of justice, most survivors want acknowledgment of what has been done to them and only endorse the incarceration of offenders who they believe remain a risk of re-offending them or others.[3] For the offender, restorative or transformative justice can include circles of support, which researchers have studied for over a decade. These circles include informal networks as well as professionals from the justice system and mental health system who provide consistent monitoring, guidance, and accountability to assist the offender in integrating into the community in healthy, safe ways.

Those who have loved ones who have abused children sexually should open their minds and hearts to the reality that we can love people and still hold them accountable for their actions. These acts of love move us beyond the silence of neglect and enabling, and they position us to align ourselves to an intervention that may include directly addressing the abusive behavior, reporting the abuse, advocating for more humane approaches to incarceration for those who remain a risk to society, and supporting the mandate for treatment, monitoring, and

2. Tali Gal, *Child Victims and Restorative Justice: A Needs-Rights Model* (New York: Oxford University Press, 2011), 31.

3. Judith Lewis Herman, "Justice from the Victim's Perspective," *Violence against Women* 11, no. 5 (2005): 571–602.

guidance. I do not enable those I love to destroy their lives and the lives of others. I resist the comfort of silence and refuse to leave them to cause harm further. As a family, community, and society, we have to go beyond hoping our loved ones who have committed abuse will change. We have to choose to love them enough to wade into the difficult waters for the safety of our children. An African proverb says, "When you pray, move your feet." Our children's lives, bodies, minds, hearts, and spirits matter. Our faith in abusive loved ones without the work of accountability leaves us all unsaved.

[A version of this essay was first published in the #LoveWITHAccountability online forum in *The Feminist Wire*, October 19, 2016.]

CHAPTER 18

Safe Space

The Language of Love

Kimberly Gaubault (McCrae)

There is a practice of erasure that happens in traditional Christian church communities. It is the systemic erasure of those who carry the weight of having sexual assault, domestic violence, gender violence, and other forms of abuse forced upon them, those whose understanding of God, love, community, and self is often structured around violations against body and spirit. This erasure makes the church a safe space for those who want to avoid the ugly reality that these behaviors and conscious decisions are often made by those we trust, in community and spaces we have designated as sacred. We are programmed to embrace spiritual rhetoric that shames and silences those who have been victims of sexual assault (regardless of gender identification). This same rhetoric is often used to fill the uncomfortable space that exists in communities where sexual assault (primarily during childhood) has occurred. It is known by clichés such as "God is good all the time, and all the time God is good"; "God won't put more on you than you can bear"; "All things work together for the good of them who love the Lord"; "Just pray about it"; and other biblically based phrases and sayings. Using these clichés—rather than engaging violations and violators head on—often discourages victims from speaking out about their abuse and their abusers.

It is important that we provide space for these conversations to happen and truths to be shared proactively, with full understanding that there will be discomfort but, through honesty and full disclosure, that there can also be hope for healing. To espouse a system of avoidance and silence is to espouse the physical and spiritual alienation of those who have been relegated to the margins of the intricate tapestries woven together to form the beloved community. The margins are the spaces that give value to the common space that is shared in the middle ground. The margins have importance and relevance to the big picture. Childhood sexual assault is too common to be treated as an anomaly. By addressing it, in community, we can open up a space for healing for those living with the shame of being violated as well as those living with the shame of having violated someone else. Love calls us to accountability in the ways we form community, and to responsibility in the ways we maintain community.

On First Times

The first time I was raped
the act was not as painful
as the accusation
the implication that
somehow
I must be at fault
almost 29 years later
I remember what I was wearing
as if it were yesterday
I never wore it again
never washed it again
never trusted my mother again
and he was light-skinned
and this was the 80's so
light-skinned was in
I was nervous
hadn't seen him before
he thought I was cute
I didn't believe it
I was dark-skinned
and skinny
and dark
and too Christian
and dark

and big forehead
and dark
and big lips
and dark
too dark to be the right shade
for light-skinned to holla at
I avoided eye contact
straightened my shirt
I remember what I was wearing
my favorite outfit
until that day
I never wore it again
I think I told you that already
I still don't trust my mother
and she don't like me
I don't think she ever has
what was we talking about . . . oh yeah
he was light-skinned
and I just kept walking
because I'm not supposed to attract boys
this is what causes problems at home
why they calling here?
you don't need no boyfriends
they calling because you just want to be fast
they only want one thing
don't bring home no babies
Maybe
I just want to be liked
at home and at school
don't feel comforted, at 17,
about being a "peculiar people"
don't want to have sex or be sexualized
don't want to always be so different
all the time

don't care so much for being the ugly girl at school
all the time
the one who can't go to no parties cause she in church
all the time
can't go to no friend's houses and can't have them come to mine
all the time
can't be in marching band because THOSE kids . . .
feeling left out
all the time
my friend and I
he and I liked to talk
we couldn't do it in school much because I'm smart
and I don't go to school to make friends
I go to school to learn
he had to get up the nerve just to call the house
because he knows the chill of ice
even when it's over a phone line
and even though it's all related
I digress again . . .
the first time I was raped
I remember what I was wearing
remember walking home from school
remember walking up the stairs to our apartment
remember being grabbed
I remember being groped
I remember being raped
I remember being raped
I remember trying to convince my mind
that this was not so bad
that if I stayed still long enough
maybe he would get bored and stop
that at least he thought I was cute
that he was light-skinned
and light-skinned was a compliment for dark-skinned

right?
I didn't scream
didn't call for help
I remember my body refusing to cooperate
refusing to allow easy penetration
I remember not fighting
not knowing how
and hating all 85 pounds of my lethargic flesh
I remember the silence of the house
how his voice reverberated off the walls of my ears
I remember what I was wearing
my favorite outfit
and believe it or not
it was not the act
but the after
that made it mourning clothes
the "you shouldn't have been wearing THAT outfit"
that turned it into shroud
and this story was never told
because I was never asked what happened when that guy followed me home
not when I vomited up light-skinned's touch for 2 days after
not when I was balled over in pain in the wake of light-skinned's embrace
not when I was being treated for the gift that light-skinned left me
not when I missed a month of school because light-skinned's visit
required hospitalization
medication
and recovery time
I was never asked why I never wore my favorite outfit again
I was never asked
so I didn't tell
and 29 years later
I still remember

how we celebrated the healing
but never talked about the hurting
and how the hurting
never fully goes away

[A version of this essay and poem was first published in the #LoveWITH-Accountability online forum in *The Feminist Wire*, October 26, 2016.]

CHAPTER 19

Unfinished

Dr. Worokya Duncan

While growing up in a Black Pentecostal church, I was tacitly trained to view God in a particular way. Like the early Christian leader Marcion of Sinope and his followers, I began to think of the Bible as having two Gods: one evil and one loving. Traditionalism and ecclesiastical rules caused me to see Christianity as a religion where pleasure is sin, human desire is automatically not God's desire, and that dos and don'ts were of more central value than the complexion of one's heart. It is not my belief, however, that this indoctrination was purposeful. Certain theologies and hermeneutics that some Pentecostal churches subscribe to cause those who are raised and taught in those circles to live in such dogmatic and legalistic bondage.

This alleged legalistic bondage tends to affect every aspect of an individual's life. Therefore, in several crisis situations, I tended to look at a situation in legal terms rather than realistically. Certain tragedies may be viewed as punishment or an example of God's sovereignty, which remains to be seen. Feminist, womanist, and liberation theology seek to redefine, reform, and realign the way individuals have understood ourselves in light of certain doctrines. These "new" theologies force us to acknowledge the assumptions that are made by certain theological assertions.

A critical example of the distortion and need for reformation is the place that is given, or not given, to women survivors of sexual assault—specifically incest—in particular churches. Also, the role that Black women have had to play in the Black church or within Black liberation theology seems nonexistent if one were to read many books and theological articles and take note of the church's teachings. This is a form of blatant sexism that, according to womanist theologian

Rev. Dr. Delores Williams, "denies black women equal opportunity in the churches' major leadership roles."[1]

Although Black liberation theology and the so-called Black church are intended to be places of respite from the onslaughts of racism in the greater society, sexism is a form of oppression that is alive and well.

Black ministers have been adamant in preaching against Paul's sayings concerning slavery and submission, but they openly preach about the role of women in a way that sounds only too similar to white patriarchy. Also, because intellectualism, whether theological or otherwise, has been identified with the public sphere (thusly separating it from women), women have been unable (until recently) to speak for themselves. White theology was unable to speak to the concerns of or speak for both white women *and* Black people. It can be concluded, then, that Black theology and a Black church that is created by and shaped by Black men cannot free Black women or truly speak in their interest.[2]

The key to maintaining any type of power, be it psychological, spiritual, or physical, is validation. Validation can be given either tacitly or directly. I believe that the dual silence of the Black church on issues of sexuality and the silence of survivors have given legitimacy to views about sexuality in general, and Black sexuality in particular.

Six. That's how old I was. Six. A super-tiny and very sure-of-myself six. All of that changed right before my seventh birthday. Every day after school, I would go to my mom's job, which was housed in a church—my church. I sat in the stairwell, did my homework, and read a book. This was my schedule. Like clockwork. What I didn't know was that someone else was paying very close attention to my schedule, and it wasn't my mom. He was young. Exuding kindness in our previous interactions and, I thought, harmless. I didn't know what grooming was, but I guess that's what he'd been doing in the months prior. I

1. Delores S. Williams, *Sisters in the Wilderness: The Challenge of Womanist God-Talk* (Maryknoll, NY: Orbis Books, 1999).

2. Jacqueline Grant, "Black Theology and the Black Woman," *Black Theology: A Documentary History, vol. 1: 1966–1979* (Maryknoll, NY: Orbis Books, 1993).

remember when it started, I was wearing my school uniform, and my hair had a red bow in it. I was reading *Charlotte's Web*. I know, that's not a book a six-year-old would typically read, but I didn't grow up in a typical household. At any rate, I was reading, and he started to touch my knee. I didn't say anything, and to this day, I don't know why. Then he began to touch my thigh, and again, I said nothing. I was six and grew up in church, and you don't talk back to your elders, even when what they're doing feels wrong. Then his fingers moved further up and pushed my panties aside. He inserted two fingers, and I finally made a sound. It hurt. I didn't even know I had a hole there until him. He removed his fingers when he heard me wince, smelled them, and went about his business. He would do this every day until right before my eighth birthday.

The way I grew up, bad things happened to people whose faith had wavered or to people who'd committed a horrible sin. I didn't know which applied to me, but I knew I had to have done something awful for God to allow this to happen to me over and over and over. When I was fourteen, I found out he had died of AIDS a few years before. I sat in torment, because back then, there was little we knew about HIV/AIDS. I was convinced I'd contracted it. I said nothing to anyone, including my mother, until I was sixteen years old. I told someone in my church because I figured, if the assault happened in church, maybe I could get healing in church too. That was a mistake.

The 2016 film *Captain America: Civil War* features a scene where the character Bucky Barnes is being held in a cage of sorts. His captor starts reading a series of words, and with each word, the audience witnesses a change in Bucky's eyes and behavior. By the time the last word is spoken, we understand that Bucky is a victim of wartime psychological programming that made him into a weapon. All it took was a word to cause him to remember everything about who he was.

I remember being in a youth group gathering one Saturday, and when someone said a particular word, all of the snippets of memory combined into a flood. Whereas through the years I had remembered some of what I'd experienced, a single word seemed to make several years' worth of assault come to the front of my mind, like a record on repeat. I began crying and screaming uncontrollably. They went into spontaneous prayer because that's what we were taught to do. When I finally calmed down, the leaders asked me what was wrong. I told them what had happened to me, and their response ripped the Band-Aid that had been placed over my gaping wound, only to pour salt into it. They quoted Romans 8:28: "All things work together for the good of them that love the Lord."

They said my being molested as a child was equally bad and necessary to make me a symbol of what God could do. They said my emotional turmoil was all part of the process and that one day I'd see that. What I thought would begin my healing threw me into pain that, for a sixteen-year old, was unmanageable. What I needed to hear was that God and someone else cared. I knew I'd never receive any legal justice; after all, he was dead. But I needed my church to say something different to me. I needed them to stop pushing a false and harmful theology, espousing violence and pain, specifically sexual violence, as a tool that God—a male God—required to teach lessons to some future people who needed to see how great he was. What about me now? How was my pain going to be addressed? Who was going to show me that God was great? Because in my eyes, you couldn't have let this happen to me and still be called anything other than a monster. In the church, accountability has to begin with what we say to survivors.

If one is going to use the Bible as the standard in the church, even when speaking of child sexual abuse (CSA), we have to rehumanize these biblical actors. Being accountable means churches admit they have sometimes been spaces of harm and not healing. Ministers can use stories like the one of Hagar, who was raped and forced to bear a child, or the one of Tamar, whose father surrendered her to a crowd to be raped and subsequently killed, to illustrate the awful, gut-wrenching, mind-fracturing, and body-breaking pain CSA survivors encounter during the act and in the aftermath, because the healing does not end. The flashbacks occur when one least expects it, and at the most inopportune moments. Accountability will not always include testifying against a perpetrator or seeking a remedy from the courts. What I would like to see is what *wasn't* done for me. I'd like to see spaces for child sexual abuse survivors to process with trained facilitators what they've endured, in church. I'd like to see ministers no longer skirting the issue by choosing to preach about every #BlackLivesMatter issue except sex crimes.

For centuries, Black women have been expected to hold up the church, whether through financial contributions, service, or both. Who's holding up these women? Who's singing their songs? "Love with accountability" in the church looks like our churches being safe spaces for crying, screaming, and cursing—and even not believing, if that's part of the journey.

[This essay was first published in the #LoveWITHAccountability online forum in *The Feminist Wire*, October 20, 2016.]

CHAPTER 20

"The Least of These"

Black Children, Sexual Abuse, and Theological Malpractice

Ahmad Greene-Hayes

The King will reply, "Truly I tell you, whatever you did for one of the least of these brothers and sisters of mine, you did for me."

—Matthew 25:40 (King James Version)

On Friday, August 26, 2016, Georgia pastor Kenneth Adkins was arrested on one count of aggravated child molestation.[1] This same pastor preached homophobic sermons and said the mass-shooting victims at the Pulse nightclub deserved to die.[2] Yet he is a child molester and a rapist. Adkins, however, is not an anomaly; in fact, he represents much of what the church stands for: hypocrisy coupled with holiness-or-hell theologies that conceal unethical sexual acts and demonize marginalized bodies.

Adkins is not alone. Many other leaders who wear sacred collars desecrate churches and the gospel with their unrelenting commitment to sexual violence. Without a doubt, our society perpetuates rape culture, but many of the church's religious leaders prey on those who often cannot pray for themselves. They also theologically nurture and coddle those who violate children, women, and queer folks, and we must reckon with the reality that survivors of sexual abuse sit in pews and preach in pulpits, often with their harm-doers in plain view.

Yet (Black) churches are largely silent. Indeed, the collective silence—from adults, from the village, from the elders—is deafening

1. Mathew Rodriguez, "Kenneth Adkins, Pastor Who Said Pulse Victims Deserved to Die, Arrested for Molestation," *Mic*, August 27, 2016, https://mic.com/articles/152822/kenneth-adkins-pastor-who-said-pulse-victims-deserved-to-die-arrested-for-molestation.

2. Darnell L. Moore, "Silence Can Be Violence, That's Why We Have to Talk about the Orlando Shooting," *Mic*, June 18, 2016, https://mic.com/articles/146524/silence-can-be-violence-that-s-why-we-have-to-talk-about-the-orlando-shooting.

even as childhood screams, hollers, and pleas to live unbothered and untouched by the perversion of child sexual abuse blare the silences.

Several visual texts, such as Kasi Lemmons's *Eve's Bayou* (1997), Michael Schultz's *Woman, Thou Art Loosed* (2004), based on the T. D. Jakes novel, Tina Mabry's *Mississippi Damned* (2009), and Spike Lee's *Red Hook Summer* (2012), explore the everydayness of child sexual abuse in Black communities. More recently, the first and second seasons of the TV series *Greenleaf* (2016–2017), on the Oprah Winfrey Network, delves into the topic of CSA (child sexual abuse) in a Black mega-church community in Memphis, Tennessee. Winfrey, a child sexual abuse and rape survivor, plays the role of Mavis McCready and gives her niece Grace the push she needs to expose all the lies and sexual traumas hidden in the physical and psychic archives of the church's history.[3] One such task is bringing her Uncle Mac to heel for sexually assaulting her sister Faith (who committed suicide) and several other girls in the church and the Memphis community. However, no one in this fictionalized account wants to talk about sexual violence, just as most Black churches and Black families want to talk about the real-life Mac I mentioned in my introduction.

Child sexual abuse in Black communities is an epidemic. Black Women's Blueprint reports that 60 percent of Black girls have been raped before age eighteen, and studies show that one in six boys is sexually assaulted.[4] We know without a doubt that many of these assaults happen in churches or in proximity to churches and their members. As such, I have several questions:

What do we do when the violence is found among those who are "sanctified?"

Where is God when Black children are sexually assaulted? Alternatively, perhaps a more poignant question is, does God condone the sexual violation of children?

3. Louise Saunders, "When Two TV Greats Meet: Oprah Winfrey Opens Up on Her Traumatic Childhood during David Letterman Lecture Series," *DailyMail.com*, November 27, 2012.

4. For more information see Black Women's Blueprint, http://Blackwomensblueprint.org; see also 1in6, http://1in6.org/get-information/the-1-in-6-statistic.

"*God Help the Child*," to quote the title of the Toni Morrison novel, but God does not help the child when the child is victim to child sexual abuse.[5]

How can Emmanuel, or "God with us," bear witness to such pervasive and unchecked evil and not be moved to act justly on behalf of the child survivor? Moreover, if God is on the side of the oppressed, as the late Rev. Dr. James Hal Cone, the father of Black liberation theology, and others have argued, where is God when Black children are hurt by those who introduced them to "God"?[6]

With regard to child sexual abuse, my work as the founder of Children of Combahee and as a scholar of religion has three aims. First, I am building a canon of thought in the study of Black religion and theology that names sexual violence as sexual "deviance" and reconsiders long-standing pathologies that situate homosexuality, gender nonconformity, womanhood, and other marginalized sexual/gender identities as not only "deviant" but also subservient to Black male cis-heteropatriarchy. Second, I am deconstructing the myth that queer subjects—both within and outside the Black church—are queer because of sexual abuse, and I am offering new ways of thinking about "pathology" and "perversion" within the Black church. Third, I contend that lived experience, personal testimony, and psychic realities are both worthy and befitting of critical theological attention and engagement, in part, because most survivor narratives never make it into academic or church archives, even as the assaults and the remembrances and effects of the assaults are archived (or repressed) within survivors' minds.

It is important to note that many of the terms used in my written and vocal work are terms that are never spoken in many Black religious spaces. Consent is assumed, but it is never taught. Rape is alluded to, but it is never acknowledged. The survivor is shunned, while the overcomer is praised. These terms, however, function as guiding principles in the fight to end sexual violence. I believe wholeheartedly that

5. Toni Morrison, *God Help the Child* (New York: Knopf, 2015).
6. James Hal Cone, *God of the Oppressed* (Maryknoll, NY: Orbis Books, 1977).

Black sexuality, gender identity, and sexual violence cannot be freely and expressly understood or discussed within Black churches until the church catches up to the mainstream discourse on human sexuality (and even the mainstream discourse lags behind those who are survivors, queer, trans, women, and femme). These words are prominent in social justice spaces, anti-rape organizations, and in other medical and legal entities, but they are often absent from the church, even as survivors fill pews and pulpits.

If we believe that the Black church is a central site of influence in many Black communities (though scholars like Eddie Glaude have argued "the Black church is dead," or, put differently, we are witnessing "church services and liturgies that entertain, but lack a spirit that transforms, and preachers who deign for followers instead of fellow travelers in God"), we must continue to question why "consent," "rape," and "survivor" are not a part of the Black churchgoing population's vocabulary.[7] We must also evaluate whether pastors and leaders in the church have the tools to work through sexual violence theologically, ethically, and within cultural context on their own. Indeed, we must interrogate both sacred and communal texts, from church by-laws to Bible study to the scripts from which the pastor preaches.

Call me heretical, but I do not believe that the Bible is a reliable resource in this regard, lest it is consulted through a womanist, queer theological lens.[8] I also contend that sexual violence cannot be eradicated until the church acknowledges the way it sanitizes biblically sanctioned rape, even as it manipulates scripture to demonize queer and transgender people, to subject women and children to patriarchal men and leaders, and to protect and cover the tracks of rapists.[9]

Victim-shaming and queer antagonism are active evils in the life of many Black churches. My work calls them both into question.

7. Eddie Glaude, "The Black Church Is Dead," *Huffington Post*, April 26, 2010, https://www.huffingtonpost.com/eddie-glaude-jr-phd/the-black-church-is-dead_b_473815.html.

8. Pamela R. Lightsey, *Our Lives Matter: A Womanist Queer Theology* (Eugene, OR: Wipf and Stock, 2015).

9. Renita J. Weems, *Battered Love: Marriage, Sex, and Violence in the Hebrew Prophets* (Minneapolis: Fortress Press, 1995).

Rather than pathologize survivors and queer people, I strive to understand how white supremacy, capitalism, neoliberalism, and the workings of the state have altered the ways Black people wrestle with racial-sexual terrorism and struggle with holistic, loving embrace of Blackness.

Many survivor-activists have pushed the Black church to think about its complicity in the rape and sexual assault of countless women, men, children, gender non-conforming, queer, transgender, and poor Christians and non-Christians, yet the Black church continues to turn a blind eye to the reality of racial-sexual violence. For example, Rev. Dr. Monica Coleman's *The Dinah Project* intervenes in a history that registers unchecked sexual violence and illicit sexual behavior as standard, if not normative, alongside patriarchy and cis-heterosexism. She writes:

> Every congregation contains victims of sexual violence. Every church with women, men, boys, girls, or the elderly contains victims of sexual violence. Whether an individual confides in the church leaders, family, or friends, or chooses to remain silent, there is no church void of the people whose lives are changed by experiences of sexual violence. Because every church contains persons affected by sexual violence, the church must respond. Because sexual violence affects every aspect of our communities, including our religious and spiritual lives, the church must respond. Because silence is a response of tolerance, the church must respond.[10]

If the church is filled with so many survivors of sexual violence, why then does the church lack urgency and conviction in the fight to eradicate the unholy and perverse reality of sexual abuse?

Perhaps it is because Black churches are more concerned with the sexual practices, behaviors, and orientations of its constituents that are

10. Monica Coleman, *The Dinah Project: A Handbook for Congregational Response to Sexual Violence* (Eugene, OR: Wipf and Stock, 2010), 4.

non-heterosexual, non-normative, or disruptive to puritanical notions of what is sacred, holy, and virtuous.[11] Among many things, "the politics of respectability," as defined by Evelyn Brooks Higginbotham, and "the culture of dissemblance," as described by Darlene Clark Hine, explicate the ways Black church people have used silence as a means of protection from white racial-sexual terrorists.[12] To mitigate the effects of white supremacist violence, many African Americans do not address intra-communal violence, and in some instances extra-communal violence, because they do not want to portray the race in a negative light or they want to be "race loyal," even asserting "race first, everything later." These patterns are deadly and send a loud message that child sexual abuse and all forms of sexual violence are not racial justice issues.

The inability or unwillingness to address sexual violence as an evil that pervades home, church, and community is steeped in larger cultural "norms," which can be traced back to the plantation where rape and torture were codified by law and the theologies of the master class. In some ways, the contemporary Black church—which grew out of enslavement—mirrors the plantation of times past, and survivors are pushing the church to consider its reinscription of master tactics—that is, attempts to abuse, silence, marginalize, shame, victimize, and dehumanize marginal subjects, or as Jesus said, "the least of these."[13]

Until Black churches are honest about human sexuality and our collective discomfort with it, sexual violence will remain unchecked, and accountability will be nothing more than a goal to be obtained in the afterlife. However, if we believe Jesus's words—thy kingdom come

11. Kelly Brown Douglas, *Sexuality and the Black Church: A Womanist Perspective* (Maryknoll, NY: Orbis Books, 1999).

12. Evelyn Brooks Higginbotham, *Righteous Discontent: The Women's Movement in the Black Baptist Church, 1880–1920* (Cambridge, MA: Harvard University Press, 1993); and Darlene Clark Hine, "Rape and the Inner Lives of Black Women in the Middle West," *Signs: Journal of Women in Culture and Society* 14, no. 4 (1989): 912–20.

13. For more on Black churches and the plantation, see, for example: Albert J. Raboteau, *Slave Religion: The "Invisible Institution" in the Antebellum South* (New York: Oxford University Press, 2004); and Mechal Sobel, *Trabelin' On: The Slave Journey to an Afro-Baptist Faith* (Princeton, NJ: Princeton University Press, 1988). For the scripture where Jesus's words are recorded, see Matthew 25: 40–45.

and thy will be done, on earth as it is in heaven—we must also believe that God is looking to the church to conjure justice for survivors right now.[14] Indeed, hell is a present reality, and heaven is too far.

[This essay was first published in the #LoveWITHAccountability online forum in *The Feminist Wire*, October 18, 2016.]

14. See Luke 11:1–13; and Obery M. Hendricks Jr., *The Politics of Jesus: Rediscovering the True Revolutionary Nature of Jesus' Teachings and How They Have Been Corrupted* (New York: Doubleday, 2006).

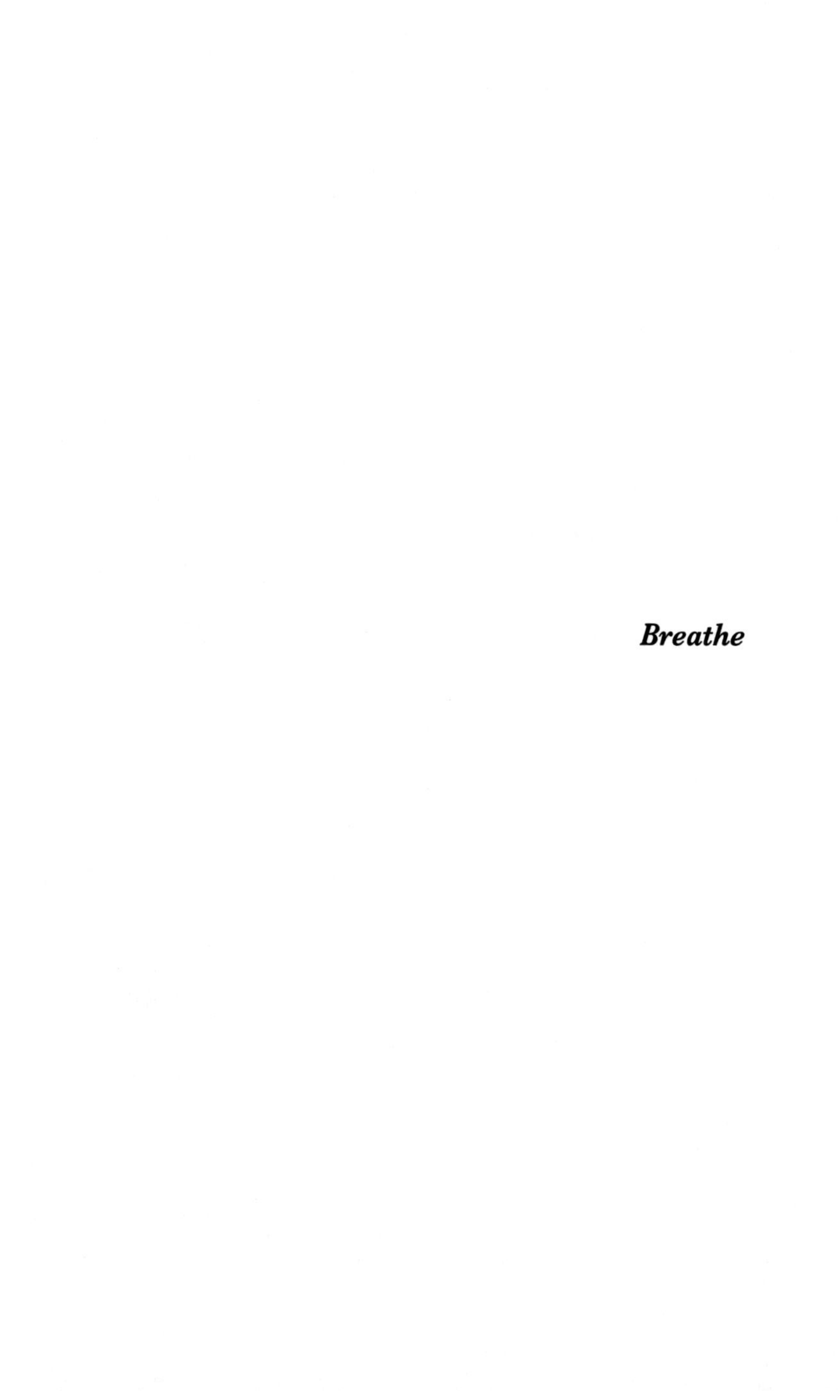

Breathe

CHAPTER 21

Who Is Accountable to the Black Latinx Child?

Luz Marquez-Benbow

According to the 2010 National Intimate Partner and Sexual Violence Survey, one in seven Latinas experience rape at some point in their lifetime. I am one.[1]

When I share my history of childhood sexual abuse, I am often asked if my brother ever asked for forgiveness or why I still engage with my family. Frankly, I never gave a fuck about an apology for such a gross and violent act. Additionally, I, like many incest survivors, struggled with the guilt that came with thinking the abuse I experienced would destroy our home life. As for forgiving myself, this is a lifelong process. Forgiveness is complicated by all the societally sanctioned victim-blaming that occurs daily. I did forgive myself for thinking that these horrific violations happened to me because in my family where my mother is a white Puerto Rican and my father is a black Puerto Rican, I was "La Prieta" (the Black One and a girl).

Despite doing everything my mom told me to do, including wearing shorts under my skirts and dresses, not sitting on any men's laps, being aware of strangers, and praying, I was still sexually abused. Furthermore, I was sexually abused and raped by people my family and I knew.

I wondered who should be blamed for my sexual trauma at the early age of seven. My mom, who failed to believe me? My oldest brother, six years my senior, the one who abused me (he was about thirteen years old at the time)? My community, for shaming and holding women and girls to blame for the sexual victimization many of us experience? My Puerto Rican culture, whose anti-Blackness deemed

1. National Center for Injury Prevention and Control of the Centers for Disease Control and Prevention, *National Intimate Partner and Sexual Violence Survey: 2010 Summary Report*, https://www.cdc.gov/violenceprevention/pdf/nisvs_report2010-a.pdf.

me "beautiful for a *negra linda con pelo bueno*" (beautiful for a Black girl with good hair)? My Black nationalist movement, which fails to acknowledge *all* of me, my womanhood, even though peers in the movement call me "Queen"?

I've been guilt-ridden for so long that I never thought about my need or right for accountability. Even as a child, I knew that to talk about accountability meant that I was living the lie that comes with double consciousness. Living in such a way is a reality for many incest survivors because it enables us to maintain familial ties even after the sexual abuse occurs. As a young person, my double consciousness allowed me to be invisible, but this, of course, made me very angry. The only way I could stop from harming others or committing suicide was to use drugs. I was angry at my oldest brother; my mother's boyfriend who molested me, the young man who raped me; and my mother. I was angry at God, the *orishas*, *y la mano de Azabache*. (Deities known as *orishas* are part of my spiritual belief system, which is derived from our West African spiritual traditions; for Boricuas and many in the diaspora, the hand (*mano*) of Azabache is a protector of children.) I was angry at every fucking being that is supposed to protect children yet fails miserably. The anger of living this reality was so overwhelming that the only release I had at the time was drugs.

For the past thirty-one years, I have lived a drug-free life, and I still struggle with anger. This is often the reality for most incest survivors because of our engagement with our families. I know it is healthier for me and my kids to cut off my family (my mom and my oldest brother) completely, but I can't entirely disengage from familial ties. Frankly, I need to navigate these dynamics because culturally, familial relationships are so crucial that it is too painful to not have them in my life. I recently made the decision to be the primary contact for my mother's care as she struggles with dementia, while at the same time completely disengaging from my oldest brother. Throughout my life, I contemplated how I would respond to my mom if she needed me, and how would I engage with my oldest brother if my mom should die. For many incest survivors, regardless of how much therapy or work one has done, family is a space that holds so much pain and love at the same time, especially in our relationships with our parents. As a child of a single parent, my relationship with my mother continues to be one that reminds me of a wound that never manages to heal.

As an institution, the family domain is a place that can cause so much betrayal, by shaming survivors and silencing our voices. This betrayal feels just as painful as the abuse itself. So I am "learning to live with the guilt" (thank you, Aishah Shahidah Simmons, for naming this reality and holding me through this process) as I create healthy space between me and my mom while also ensuring she is cared for in her time of need. My mom's dementia has caused me to grieve for any dream I ever had of working to strengthen our relationship. If she had only believed me, it would have been everything for me. I will never know the closure I would have felt, the growth that comes from healing with a parent. As a mother myself, I am also trying to be accountable to my own children. I have not always gotten things right with them. However, my relationship with my children is less about getting things right and more about how we journey through life, grow, and navigate the world. Who is accountable for these contradictions?

As a little girl, I believed I was unlike most kids because I was sexually violated by various people and at different ages. As an advocate to end such abuse, I know this type of violence against children is more rampant than we care to acknowledge in society. National studies report that 90 percent of sexually abused children know the perpetrator. Furthermore, the impact of child sexual abuse can last a lifetime and is often intergenerational. Who do we hold accountable for the childhoods that are lost because of child sexual abuse? Who is accountable for the impact of child sexual abuse on our kids and the generations to come?

After I became a mother, I promised my daughter and two sons that I would protect and listen to them. I was intentional with sharing information about their bodies. I believed that even if I couldn't protect my kids, 'cause child sexual abuse is some insidious shit, I would always believe and support them. While I broke the cycle of child sexual abuse, I want to know who is accountable for the conversations I had to have with my children. These are the conversations that many in the Black diasporic community need to have with their children. Who is accountable for these difficult yet necessary discussions about the realities of living in a world that views most Black diasporic people, especially our children, as disposable? This is evident through rampant policing and other forms of state-sanctioned, white supremacist violence perpetrated in our communities every day. Our school classrooms are not even safe for Black diasporic children. On top of the over-policing and the violence, there's the pandemic of child sexual abuse too.

Who is accountable to the Black diasporic child?

As a Black diasporic community, we need to have critical dialogues and action strategies about our responsibility to end child sexual abuse, not because it's any worse than in other communities, but because we must hold ourselves accountable to ensuring the safety of all our children. We have placed race at the center while women, children, and LGBTQI (lesbian, gay, bisexual, transgender, queer/questioning, intersex) people and other critical realities are too often on the margins in our community. Liberation for our people must include standing up against misogyny, homophobia, and the notion that women and children are property. In the name of radical love, I need my Black diasporic brothers to take responsibility to tackle the issue of masculinity and the sexualization of our children, of girls and women, and to mentor young brothers. I need for brothers to do this organizing work with the same rigor that they take in their other efforts to hold white Amerikkka accountable. Brothers can't continue to be blinded by the same patriarchy they benefit from while also blaming the women in their lives for emasculating them.

Who is accountable to Black Latinx girls and women?

Professionally, I've explored the notion of sisterhood/siblinghood. What does a healthy bond feel like with another human being, where everyone holds each other, especially at our worst moments or during transitions? During my time in the mainstream anti–sexual violence movement and disability movement, I inquired about this concept of sisterhood within women of color (WOC) spaces and while supporting Black and Latinx young adults with disabilities. I also learned, from my late other brother, Dave, who lived with a physical disability, that so much is possible when intentional support exists.

As a 2016–2019 Just Beginnings Collaborative fellow, I am reimagining the concept of siblinghood together with other adult survivors of child sexual abuse in my Black Latinx community. My project Black Latinidad: Building to End Child Sexual Abuse is about creating a space for Black Latinx adult survivors of child sexual abuse where we can build in deep community and speak our truth while expanding our capacity to create systemic political and cultural change.

From a Black Latinx cultural perspective, the term "sisterhood" denotes a powerful connection to our historical African traditions as women leaders protecting and teaching the African ways of healing and protecting ourselves. My innate being has always believed, upheld, and explored the sisterhood within myself and other movements. Presently, I am interested in expanding on the meaning of "siblinghood" by applying this traditional value as a culturally specific response to supporting adult survivors within my own community.

This concept of siblinghood was the foundation for the development of a group I cofounded over ten years ago: the National Organization of Sisters of Color Ending Sexual Assault (SCESA), the country's first national WOC-led, anti–sexual assault organization. In the late 1990s, women of color working at state sexual assault coalitions across the United States came together to address the lack of our representation and leadership at state coalitions. This organizing work led a collective of sisters to form a WOC leadership project. To be clear, we were more focused on increasing the numbers of WOC leaders than we were on leadership development. The collective grew and evolved into SCESA. It is with a renewed commitment and the inclusive language of siblinghood that the next phase of my work is unfolding.

The experience of child sexual abuse can change how we love, how we parent, and how we form relationships. Moreover, white supremacy has harmed us as people of color to such an extent that many of us struggle with continuing to live in our traditional collective communities. As Black Latinx communities, we too are struggling with living in relationship with each other. Given this reality and the harm of child sexual abuse, I believe it is, as the revolutionary Assata Shakur asserts, "our duty" to rebuild our communities' capacity to provide intentional support. The late human rights warrior Grace Lee Boggs once stated, "We have to change ourselves in order to change the world." This was necessary for her not because something is wrong with us, but because she understood that the revolution begins with self and in community with each other. Black Latinidad: Building in Siblinghood to End Child Sexual Abuse gives voice to our truths as we dispel the shame and guilt many of us live with, and allows for collective support in our communities.

A child is not capable of causing anyone to violate them sexually, nor should a child be held responsible for their own safety from such abuse. When we, Black diasporic people, are not accountable to each other for ending child sexual abuse in our communities, we burden Black children's bodies and psyches with the responsibility of carrying their unacknowledged sexual trauma as they simultaneously spend a lifetime carrying all that vile, white supremacist toxicity. This was my reality as a seven-year-old Black Latinx child. I didn't think that I was worthy of holding anyone accountable for my safety, including my family, while also navigating a toxic world.

[A version of this essay was first published in the #LoveWITHAccountability online forum in *The Feminist Wire*, October 27, 2016.]

CHAPTER 22
Reclaiming Our Voice

Tanisha Esperanza Jarvis

The universe has a way of aligning everything in its perfect place. You will find your spirit's wants and needs always align. There is no coincidence that your eyes have wandered onto this page.

I share a message with you. I speak into existence the healing of our souls; and like the griot of western Africa, the words on this page sing the songs of my ancestors with wisdom about the future. Sisters, brothers, and siblings, in my narrative you will find the woven stories of trauma, survival, and healing.

Memories of my childhood home are enmeshed with the smells of empanadas, with the sounds of salsa vibrating from the radio. Have you ever been to a West Indian market on a Saturday? That is the sound of my family; loud, jubilant, and hearty. Their bosoms would rumble with laughter as their hands molded food to life. The center of a Panamanian household is the kitchen, and there you will find the matriarch. She is the Afro-Latina who holds the magic and fire of our history, but wrapped in her essence is a sadness deriving from the exploitation of our people. Our culture is matrifocal, but we have been conquered by patriarchy. This has cultivated a cycle of violence and avoidance.

Detrás de la puerta stands the *tío* (*behind the door, stands the uncle*). He is a creature of myth and lore. At night, communal voices whisper of the devoured souls of his victims. He often presents himself as a male, but it is not uncommon for him to take the form of a woman. Sometimes he is an uncle and others a neighbor, but what grounds his existence is the code of silence held by the community. The boogeyman is *not* chased from the village by pitchforks and fire. No. His victims are buried alive in a shallow, unmarked grave. Repeatedly, stones of slut-shaming and victim-blaming are thrown their way. How do we survive?

Unlike in the popular narrative that circulates in the media, the one of a stranger creeping into the rooms of little children, I was violated in the home of someone familiar. My story is not unique. Down every road and city block, a child weaves a similar tale. In conjunction, there is an adult who turns an eye.

When a child gets a physical cut, we rush to bandage the wound, but what do we do for the emotional wounds? If it is not tangible, does it not exist? Is it easier to deal with temporary cuts and scrapes, but what will suffice for the complex trauma of childhood sexual abuse (CSA)? A feeding tube? I hurt. I scream out through my rebellion. I am not a fast girl or a prude. We are not confused about our sexuality, nor are we not "man enough." We are dying inside. How do we survive?

At the doorsteps of Spelman College, my voice found me. She was hidden within the library of intellectual, social activism. There she was in the classroom, following the echoes of Toni Cade Bambara and Audre Lorde. With a microphone in hand, she yelled the piercing sounds of a warrior.

Social justice tightly grabbed my hand and led me to the microphone of action. Through my Social Justice Fellowship and Bonner Scholarship, I was tasked with creating an initiative and, with other Spelman students, implementing it into the school community. There I founded the Survivor's Network, an organization created to implement a safe space for survivors of sexual trauma and bring awareness to preventive measures. This journey guided me toward recovering survivors, grieving parents, and perpetrators. In my work, I realized healing must be holistic.

The aftermath of CSA is like that of a hurricane that has destroyed an entire community. One whose winds tear away the sidings of childhood innocence. Shattered realities lie scattered on the ground, and foundations cease to exist. How do we survive? The same ways our predecessors have been doing for centuries: as a community. We have survived the treacherous voyage of the transatlantic slave trade and the continued bondage of white supremacy. At every step, we leaned on our communities for our preservation. In numbers, we heal. As a community, we rebuild. As a collective, we demand accountability through restorative justice. How do we survive?

CSA leaves nobody untouched. The individual, the community, and the perpetrator must restore harmony together. Including preventive and intervention methods is a necessity. Preventive measures include discussing what sexual abuse and trauma looks like. If we do not speak on it, we cannot heal. Through a paradigm shift, a new society must be created, one where our children hold a space to share. Before we seek justice, we need to believe in the confessions of our young people. Centuries of trauma are built on exploitive lies. A child cannot consent to sex. A child cannot "tempt" an adult. The moment a child reveals their trauma, they should be believed. We must let go of our egos and guilt around the incident(s). Sometimes we are unaware, too entangled with our own pain. Your pain is valid. Let us heal together. I personally believe the moment we become aware of a predator among us, the person must be expelled from our village. We cannot protect our children by locking the door. We must remove the boogeyman from the house. However, this is not to say we disregard them as we would trash. On the contrary, we hold them accountable for their injustices. If the victim needs to scream and combat the "monster," then we give them space. At every intersection, the community is a united front, reestablishing that there will be no tolerance of abuse. A solution and reconciliation may not come to fruition, and acknowledging that reality is also an authentic expression of healing. Only when the person has been held accountable and atones do we open a channel of communication. Then we can sit at the table, as a collaborative, envisioning a healthier future together.

For many centuries, we have shed invisible tears that have been denied by our communities and oppressors alike. In our hearts lie secrets and pain, which we harvest like a collection of charred photos.

"As diasporic Black people, we must be unbreakable."

"As Black women, we must be resilient healers."

"And as queer bodies, we must be silent."

These are all fallacies!

Today you take your first breath. As you heal with me on this journey, we find a new voice. The passage reveals a new world, filled with the piercing shouts of warriors and healers. We will reclaim our voices.

We join together, feeling the interconnection of our existence. With our shared force, we vibrate positivity toward our children, healing the child within us and the children we love. From our yell, a collective voice emerges. A phoenix rising from the ashes blocks any force that tries to dismantle our connection.

The words on this paper will come to an end. Yet the conversation is not over; the table has just been set. I forward the mantle toward you, placing the pen in your hand. Will you write the next chapter?

CHAPTER 23
Network of Care

alicia sanchez gill

From the moment I experienced the first daggers of sexual abuse, until last night, when I responded to an email from a stranger requesting resources for a child sexual abuse survivor in their life, my work has centered on my own experiences of harm and the experiences of survivors who are a lot like me. As a queer person of color, a survivor of child sexual abuse living at the intersection of many identities, and a social worker whose life has focused squarely on anti-violence and healing outside of carcerality, I often think about the ways survivors heal and resist together. In a world that tells us to shrink, a society that tells us we don't have a right to exist or do this work or be the experts on our own lives, we are still here. We create meaning with one another and find hope in our interdependence.

My understanding of interpersonal violence is deeply shaped by my own values, experience, and narrative but also by the stories of the hundreds of hotline calls I have answered, folks I have worked with in support groups, friends, and friends of friends who have bravely and sometimes desperately shared their stories with me. Looking for answers. Hoping for healing. Searching for a more just world, however they might create it. The stories of survivors are woven together in a web of mutual care. What I have learned is that our stories become catalysts for change. *What I have learned is that our individual and collective healing relies on a network of care and support, and on speaking the unspoken.*

The first time I was sexually assaulted, I was seven. My half-brother moved in with our family at the age of sixteen and almost immediately started abusing me. As the primary after-school caretaker to a latchkey kid of parents working hard to make ends meet, he had complete access to me and to the privacy needed to assault me on a regular, almost daily basis. He began his grooming behaviors by forcing me to watch pornography and to mimic behaviors under the guise of "playing house." And when the sexual abuse became so violent that I threatened nervously to tell *someone*, he told me that no one would believe me, that I was dirty, and that it was my fault for being so curvy anyway. And I believed him. No loving adult in my household or in my life had ever had a conversation with me that would indicate otherwise. I also know that we were Afrolatinx in a community where anti-Blackness was vitriolic. And while I didn't have the language for my fears, I knew that if I told, my brother could be in the kind of trouble that devastated families like ours. When I was thirteen, my brother committed suicide. I sat silently at his funeral, holding both my anger that I'd live with this forever and he wouldn't, *and* my relief that he couldn't hurt me anymore. I was sexually assaulted many times after that. By another family member, by a family friend, and by a person I dated. I wouldn't tell anyone about the abuse until I was twenty-one.

Child sexual abuse, by its very nature, demands shame and isolation. Often our abusers have manipulated our voices through violence and coercion. They have counted on our shame and silence and the silence of those around us. For many of us, our relationship to concepts of disclosure, justice, and accountability have been complicated by our relationships to our abusers. So many survivors, like me, were harmed by the folks closest to us—the ones who were supposed to keep us safe. The ones who look like us and speak our language in a world where we are so often "othered." It is confusing because our abusers hurt us and then helped us finish science projects, or took us to church or bought us ice cream. It hurts because our abusers are still here, at Sunday dinners, at graduations, at holiday gatherings. For many survivors, having to choose between speaking our truth and losing loved ones, or remaining silent and keeping them, is a devastating form of negotiation we should never have to go through. The radical, loving choice for those around us is to dismantle our *"culture of quiet."*

I have a vision for a place where children are protected from violence, a place where they are supported the very first time they experience harm. A place where families have conversations about consent, boundaries, and healthy masculinity before abuse happens. I have a vision for a place where parents and teachers have paid sick leave, living wages, and time to be attuned to their children's and students' needs and behaviors. A place where families aren't ripped apart through deportations, policing, and the prison-industrial complex. A place where the protection of children is community-led and not institutionalized. Where child safety, health, and well-being are not placed solely on the shoulders of women and femmes.

Networks of care for our children, and for the adults who have survived, mean creating community-based prevention and responses to violence. Responses that do not engage in punitive justice but hold perpetrators accountable and keep survivors safe. These allow us to wrestle with dichotomies of good and bad and the various complexities and nuances of the communities with whom we are a part. This may involve affirming church communities; it may involve family and friends.

We—you and I—are often the first people to whom child sexual abuse survivors go when they share their experience. Whether as children or as adults, they tell their families, friends, partners, coworkers. By believing survivors, being prepared for crisis, and utilizing all our resources in a coordinated, safe way, we can help survivors feel seen and heard, and protect the children who have yet to come. In our networks of care, violence prevention will not happen through dependence on policing but through divestment in any system that seeks to dominate, coerce, or control our communities. It will depend on each of us to interrupt violence.

Recently I watched a fascinating video of fire ants in action. Fire ants work together in such a closely coordinated way that when in danger they can become a moving, protected, semisolid structure. Yet when a barrier falls in their way, like a tree branch, they are able to navigate around the barrier in a way that behaves almost like water. And not one ant gets left behind. What if all our networks of care could be like the fire ants? Solid and coordinated but adaptable and responsive to need? What if they all centered on safety, rehabilitation, accountability, and healing—creating communities where child sexual abuse is not just no longer tolerated but is also eradicated? Where those of us who have survived are not left to pick up the pieces of our shame alone but are met with a chorus of "we believe you" and "it's not your fault." Where people recognize that when violence happens, the whole community needs healing.

For those of us who never told, or told and weren't believed, for those of us who were left unprotected, we know the swelling of betrayal that rises up in our throats. Our stories are powerful calls to action. Our stories allow us to connect to one another and name our abuse and our abusers. Our stories are grounded in love for ourselves and our communities. Our stories help manifest the world we want to see. It is through these deep and meaningful connections, these networks of care, that I was able to come back from my darkest edges and begin healing. *What I have learned from survivors is that, like fire ants, it is our interdependence that will save us.*

[A version of this essay was first published in the #LoveWITHAccountability online forum in *The Feminist Wire*, October 21, 2016.]

CHAPTER 24

The Fear of Believing Survivors

Rosa Cabrera

Many times, my mama describes to me the moment she knew my dad was plotting to kill her. The details are always consistent: the way his lips turned white, dried up, and quivered. The quiet and the chill of Riverside Park, New York. Even though my dad used to beat my ass, for me the possibility of losing my mother was too frightening to believe. It couldn't be real. Not me. Not her. Not him. Not us. But she keeps repeating the story, the knife she felt in his pocket, the cold, his lips. How she said she needed to use the bathroom and quickly walked away. Each time she tells it, I feel her desperation to rid herself of the story, to offer me this thing I don't want. Each time, she tells it with her chest jumping and falling, her voice running through details with enough rage and volume to fill up my head and an auditorium full of listeners, but not without expressing how scared she was. Is. Something in her silently demands that someone else also be enraged at how she is forced to feel. Telling it is how she attempts to expel it. It's too overwhelming to let it to consume me: her anger, her fear, the thought of my dead mother, and the possibility that I could one day be an angry, scared, or dead body too.

In *The New Jim Crow*, author Michelle Alexander describes the way we "know and don't know" that the system of mass incarceration imprisons more African Americans today than were enslaved right before the civil war; how we "know and don't know" that we're moving about our lives, business as usual, without responding to this atrocious social crime. The horror of this reality leads to our justifications of systemic racial inequity: "Well, they did the crime, they do the time," or, "Those people just need to learn."[1] We deflect complicity or

1. Michelle Alexander, *The New Jim Crow: Mass Incarceration in the Age of Colorblindness* (New York: New Press, 2012).

any acknowledgment that our inaction is permitting the system to take away people's lives, people who commit the same crimes white and wealthy folks perpetrate at the same rates (if not higher rates) without facing the same hefty consequences. We're too scared to admit to our grotesque denial. The notion is so overwhelmingly frightening that we convince ourselves that it cannot be true.

It is this same willful, self-serving, and low-key protective lack of vision that often impedes us from not believing survivors when they speak, especially when the person that causes harm is someone we love or recognize as a leader, a family member, a celebrity, or clergy member. It hurts to believe that someone would do something so wild and "out of their character." It hurts to consider that we might have been exposed to harm ourselves. It hurts to feel betrayed. It hurts to feel fooled. We make up explanations or place blame in ways that align so comfortably with oppressive practices that have settled in us over time. Usually that means blaming adult and children survivors, the same way we blame Black and Brown folks for the identical crimes white and wealthy folks commit but are excused for.

Throughout my youth, I was angry with my dad for so often gaining my trust only to break it. After beating my ass, he would ignore me for days until he broke the ice with the offer of money or anything else I might want but not an apology. Never an apology. Still, he would regain my trust, over and over again, because I wanted him to love me. I would blame my mom for letting him humiliate her, for letting him hit me, and having my siblings and me all walk on eggshells so as not to ruffle his feathers. Why didn't she clap back? Why didn't she grab his hands? She was an adult just like he was. Why did she let him scare her? Nevertheless, my mama demonstrated love for me in different ways. She caressed my head in the dark, spoke to me with clarity but compassion when I acted selfishly, and cried when she read my runaway letters. Because of her emotional perceptiveness, it was easier to place blame on her than to demand an apology from my father. I saw my father as a threat. An impregnable wall. On the other hand, my mother was safe, and accessible. Through this dynamic a hierarchy was maintained, and it didn't just make my brother, my sister, my mama, or me more susceptible to harm, it also made us susceptible to blaming each other (and we did) for the harm my father perpetuated. This dynamic also brought me the furthest away from the language I needed, and the closest to shame when realizing that I had lost my virginity before I fully understood what virginity was.

But even as I watched him emotionally brutalize my mom and physically hurt me, I wouldn't believe that he would try to end my mother's life. I thought that was a boundary he would not cross. I justified my own disbelief. I told myself, and her, that she was paranoid or so distraught by my dad's abuse that it was causing her to see and feel things that weren't real. Imagine that: abuse causing someone to imagine abuse. On numerous occasions, she mentioned to me the times she saw my dad following her in public and hiding behind cars, walls, and bus stops. I thought, my dad is a jerk, an asshole, but he wouldn't do something as goofy as stalk my mom, his own wife, despite the fact that he would verbally shit on her in front of her kids. He was so steadfast in his ability to control others that he frequently reminded my sister and me that he owned our bodies and our belongings, so I couldn't imagine him ducking and diving from any of us. It wasn't until I turned twenty that I believed her—not because I learned how to become a better advocate for my mom but because I caught him in the act.

I found him hiding beside the wall of a college campus building, where my mom took English classes as part of a community ESL program. These were classes he so vehemently didn't want her to take. I was proud that she insisted and took them despite his disapproval. But the day I caught him, I was overcome with embarrassment, surprise, and anger. I was surprised that he was actually hiding from someone he had controlled for such a long period—longer than my own lifetime. It had disrupted my image of him as someone so secure in his dominance. His humanity confused me. I couldn't see it then, but despite the fact that his dominance brutalized me and my family, he was also the closest example of what the opposite of self-confidence looked like. In this single moment, the façade told on itself. He looked so vulnerable. I felt angry at the fact that he had always stalked my mama. In a single moment, her descriptive delusions turned to reality. I wanted to punish him.

That summer day, with ice cream in hand, I decided to surprise him in the act. When I approached him, I wanted to see something different than a hardness on his face, so I asked, "What are you doing?"

"Protecting your mother," he responded, stepping away from the raised lawn by the building, placing himself in full sight.

"By hiding? In broad daylight, though?" I asked, licking my ice cream, reveling in the crumbling image of himself. I castigated him, just as he and the nation as a whole had taught me. I turned toward the building's entrance, and when I looked back, he was gone. As I waited for my mama alone, I felt overcome with shame for not believing her. The shame deepened when I explained to my mama what I saw and she responded, "Didn't I tell you?"

The family had dinner at the apartment that night. Nobody talked about what happened, what was always happening. I didn't want my dad to keep lying about protecting my mama, or to remind us that he owned us. I didn't want to make my mom to have to retell her stories aloud or secretly in her mind, in my dad's presence. I didn't know how to hold all those possibilities, as well as my own rage, and turn my dad's defiance into regret. I couldn't be a good advocate for my mama. I couldn't get my dad to admit to causing harm.

Aggressors sometimes won't believe the level of harm their actions are causing survivors. Their gaslighting and denial is sometimes the product of an unwillingness to see the abhorrent within themselves. Like the bystanders (both those who actually witness the abuse and those whom survivors open up to), the aggressors are frightened of the possible level of torment and harm they cause survivors. Like bystanders, they place the blame on victims. Phrases like "I didn't hit you that hard" and "You provoked it" are common messages fabricated to cope with the possibility of being a monster.

My dad always used to tell me, and still tells me, that I'm always going to have conflict in my life. I "talk back" too much. I don't respect authority. He once told me that I would end up with a lover that would hit me because of "that attitude" of mine. *Necia. Comparona. Sinvergüenza.* Our mouths are filled with rhetoric whose purpose is to silence survivors and normalize abusive behavior by not calling it abuse and, similarly, not accurately describing resistance to that abuse when it happens. We are expected to be still as children and never outgrow that stillness.

Nope, I don't sit quiet when I'm forced to accept actions against my own well-being. Yup, I move with rage when I'm cornered by power. And, yes, I did date a lover for two years who both literally and figuratively pushed me, cut me, and made me bleed. But fortunately, unlike my mother, after finally understanding the situation I was in, I had the material resources and emotional capacity to leave. My resistance to and distaste for injustice against myself is not the cause of my conflict. For my father to absolve others of behaviors like his own is to uphold his own innocence. This is easy for him to believe, because he's echoing the rhetoric that bounced around the Dominican Republic when he was a child and was confirmed by American patriarchy when he was as an adult. This is how to uphold abuse. We justify it, validate it, create "coded language" around it, and even reward it, because we're scared of acknowledging the ways we enact and enable it.[2] In any situation, that would turn us into monsters.

These coping mechanisms, meant to turn our thoughts away from harm, actually perpetuate it. We cope by embracing stories with protagonists that cause harm but lack a complex internal landscape that is capable of a self-reckoning. We cope by fantasizing about and fetishizing violence in American movies, music, and sensationalized news programs. We tell ourselves, if it is external to us, if it is "those people," or that impossible or hilarious scene or plot, then it cannot be our beloved or us, even as we witness our beloved or ourselves cause harm.

I'm not above it. I was born and raised a Dominican American. My home—this country and my parents' country—have taught me

2. Toni Morrison, "Black Matters," in *Playing in the Dark: Whiteness and the Literary Imagination* (New York: Vintage, 1993).

how to cope by not believing and not seeing and, ironically, by also believing that the quickest and most potent way to access some version of power, and to feel heard and seen, is to translate anger into violent expression and action.

It hurts to see that in order to survive, we refuse to recognize abusive power. I bury the fact that I have been and could again be subjected to harm—I do that so I can engage in relationships. So that I can show up for work, I bury the fact that the lack of fair compensation for the work I do is not unrelated to the coercion of bodies and minds in instances of sexual assault. So that I can step outside my home, I bury the awareness that on any day, my life or my child's could be taken away because of someone else's willful ignorance. In similar ways, we bury the harm that our beloved cause when survivors force it into our awareness.

Patterns of abuse are upheld through one-dimensional thinking. We're monsters when we silence survivors who cause us discomfort, we're monsters when we enable and defend those who cause harm, and we're monsters when we cause harm. We can't break toxic patterns of abuse until we start avoiding depictions of ourselves as monsters. Abuse isn't one-dimensional, because people aren't one-dimensional.

I added to my mom's isolation by not believing her. I had to learn how my avoidance of parts of my trauma, by refusing to acknowledge how bad it was, was enabling abuse against her and me, and how my attempt to dilute my mama's pain was retriggering and deepening it. Now I believe my mama when she tells me she's afraid. I believe her rage is fully rational. I want my father to acknowledge that his actions were harmful and to honestly reflect on how the violence he witnessed and experienced as a boy forced him to mirror those dangerous actions and behaviors.

I imagine how agonizing it is for my mama to remember. I imagine how isolated and betrayed my father may feel reading this essay. My own rage, my father's pain, my mother's fear are all braided into my consciousness and haven't escaped this essay. I can't think of a more important step to take toward healing than to stop attempting to cancel our own experiences and stop using our own experiences to cancel those of others. One experience doesn't make the other non-existent. How else are we going to heal the wound than to identify its source and use pain and rage as marking points? This is how I want to love and be loved: to believe and be believed.

[A version of this essay was first published on *Medium*, July 2, 2018.]

CHAPTER 25

Colliding Traumas

Esther A. Armah

We're taught to put a lot of pain in the shadows—we're taught to do that as African women . . . what's that thing that is in the shadows.

—Peres Owino, *Bound: Africans vs African Americans*

Giving without receiving isn't love. It is hatred of the giving self.

—Ayi Kwei Armah, *Two Thousand Seasons*

Sifting through the broken glass that held my promise and my dreams
I'm just gathering pieces, To get here
I'm just holding myself, To get here
I'm livin' on stolen breath.

—Imani Uzuri

Esi. She was turning fifteen. She danced the shaku, shaku. She lived in Teshie, a busy suburb in Accra, Ghana's capital. She liked her hair cut just so. She headed to the barber to get her hair done. He was her regular barber. He was her pop's friend. She knew him. He knew her and her family. On that day he locked the shop door. He raped her.

Esi told her pop.

Esi, her pop, and her family gathered. Some stood. Some sat. The barber and his family came too. The barber stood. His family sat. They had gathered before. Esi's barber had been in her family's home many times. He and her pop shared a Star beer on a Friday night. They laughed together, shared stories of the craziness of Ghana's politicians and the latest rants on Joy FM radio—their morning radio station of choice. This was a familiar family ritual.

This gathering, though, was different.

The barber didn't call Esi a liar. He said he "had sex" with Esi.

***

It wasn't sex. It was rape. In Ghana, that is classified as "defilement." Right now, I live in Ghana, and I hear that word "defiled" a lot. It is how rape of children under the age of sixteen is described by our antiquated laws. Dictionary definition: "sullied," "marred," "spoilt," "ruined," "tainted." Defile: "to make unclean, unfit, or impure," "to corrupt the purity." The twenty-first-century interpretation: victim-blaming and -shaming while perpetrator-shielding.

I don't know the barber's name. In the media, it was only hers we learned. She was underage, then. She is not now. A reporter wrongly included her name and age in the story. He was chastised across social media. It was too late. Her name was out there. His was not.

The two families gathered. Drinks were offered. Some "small chops" were served, as we call snacks in Ghana.

The barber appealed to Esi's pop to think of their long friendship, his family, his business, and his future. Her family nodded and murmured.

Esi's pop agreed. We don't know what her mother said. We know she was there. Esi was not asked and did not share the impact of the rape on her body, mind, or soul.

The result? The two families protected the barber and the friendship. They didn't report the rape to the police. That was the end of the matter.

In Ghana, through a complicity that is cultural and communal, families—men and women, representing both the victim and the predator—come together and exchange something to make the accusation, the rape, the sexual violence go away. This is common. Reporting it is not. Such is the process and practice for dealing with sexual violence outside of court. In this process, admission is common. What follows admission is a call to action regarding the future of the perpetrator and an insistent pressure on the victim—so often a girl or young woman—to accept an exchange. It is often money, sometimes it is schnapps. In Ghana, during these family gatherings, they do not say it did not happen. They do not call the victim—usually a girl or woman—a liar. They may sometimes, but often they do not. They exchange goods, money, sometimes apologies and pressure. The pressure is almost always inviting the victim's family to see how the life of the violator would be irreparably damaged by her accusation—not by his action. We portray the violence as unintentional, we diminish its impact, we cajole, we call on Jesus, and where that doesn't work, we may lean back on juju. We rarely seek justice via the courts, which usually means acquittal and only in rare cases conviction.

It rarely looks like justice for the survivor. But life continues for the perpetrator.

I was told about a fourteen-year old girl in Accra's Nima area. Her birthday gift from her classmates was gang rape. They made her pregnant. Months before her fifteenth birthday, she gave birth. Her education was over. The boys told her no one could touch them. They were right. Their names were known, their locations too, but the police waved away consistent calls by her family to arrest the boys. She became a teenage mother, a statistic described and named by a government that, according to its policy, would say that she needs better self-control and tools and morality and Jesus to not get pregnant. It would not classify her "circumstance" as rape. The girl ended up in a series of multiple psychiatric wards, her dreams of studying science stolen and broken. The boys would go on and complete school. Seven years would go by. Her life forever changed, theirs untouched.

Here in Ghana, social justice organizations, policy folk, and child sexual abuse counselors preach the "just say no" mantra of sexual-violence prevention to girls. They offer ways of saying no. Make it authoritative, make it clear, and make it aggressive, they say. The girls do. The girls did. The girls have. And they are then confronted by society's communal, family-led out-of-court settlement or the judicial re-traumatizing process.

Reporting is rare. Justice through the courts even rarer.

In Ghana, sexual violence is casual conversation. It is unremarkable. It is dropped onto the bodies of teen girls and growing numbers of boys, with undiscussed and unexplored consequences within those lives.

My global call is for "emotional justice."

That means creating a process and practice to articulate, deal with, and heal from the legacies of untreated trauma created by our global history, in which sexual violence is prominent. That is our work.

We have intersectional traumas: our traumas are not singular or individual; they connect and they collide, they collude and they are communal. They manifest in ways that cause hurt and harm beyond the incident of sexual violence. We never seek emotional justice. We know how to create chaos, but we don't know how to heal and build through the carnage into something else.

In the United States, "school-to-prison pipeline" is a well-known phrase. It describes the stages children of color are put through, moving along a direct path from classrooms into cellblocks.

In Ghana, we have a sexual violence pipeline.

It begins in junior high school and advances through senior high school to university. School is a playground for predators. But we don't use that word. They are teachers. No checks. No background verification that these authority figures can be around children. No. In Ghana, teachers are often among the top three professions held by child sexual abusers.

As I write this, Faith is fighting to stay in high school in Ghana. Her head teacher is chasing her body. He has been for more than two years. She is chasing grades. It looks as though he might win. I am in Accra. Two others and I have driven for more than two hours from the city of Accra, past wild green fields and discarded objects that the weather has transformed into something unrecognizable, to arrive at Faith's school. Her town is more a village than a town. It is in the Volta region, one of ten political regions in Ghana. Small shops, a local hospital, washing hanging on lines to dry. Paint peeling on shops stacked with soda, boxes of Ceres juice, bottled water, prepaid cell phone cards, and biscuits. There are groups of young men, dark-chocolate skin gleaming, seated, watching cars like ours go by. We drive past the taxi stand. The drivers are cleaning their cars, complaining about the lack of business. The town may be small, but the head teacher is not. He has turned the corridors of his school into a predator's playground, Faith and her classmates tell us. He roams hallways and classrooms. He grabs at girls' breasts and their butts. That's what they will tell us. We arrive on School Sports Day. The teacher, whose voice I know but whom I have never seen, greets us. The to-and-fro of students from multiple schools creates easy cover for us. Chairs are pulled under a tree. We welcome the shade. There are three of us. There are seven of them—students and survivors. One by one, teenage girls in school uniform approach us. "Good afternoon," each says. Then, they tell their story. They recount incident after incident of sexual abuse and harassment at the hands of their headteacher.

This is not his first time. Nor the first allegation. We would learn allegations stretch back to 1992. At that time, he taught science. His lab was his rape den. He likes the smart girls. Always smart girls.

Under that tree, seated on classroom chairs, slices of sunshine hitting the hard ground, we listened. The girls' stories, the teachers' corroboration, the faux investigations, the lack of change or result. Coalition Against Sexual Abuse (CASA), of which I was part, then petitioned government ministers, the Ghana Education Service, and the Criminal Investigation Department to temporarily remove the head teacher and for a thorough investigation to be conducted into his alleged conduct. Consistent pressure yielded results. He was asked to go, temporarily. An investigation began. The Ghana Education Service conducted their hearing, at which the girls alleging the sexual harassment were invited to speak. They were asked to have "credible" evidence with them and to bring a friend or counsel. The hearing took place more than three hours from their town. To get there, the girls had to cross a river by boat and use several cars due to the lack of reliable public transport—all at their own cost.

Faith is nineteen. The other schoolgirls, Jemila, Jocelyn, and Monica, are aged between sixteen and nineteen.[1] As I write this, the girls' hearing has taken place, and they are waiting for the ruling.

Ghana's media landscape is loaded with stories of teachers and head teachers committing sexual abuse, harassing, extorting sex for grades or school fees, and raping their students, many of whom end up pregnant. Pastors are a powerful predatory presence too. On the global stage, from Ghana to the United States, we have process and practice around sexual violence. But what is that process? What is that practice? How does it manifest? Who does it serve?

For too long, we have not been held accountable for unexplored and uninvestigated wounds. We have walked with the manifestations of those wounds but not created process or practice to build with them, through them, and beyond them to a sustainable emotionality that defines and centers healthy love.

It has been argued that in the healing processes to recover from sexual violence, survivors' testimonies should be centered and held as the highest priority. But what if those who are survivors are also perpetrators? Where do we stand? What do we do? In the area of emotional justice, these are what I call "colliding traumas."

I think of Junot Díaz and Zinzi Clemmons.

Díaz, a Pulitzer Prize–winning writer, authored a *New Yorker* piece, "The Legacy of Childhood Trauma," that made global headlines. In it he documents being a survivor of rape and not telling anyone or seeking healing or help, which, he writes, resulted in him crashing through his own life and others' in varying ways. He also documents the ways he loved and hurt and harmed, and the moment he became a silence breaker. The piece was followed by the critically acclaimed novelist Zinzi Clemmons accusing Díaz of sexually assaulting her. Zinzi Clemmons is a critically acclaimed writer, whose first novel is *What We Lose*. Her accusations ignited a storm that brought a number of academics, educators, activists to various tables.

What resulted was a gathering of minds that, over the course

1. Names have been changed to protect identities.

of time, included the publication of two open letters. One of them, signed by prominent academics and writers, lamented "the ways in which the press and those on social media have turned tweets made against Junot Díaz into trending topics and headlines in major newspapers both inside and outside the United States." It continues:

> The (at times uncritical) reception and repetition of the charges have created what amounts to a full-blown media-harassment campaign. They have led to the characterization of the writer as a bizarre person, a sexual predator, a virulent misogynist, an abuser, and an aggressor. Within less than 24 hours after the tweets, scholars and writers called for a boycott of the Pulitzer Prize winner and for his withdrawal from Voices of Our Nations Arts Foundation. . . . Our concern is with the sensationalist register in which the media and some social-media users have portrayed the accusations of misconduct leveled against the Latino author. . . . The issue at hand is not whether or not one believes Díaz, or his accusers, but whether one approves the use of media to violently make a spectacle out of a single person while at the same time cancelling out the possibility of disagreement about the facts at hand.[2]

Responding to that letter was a group of junior scholars, academics, and gender non-confirming and trans faculty of color from different levels of academia. In their "Response to the Open Letter," they wrote, in part:

> We write first and foremost as an expression of solidarity with survivors who have shared their stories, those who have not yet come forward, and those who never will. . . . Our intention is to encourage our colleagues, mentors, students, and our

2. "Open Letter against Media Treatment of Junot Díaz," *Chronicle of Higher Education*, May 14, 2018, https://www.chronicle.com/blogs/letters/open-letter-against-media-treatment-of-junot-diaz.

> communities, as well as the larger media, to more carefully consider how survivors are impacted by narratives that center perpetrators of misogyny and those that support them. We feel compelled to respond to the "Open Letter Against Media Treatment of Junot Diaz" and the climate of suppression, silence, and potential punishment of survivors it has fostered.[3]

The Díaz piece, Clemmons accusations, and the two letters that came in response are a specific example of colliding traumas. These are also intersectional traumas. They reveal our need to create new language and new process and practice to deal with this set of complications.

They are survivors. Clemmons and Díaz both. They are silence breakers. Clemmons and Díaz both. One is both survivor and perpetrator. Their silence breaking launched colliding traumas. We are in the midst of these colliding traumas.

That collision manifests in our movements, our families, our policies, and our institutions. That manifestation protects broken, fragile, wounded community and condemns us to build from those spaces. Then they implode. And the cycle of colliding traumas begins again.

We articulate an ideology of freedom, but we practice emotional patriarchy. What I mean by that is women of color have been taught to privilege the trauma and its legacy on men. That is what we practice even as we articulate ideologies about dismantling harmful structures that we recognize cage rather than connect us. Institutions and individuals within them dispatch structures and systems to protect and support the perpetrator even if they are simultaneously articulating the importance of survivor testimonies. Intellectual brilliance, ideological and political progressiveness, and emotional illiteracy can stand, live, breathe, and be built up in the same body. What they cannot do is thrive beyond a particular point. They are built up, and they break.

3. "In Scholarly Debates on #MeToo, Survivor Support Should Take Precedence," *Chronicle of Higher Education*, May 25, 2018, https://www.chronicle.com/blogs/letters/in-scholarly-debates-on-metoo-survivor-support-should-take-precedence.

That cycle ends with the practice of emotional justice. For me, we are in the emotional justice iteration of our global Black liberation movement.

It must be built by creating process and practice.

It is a public first, but it may offer us space to untangle webs of hurt and harm that followed hurt and harm. We say that we cannot continue to practice a politics of disposability. That means our healing tables will always be complicated. Healing rejects absolutism and engages complexity. Trauma's truths are hard to tell.

I have shown how Ghana's gathering spaces around sexual violence privileges the perpetrator and his (it's usually his) future, fortune, and likelihood of being forgiven. In the United States, the language may be more eloquent and the gathering may be virtual, but the outcome is still emotional patriarchy masquerading as progressive politics and ideology.

This is hard. It is peculiarly and particularly hard.

We are not all right. We are all right. Junot, Zinzi, the contents of the first open letter, and the response within the second. Being right does not allow us to be healed. We need different language and to walk down unbuilt paths for this particular work to happen.

How do we do that? By dismantling emotional patriarchy.

We start by acknowledging that this EJ healing table is complex and complicated. Who gets to sit at it? We are family. We protect family. We practice emotional patriarchy. Women of color particularly go out of our way to protect men.

That is what the Junot Díaz scenario reminds us. That is what happens in Ghana. That is what happens across the United States. That is what happens globally.

So how do you dismantle emotional patriarchy?

First, recognize it. It is our emotional inheritance passed from one generation to another. It shape-shifted untreated traumas, which made their way into hearts and souls and minds and tongues.

Though we have done much work, we have not done *this* work.

As Black women, we are expected to filter our feelings, to pass them through multiple sieves. Our pain is not met with empathy, nor our anger with understanding, nor our disappointment with compassion. Policing emotionality creates struggle; it means having internal fights with how you feel in order to negotiate society's resistance and rejection of your humanity.

In this world, emotionality became the graveyard for untreated wounds due to injustice. We all sustained wounds. Some we buried. Some buried us. Stuff has to go somewhere. It has to. It is not that you don't feel; it is what gets done with those feelings. No space to speak your truth and have it heard in the language in which you spoke it. So your anger can never be temporary; it is a characteristic that condemns you in a workspace, in the eyes of men, and it is a label that you seek to avoid by folding yourself in different ways.

In Ghana, the gatherings are not a healing space for survivors but a freeing space for the perpetrators. They are a space that makes a victim feel haunted and hunted, where they are rarely heard and almost never healed but instead re-harmed. They also do not create the kind of intimate reckoning required for perpetrators to confront their own actions. Mothers vociferously defend their sons who are perpetrators; fathers are equally vociferous in defending daughters who are victims. Mothers pressure their daughters to accept the exchange that paralyzes the trauma and allows the perpetrator to return to his life. Fathers do the same. It is not healing, it doesn't serve change, and it protects the perpetrator and entrenches trauma within the community.

With the Díaz and Clemmons scenario, the gathering was scattered: it occurred across social media and with the writing and publication of letters by academics, activists, journalists, and educators.

This collision of traumas is unchartered territory in our movements. We must articulate what is creative chaos, what is silence-breaking, what is the legacy of childhood trauma legacy, what is adult-traumatizing reality. The traumatized and the traumatizers may live in the same body, so what forms of language and processes are we building to do the work of intimate reckoning in order to continue our movement work?

Globally, we practice "emotional patriarchy." Globally, we can end this practice and in its place create a process and practice of emotional justice. That means a healing table with paths, pacing, and preference. In this approach, survivors are heard first. They do not simply speak first, they are heard first. To be heard invites an opportunity to engage in the aftermath of the sexual violence, attempts to understand and offer resources to mitigate any further harm.

Global Black love has never been unconditional, but we can use emotional justice to make it accountable.

Ghana and the United States. We are stories, you and I. We are family too. Snapped branches from a bent baobab. Disconnected family, connected and colliding traumas.

Our branches point accusatory, finger-shaped leaves. We scream silently. Unheard by each other. My Black. Your Black. Both unheard by families focused on arranging for silence to spread, corners tucked into children's souls while predators say grace, pour libation, adjust church hats or straighten kaba and slit. Our pastors look alike—different accents but same hypocrisy, shame, and judgment. Neither recognizes what has been taken.

We have made ourselves accountable to the wounds. They shape our narrative as we drown voices with others denials and justifications.

We have too long side-eyed each other's Blackness, eyes running up and down a panorama of Black and Brown form.

We carry a shared truth. We did not get to grieve. We don't always know how. We are learning what it means to hold space. We do not know what it feels like to be tender and have tenderness directed at our hurt spaces. All these firsts are what occurs at the healing table, and they begin with survivors. This is our process and practice. The healing table cannot be deadlined or sidelined. It is ongoing; it is a place to which we return again and again and again. Part of tenderness means traveling through a gamut of emotions to get there; we may sound punitive, we may rage and rant, we may scream, we may be silent, we may wail and wonder—we may need all of these to get to tenderness. With emotional justice, our healing table makes space for all of this.

Emotional justice means colliding and intersectional traumas, and dismantling emotional patriarchy. We acknowledge that it is unchartered territory. It is scary. But it is not nearly as scary as the silence of survivors, the privileging of perpetrators, and the expectation that liberation can come through progressive politics and ideology alone.

Emotional justice is ours. Let's build our healing table. Work with us. Walk with us.

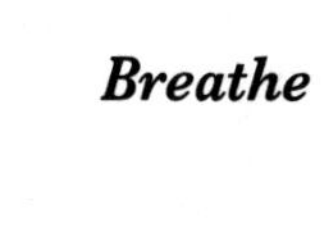
Breathe

CHAPTER 26

Kissing, Forgiveness, and Accountability

Farah Tanis

When I was five years old, my uncle—already in his twenties at the time—would grab me out of sight and bring me into corners of the living room, the backyard, the kitchen, and the bedroom. Once he even cornered me in the bathroom to force his big mouth upon mine and force his tongue inside my five-year old mouth, kissing me through muffled screams and gags as my body convulsed in repulsion. I was a child consumed with anguish and fear. My loneliness engulfed me in a constant state of dissociation. One time, he pushed me onto the cold tiles of the bathroom floor to do this thing he called "kissing." Lying on top of me, fully clothed, he would grind himself on my little body, until I was drenched in his release. Each time he did this, I would beg him before he began, "Don't pee on me," not realizing until years later that what he expulsed at the end of his grinding himself over my clothing was not urine at all. This experience traumatized me for decades. I became repulsed by kissing, for what I thought would be forever. Scarred for decades, I lived at the intersections of pain, having survived depression and struggles with anxiety—a survivor with additional compounded traumas and volatile relationships, disconnected, unable to cry, and hating kissing. With *my* beautiful lips, hating kissing.

Then I my met the woman who would become my wife. I was already thirty-three, my disposition cemented, my disconnection from myself welcomed and almost complete. During our online courtship, our late-night conversations, her on the West Coast and me on the East Coast, she talked and talked about me, about herself, all her favorite things to do, and she talked of one thing that sent her into ecstatic joy—kissing. Kissing, full, deep, wet, soft, hard, transcendent open mouth kissing, kisses she said would tell her everything about me. She talked about kisses through which she would speak to me of love, of tenderness, of happiness, of strength, of bravery; kisses through which she would transfer all the gifts of her heart to everything that is me. It went on like this for weeks until finally we said, "It's time to meet."

It wasn't long before she traveled to the East Coast and we met. Hell-bent on being liberated, longing to know what freedom could mean for me, to make love and be locked in long kisses, to sit on the couch locked in kisses, to be in safe, queer-friendly spaces locked in deep, warm kisses with my lover. I remember it so vividly now. When I laid eyes on her for the first time and she smiled. I could notice almost nothing else but her lips. Bare naked lips. Perfectly pink and perfectly violet. I tried not to look, but I couldn't resist, until finally I allowed myself to look. We sat in the car on the way back to my place, and all I could do was imagine how they would feel on my own lips, on my body. The evening back at my home was peaceful. She had taken a red-eye from Los Angeles. She brought gifts, and I spent the previous night unpacking boxes and cleaning the house I had barely just moved into.

There I was. There we were at this place of impending transformation together, a place of reconciliation and restoration, first and foremost with myself. Lying on my bed on our sides, facing each other in a perfect fall evening as the sun went down. I can still smell the cinnamon and pine and brown sugar, pumpkin seeds and hot chocolate. We were drawing closer together, and before you know it, our lips met. It was perfection, but I drew back. I drew back from perfection. Not wanting to go further. I hadn't given myself over to a kiss in years, if not my whole life. How was I going to relearn in one evening, in one night how to kiss again? How could I give myself over to the kissing and the softness, the wetness, the feel of her lips on mine, entering mine? I wanted exactly that, needed exactly that and so, I pulled closer, of my own volition, my choice, thinking of my wants, my needs, meeting her lips again; and this began a session of kissing like none I could have ever imagined. The best erotic, transcendental experience of kissing and love-making before the actual love-making began with kissing. For the first time in I don't remember, if ever at all, I experienced a kissing that I had heard could immerse you in ecstatic joy. Kissing, full, deep, wet, soft, hard, transcendent open-mouth kissing. Kisses that did indeed tell her everything about me and kisses through which she would speak to me of love, of tenderness, of happiness, of strength, of bravery; kisses through which she would transfer all the gifts of her heart to everything that is me even now, thirteen years later. Kisses that were my salvation and my healing and liberation.

My uncle is long dead now, and I have worked hard to forgive him postmortem. For that to be possible, there had to be a forgiving and a welcoming of myself to myself. The self I know I could have and should have been had he not put his hands and his mouth on me, grooming me for what I know now was rape.

Moreover, there had to be an accounting, a reckoning, and since my uncle was already six feet under by the time I found the courage to tell, I decisively disclosed his abuse to a room full of grieving family after his funeral. I told great-uncles and aunts, and I told my grandmother and all those who made him into what he was, those who perpetuated the misogyny and violence he embodied. I remember at the age of nine, I walked in on him raping a young woman who lived in our home. I told the family members he was a rapist. I told them I didn't think they should mourn only the part of him that was the "loving" uncle who tried to help everybody, but also sit in acknowledgment and contemplation of the part of him who practiced rape. An accountability process had to be engaged. I longed for a life of liberation from the pain of sexual trauma, and I longed to forgive with the sort of forgiveness that at this point was impossible for me to extend to my uncle, except maybe if it extended only to his spirit. I believed that spirit still roamed the earth and our neighborhoods; it was inside young men who made it their purpose to desecrate, abuse, and break Black girls.

Inherent to the process of forgiveness is holding the harm-doer accountable for wrongdoing. Whether it's what Everett L. Worthington Jr., in his book *A Just Forgiveness: Responsible Healing without Excusing Injustice*, refers to as "decisional forgiveness," in which "we control our behavioral intentions toward the harm-doer," or what he calls "emotional forgiveness, in which we experience emotional replacement of negative, unforgiving emotions with positive, other-oriented emotions," forgiveness activates mercy and makes a demand of harm-doers to authentically act to right the wrong. Forgiveness is not exoneration. Forgiveness is not justifying or excusing one's behavior. It is not saying, "What you did is okay." It is not saying, "The act you committed isn't important" or "You didn't really hurt me" or "I'll let you off the hook this time."[1] Within the spectrum of what can result from compassionate accountability, to me, forgiveness is the zenith.

Despite the fact that he was a serial rapist, it never crossed my mind that my uncle should be in prison.

I've been in the anti-rape movement for over twenty years. I founded Black Women's Blueprint and led the Black Women's Truth and Reconciliation Commission (BWTRC), held in New York at the United Nations in April 2016.[2] The BWTRC focused on truth, healing, justice, and reconciliation with a focus on the restoration of survivors to themselves, as well as what it would mean to restore harm-doers to their own humanity.

I have said this: I envision a world where if prisons still actually exist one hundred years from now, healers should replace the prison guards of the harm-doers we put there. This is what a country where

1. Everett L. Worthington, *A Just Forgiveness: Responsible Healing without Excusing Injustice* (Downers Grove, IL: IVP Books, 2009).

2. Black Women's Blueprint is a transnational Black feminist organization that celebrates and seizes the opportunities of the African Diaspora, all while mourning the violent conditions that created it. For more information, see http://Blackwomensblueprint.org. Launched by Black Women's Blueprint in 2010, the Black Women's Truth and Reconciliation Commission (BWTRC) carried out its mandate over a six-year process. An independent body led by and composed of members of civil society, the BWTRC examined the history, context, causes, chronology, and consequences of rape and sexual assault on women of African descent. It focused on women of African descent with legacies linked to the transatlantic slave trade and enslavement in the Americas and the Caribbean. The BWTRC was the first of its kind in the United States to focus on the historical and contemporary experiences of rape, sexual assault, and reproductive violations against Black women with its mandate aimed at truth, justice, healing, and reconciliation.

accountability for rape and child sexual abuse that is not steeped in punitive justice could look like.

I constantly dedicate my work in the transnational Black feminist movement to my father, to my mother, to my experiences alone, and to the collective community. I ground it in forgiveness, in the practice of forgiveness as an intentional act of resistance. For Black people, for Black women in particular, for all people of color, for all women, this practice involves engaging in extraordinary acts of freeing oneself, extraordinary leaps toward healing, extraordinary steps in revolution and forms of liberation where even those who've caused harm must come along when the ring shout of freedom goes out.

I don't tell my story to forgive all the rapists. This is not a story about forgiving all the batterers. It is not a story about forgiving all the traffickers. This is a not a call for all to practice forgiveness and then all will be well. As Black women we are often trained and even coerced into forgiving and just surviving. Even as girls, we are conditioned to protect those who do us harm. So we know that forgiveness is an individual and complex process, even when it is communal. It is a multilayered process, requiring profound meditative thought and a conscious series of decisions, as well as inner and outer confrontations.

However, we need to think of moving, bolder and braver, into a future that centers the harm-doers as human beings. They need to be asked about solutions and given the opportunity to speak of what could or should have been different in their lives. They need to tell us what would have stopped them from raping. Is there such a study? I'm not referring to one that asks, "Why did you rape?" but instead one that asks the following:

1. "What would have stopped you from raping?"
2. "At what point in your life could that action—or series of actions, or change to prevent you from raping—have occurred?"
3. "What happened that you never received these things?"

The answers I imagine we could receive, in order to bolster solutions to prevent rape in the future, could be astounding. And they could transcend what we already know from offender-management programs, because we would hear from those who don't make it to such programs but who simply end up in prison or remain in our communities, on our campuses, in our houses of worship, and in our homes.

Just as many survivors talk about feeling human again, reconnecting to their bodies and their world, is it possible that harm-doers can also connect to their humanity again? And fully understand, connect with, and internally acknowledge the humanity of those they harm, as well as the communities and future generations affected by the ripple effects?

What then is the work we need to do to make Afrofuturistic visions hu*manifest*, to take back our lives, own our rage, move through it, and heal from it? We need to come face-to-face with what we fear most. We need to get at the answers from harm-doers themselves—not the first answers, which will undoubtedly make us cringe, like "she deserved it," "she wanted it," "I don't know," or worse. We need to come face-to-face with the harm-doers. We need to get the solutions we know are possible by entering a period of targeted inquiry and discovery. This includes a process of accountability and humanizing the harm-doers, which, for many of us, are our family members and our romantic partners. For too many of us, they are those we cannot stop loving. The past is ever present in the structural and intergenerational dynamics in our community. However, what is also ever present is the blueprint that can inform and transform future strategy into a practice of what I've come to call "liberatory prevention," in which we use and honor the past not only to liberate ourselves but also to demand that communities liberate themselves from the chains of complicity. With liberatory prevention we create new participatory processes for engaging harm-doers in the work to end the violence they commit, thus ending violence in our time and for future generations.

CHAPTER 27

This Is My Return

"The Soul Is Covered in a Thousand Veils"

Sevonna M. Brown

Beginning Again: My Soul Reached Up and Carried Me from My Sleep

I was in college at a women's retreat, the first sleepover I had done with a group of grown women in my entire life. I had been a Girl Scout growing up, and so camping and cooking over the fire were among my favorite pastimes. This was exciting, the beginning of my development as a leader and what would be a major stepping-stone in finding my own voice in my life's work. We were in a mansion in upstate New York that sat in the middle of the woods and functioned as a creative and artistic space for social justice organizers and advocates to plan, process, and retreat. We gathered as women of color proposing our own change projects for navigating a freer and more liberated world for women and girls. We meditated on the legacy of Audre Lorde, the poetry of Alice Walker, and the prose of Toni Morrison. We sipped on the harmonies of Sonia Sanchez's wisdom and curled under the classic stories of Jean Toomer and Zora Neale Hurston. We were made and then made over by the gems we each dropped and planted in the space.

After a day's work of visioning, manifesting, dreaming, planning, and mapping our individual and communal goals, the power cut out just as we had put the dishes away from dinner. By this point we had spent the full day bonding, unearthing our personal charms and practical rituals, stirring large pots of spaghetti, building altars, setting profound and necessary intentions, and unpacking both the weekend's wears and our life stories. With the power out, the mansion was incredibly hard to warm up. We were retreating in the midst of March breezes and crisp air. The wooden walls were aching with the cold, so much so that we gathered around the oven wearing our jackets over our pajamas, continuing on in sisterhood and organic bonding that lasted for several more hours.

Once we were full from laughter and conversation, and every snack we would find in the mansion, we finally retired to sleep for the night, bundled in two or three blankets each to manage the cold. It was hard to complain given how rich and invaluable the entire experience had been. The cocoon of the blankets nearly sedated me, and I fell into a deep sleep, moving through a dreamscape for hours. Morning broke around six, and I felt the lightness of the sun break through the windows and the cracks of branches that surrounded the mansion. In a lucid state, I felt like I was underwater. My legs melted into the mattress, and I could only shift my weight from side to side.

As I tried to sit up, memories triggered me back to my six-year-old self, who was an avid bed-wetter. Nearly each morning I would wake up with urine soaked in my pajamas and down to the mattress. Soaking in grief and in shame, I would lie stuck to the bed unable to move, feeling stuck and pinned by my own mistake. My harm-doer lived in the house where my experience of child sexual abuse took place between the ages of two and eight. This loss of control over the body is a common symptom for child sexual abuse survivors. The out-of-body experience of floating and sinking all at once is a major part of the impact of child sexual abuse on the somatic experience and the cellular memory of the body. While I had not wet the bed at this women's retreat in a middle of a power outage in the woods, I could remember the feeling—the distress of the cold, the wetness, the inescapability, the fear that he might come in that morning looking for me.

This time I woke up swimming—drowning, in fact—in the faculties of my own survival. I could feel my soul pick itself up. I thought to myself: this is my return. My return to that which I do not know, that which is boundless, that which is a six-year-old coming of age threefold. It is that of a jaw dropping, a heart melting, a needle spinning around a record while my mother's hips sway, both her hips and the needle going everywhere and nowhere all at once. This is my return. That which is sacred only to me and that which is my own. A layer of my soul peeled back and looked at me.

But what I did not know was that this would be one of many returns. Returns to self, selflessness, self-fullness. I was unhinging—beyond suffering. This re-remembering was necessary for me, as I was crossing over into a new threshold of my leadership. If what Hazrat Inayat Khan says is true, that "the soul is covered in a thousand veils," then that frigid March day chose me. It chose me to uncloak and pull one of a thousand veils off.

Seer, Seeker, Broken Open

It was another March morning, years later, that had me at a another crossing in my life. I had just suffered two major accidents. In the first, I was coming out of a Just Beginnings Collaborative roundtable on child sexual abuse in Washington, DC, and I was hit by a six-hundred-pound door in the entrance of the Office of Justice Programs. This was not only devastating but incredibly triggering for me, and two weeks later, with major shoulder injuries and a balance disorder from the door incident, I fell down a flight of stairs and suffered a concussion. Both of these accidents could of been catastrophic, but I survived them in totality with the support of family and friends who surrounded me with deep love and compassion. It was on that March morning in the midst of recovery that I experienced a rite of passage I felt had been a long time coming. My recovery was rapid. I rose much taller than I was before, and I witnessed the power of my ability to heal myself and decide on loving myself. This rite was so vivid and so utterly present for me. It was shaping my every move and every thought. I could see it in my patterns, my thoughts, and the way I moved around the world.

Physically, I felt incredibly strong, beyond my capacity to even understand. Spiritually and emotionally, I felt overwhelmingly connected and settled into what I believe seers and oracles feel: possessing super vision and the supernatural capabilities to see love in every single being—even those who have harmed you.

I called my sister and told her what I thought might be the only explanation for the way that I was feeling: I must be pregnant. Not waiting any longer, I went to take a test, and double lines popped up on the kit. I laughed to myself, but above all my spirit body said, "Get ready." My conscience spoke back to me, clearing it with my soul, stating that my justice was coming. Not in the birthing of the baby but in the birthing of myself.

I knew that I had to move beyond my relationship with my triggers to go forward with what I thought would be the most challenging re-veiling of the self: giving birth. It would be a source of connective tissue between me the survivor and me the soul covered in a thousand veils, a way to utilize my own suffering for the manifestation of my own power and joy and divine love. This transformation is what justice means to me. It is a healing and an unburying of the self that is deeply invested in the radical politics of self-love.

Compassionate Accountability

Some of the self-work that I did to arrive at my own self-love and self-justice through compassionate accountability involved being in conversation with my harm-doer.

As a survivor, I have a strong connection of the ways the body is impacted by violence. I have not only lived through it but have also studied it closely and with detailed attention to the impact of trauma and violence on the cellular DNA of survivors. One of the most valuable gifts I have ever given myself has been to research and understand the ways, beyond triggers, that we hold and carry the material consequences of living inside of traumatic memories.

I felt personally responsible to not only save my own life through learning, but to also acknowledge that the state of my mind and being impacts my cells. While I was carrying my son, I realized that my cells, my DNA, and my soul-body's memory would be transferred to him. In fact, I knew that we were sharing a veil, that on the day when the earth would decide he should arrive, that that veil would peel back. Sitting with this, in deep meditation and contemplation, I sought to purify this cellular memory of mine—not to rid myself of it, but to clarify and reconcile the memories that needed to be transformed. This would need to happen through my own strength.

As I began to deepen my learning and peel back the layers of my own experiences through this studying, I not only found a deepening of my healing process but also realized that for me the journey of healing and justice was a high-risk issue. I needed to speak to my harm-doer and confront the damages that left me feeling underwater for so many years of my life.

When you have endured repeated trauma for eight consecutive years, there is a great undoing and reclaiming that needs to take center stage in your healing process. It is a jambalaya recipe of healing, rituals, practices, accountability, self-love, healing, intention-setting, and cleansing. This, unlike most approaches to seeking accountability, involved no third party—simply him and me. This was incredibly difficult to do alone, but for me it was necessary to work through the hardest parts in order to live inside of my own resiliency.

Re-veiling the Self: Labored and Delivered

I woke up, water breaking between my thighs. Amniotic fluid rebirthing and baptizing grown-woman legs humming toward the moment of birth, of breaking and of becoming.

I was waking up in the middle of the night to grab a glass of water when I did a child's pose (a yoga pose one can achieve by kneeling in a wide-knee formation while bowing one's head to meet the surface beneath) and felt my water breaking.

My favorite part about feeling my water break was realizing that I was not going to be the same after that. And that is something incredibly humbling—the notion that you are changing but do not know what or who you're becoming. There is something restful there, where you can know everything and nothing all at once.

I knew that I was going into labor. I knew that my water was breaking. I knew that everything was going to be just fine. Yet at the same time I knew that the outcomes could vary. I was aware of each and every thing that could go right, and that which could go wrong. But what I knew for sure was that I was going to have to evolve. That, in and of itself, was so very freeing.

One of the biggest lessons I learned was the gift of surrender. Which I actually didn't think was possible for me. As a survivor it is incredibly hard to visualize myself letting go. For so long I lived clenched up and tensed up from the fear of losing my guard or letting it down. And now, when I think about what it means to surrender to an experience or moment or transformation in my life, I think less about letting go and more about noticing that the process of surrender is utterly irresistible. You cannot help but join in when surrender invites you. It is like there is an open door, and there is nothing more painful or less painful on the other side. And as I went through every contraction thereafter, I knew a new metric for understanding time and suffering.

When you surrender, you get to see yourself brand new and reborn. You get to greet yourself and say "Hey, old friend," and that's really liberating. It is liberating when you surrender because you might find that you are more capable than you had ever set out to be.

A wise birth worker once told me that the same muscles that are impacted by trauma must be used to pass a child through a woman's body. In her book *With Harp and Sword: A Doula's Guide to Providing Trauma-Informed Birth Support*, Kenya Fairley takes stock of the lives of pregnant survivors in the second part of the book. As she writes in the book's introduction, "For pregnant survivors, the impact sexual violence may have on women's pregnancy and labor can include: disbelief about the pregnancy, increasing anxiety related to her ever-changing body, unfamiliar sensations in the pelvic and vaginal areas [that] may reactivate trauma, emotional disconnection to her growing baby, trepidation and fear about the birth and experience, flashbacks, nightmares, disturbed sleep patterns, harmful coping practices, delayed access to prenatal and maternal health care."[1] This is not even an exhaustive list of all of the things that pregnant survivors can encounter emotionally, spiritually, and physically.

The high level of disturbance to the body and the psyche after trauma occurs in pregnancy and extends to labor and delivery. Fairley writes in depth about the triggers and problems that can arise, stalling labor, and sometimes leading to unexpected outcomes. She posits trauma-informed care as a beneficial strategy for all women given the high prevalence of abuse and violence against them.

As the author so eloquently writes, trauma echoes are the experiences pregnant survivors come up against that are related to their sexual assault or experiences with ongoing violence. This is so important because "survivors may feel out of control of their body and/or mind." Fairly writes that, "standard positions for birth may increase vulnerability, exposure, and loss of dignity and modesty, [and] use of dim lighting or closed doors, [and] small spaces may trigger painful memories."[2] The book offers this knowledge so that doulas can be prepared when survivors request guidance, want practical suggestions and assistance, and need greater planning to support trauma echoes.

After this level of surrender, I have come to know that I have touched the miracle that I am alive and living in. Revealing or "re-veiling" the self has become my life work of resiliency in the afterlife of child sexual abuse and trauma. What I have learned is that my trauma has not killed me; instead, it allows me to be reborn over

1. Kenya Fairly, introduction to *With Harp and Sword: A Doula's Guide to Providing Trauma-Informed Birth Support* (self-published, 2016).

2. Fairly, *Harp and Sword*, chap. 3.

and over again. The domain of our inheritance is sacred and divine rebirthing.

Measures of Accountability, Justice-Making, and Reconciliation

It is the stories of the women and girls, and the several hundred whose names we do not know, that have inspired the human rights initiative, public tribunal, and historic truth commission known as the Black Women's Truth and Reconciliation Commission (BWTRC). I came to the transnational Black feminist organization Black Women's Blueprint as a member and then was brought in to do the work of the BWTRC. On the other side of the commission, we are still reclaiming our mothers' bones, singing our praise songs, and asking critical questions about a new vision for justice and reconciliation. How do we as Black women continue living in the same world that we were raped in? We look back at those stories to conceive of new ways of looking toward the future; however, that is not enough—we also have to live in this present moment of terror, crisis, and urgency.

From April 28 to May 1, 2016, hundreds of Black women gathered in New York City for the BWTRC, the first-ever public platform for victims of rape and sexual violence. We convened this groundbreaking four-day event where survivors shared their stories in a public truth-telling forum, envisioning justice for ourselves and our communities. Although the BWTRC had been in development for close to six years, the narratives of Black women and girls who sparked this movement began decades, even centuries, ago. The culmination of public education, historical documentation, and narrative collection, all overseen by BWTRC staff, board, and community members, as well as senior advisers of Black Women's Blueprint, the BWTRC hosted survivors from across the world, gathered together to reflect upon sites of memory, labor in love, and mourn in solidarity.

Hundreds of us organized to witness the testimonies of Black women survivors, elevate public deliberation about them and the policy recommendations on their behalf, celebrate the rights and futures of Black girls around the country, and seek healing and reconciliation for survivors, their families, and their communities. Commissioners for the BWTRC included racial justice leader and cofounder of #BlackLivesMatter Alicia Garza and reproductive justice advocate and former executive director of SisterSong Loretta Ross.

The BWTRC was created because Black women have never had the opportunity to publicly deliberate about this human rights issue—the pervasive issue of rape—that affects more than half of us even before the age of eighteen. Over four days, the BWTRC showed us that we know of a God who bleeds like us, and that God lives in each and every one of us. That the sacred temples of Black women's bodies hold a God who bleeds, who understands our wrath, our encounters with injustice, and our resistance.

The BWTRC showed me the ways that our bodies are the site of our rage and the home to our beauty, our peace, our resilience, our truths. The testimonies of Black women and girls who share the struggle and survivorship of rape speak of the miracles we have created and built between diasporas of memory. This BWTRC was born out of the faith statements of Black women and girls. It was also conceived in a moment of political unrest and a moment in movement history of increased demand for the voices of Black women and girls. What I witnessed over those four days of the BWTRC was a nation of Black women giving birth to themselves, their voices, and their strength. We did what some womanists would call the inner work—accessing our own innate divinity in order to receive more light. It's the work of water breaking, of bone moving back into its rightful place, of earth surfacing, of veils peeled back.

Sacred are the texts of Black women's lives—the sacred stories we share in their own voices, and the sacred women whom they birth from themselves in the process. We have been speaking our truths, at the kitchen table and late at night in our bedrooms, and see ourselves in the quiet moments of solitude. We have all acted as the spiritual midwives of these stories, ushering them from the spiritual vessels of our bodies to come earthside, return to the ground and to the earth. We have labored through the process of bearing witness, and now we must put forth the care and carry out the process of healing going forward. The sacred is political, and preserving our sacred lives, bonds, kinship ties is an act of political warfare.

Reclaiming our rituals, our song, our recipes, our memory is the first step in healing and reconciliation. We are owed our mother's blood, we are owed our grandmothers' stories, we are owed our great-grandmothers' names, we are owed the hymns and prayers of our ancestors. Those sacred memories inform our political orientation and call our liberation to justice. It is through the reconciliation of our relationship to the continent that was robbed from us that we can begin a new political alignment. It is through the ripples in the waters of the transatlantic slave trade and the nightmares in the waves that we can begin a process of re-memory and healing.

My Soul Looks Back

I recall going into labor, and bathing in rose water, soaking mind-body-spirit to bridge a connection that would allow just one more veil to fall back. I remember releasing large, heavy pieces of the past into the water, engaging in a reclamation ritual and declaration. I came to define my own capacity for joy and for healing. This would be one of many crossings.

The smell of life and death came to me in nutmeg, cinnamon, rose, lavender, and earth. I was wrapped in truth and cedar—in wool and water.

The reconciliation within my own body declared unto me: The time is now for us to reclaim our bodies, our spiritual homes, and the sacred temples we choose to love in spite of trauma and violence. The project of truth telling and testimony cannot end here. It has to continue, as there are thousands and maybe even millions of stories still to come forward. This is only the beginning of our work as truth bearers, holding the stories of Black women close to our own spirits and the traumas that we ourselves hold. In this moment I believe in truth telling, honest recognition, painful confession, and the beginnings of reconciliation.

The breaking of waters, the shedding of truth, and the floating and sinking all at once were a remarkable component of my own devotion to my healing and the justice needed within. Once again, one of a thousand veils peeled back.

CHAPTER 28

Violation and Making the Road by Walking It

Zoë Flowers

They were my favorite shorts. Blue with a white strip down the side.

One: Violation

When I was a little girl, my grandparents' house was like a castle. It was a Victorian-style home with many oddly shaped rooms. Because my parents worked, they would send me to that house every summer. I spent most of my time either reading or playing in the backyard.

My grandmother's backyard was massive. It had huge oak trees and wildflowers that grew in all directions. It was my magical kingdom. My older cousins hated getting dirty, so I had the yard all to myself. It was just me, the ladybugs, and the frogs. On hot days, I'd run through the sprinkler and then collapse on the dirt, letting the sun beat down on my drenched body.

After a while, I'd reluctantly return to the house, damp and covered in dirt.

Nighttime was the only time my cousins and I played together. We would play hide-and-seek, truth-or-dare, anything we weren't supposed to do. As soon as my grandmother went to bed, we'd go out and play.

My grandmother was not as strict as my parents were. Her main restriction was on laziness and boredom. I'm from a traditional West Indian family that firmly believed that idle hands were the devil's playground. Laziness was a trait she would not tolerate and was reason enough for a swat across the legs. In her eyes, children had no reason to be bored—ever. If she caught us lying around, she would find something for us to do. There were always dishes to wash, rooms to clean, or books to read. That was another good reason for me to stay outside.

Physically, my grandmother was a very attractive woman. People who met her could not believe she had twelve children and sixteen grandchildren because she had such a youthful glow. She had jet-black hair that she wore in a tight bun. At night, she would let it down and I would brush it out for her. It was long and soft. She was a big-boned woman who was effortlessly gentle . . . until she wasn't. Her dark eyes were often steady, and they seemed laser-like when she regaled me with stories about growing up in Jamaica. Her stories were not for my entertainment. They always had some moral that related back to the necessity of being an obedient child. She'd talk/lecture to me for hours while I braided her thick black hair. Still, our ritual was the one chore that I didn't mind.

Most of my relatives lived very close or visited her often. The house was never empty. Food was always on the stove, with grandmother standing over it. She didn't drink, but everyone else in the house did. Liquor was a constant in my family. The adults could always count on getting a drink, a meal, and good conversation. There were many nights that I'd sneak out of bed, sit at the top of the stairs, and listen to the grown-ups. I loved listening to their loud voices debating, arguing, and making fun of one another, often drowning out both the television and stereo. At times, it was difficult to know if they were arguing or joking.

One of my favorite people in that house was my "uncle." He was different from my other relatives. I could talk to him. No matter what the question, he would answer it honestly. Like my grandmother, my other relatives believed children should be seen and not heard. He wasn't like that. I thought my uncle knew everything; he'd been to places I'd never even heard of.

He and my "aunt" lived with my grandmother for as long as I could remember. In almost all of their pictures there were exotic women flocked around him. His pictures portrayed a confident young man, tall and muscular, with a smooth, dark complexion and dark curly hair. I guess he would have been considered attractive in his day, but for as long as I could remember, he'd been old and wrinkled. The only remnant of the young man in the pictures was the mischievous twinkle that never left his eyes.

I was seven years old the first time he fondled me. It was a typical day. It was summer. The adults were in the kitchen laughing and enjoying each other like they always did. He called me into his room. We'd often play checkers or dominoes, which we played to the death. He never let me win; he said it was not good for children, especially women, to get special treatment. I raced up the stairs as I always did. When I got in the room, the board was not in its usual place. I asked him where it was, and he told me it was under the bed. I remember getting down on all fours looking for the game. Suddenly I felt his fingers frantically tugging at my shorts. They were my favorite shorts. Blue with a white stripe down the side (blue has always been my favorite color). They were tight, but I loved them so much. I maneuvered myself around and looked at him as he pulled me toward him and clamped his hand over my mouth. I was a chunky kid. The shorts were tight. He was having a hard time getting his fingers in. I didn't know what was happening. I can't remember if I knew it was wrong. I can't remember if I wanted to get away. I just remember him saying, "Shh," in that raspy voice of his. I remember he was almost smiling. One of his hands stayed on my mouth while he penetrated me with the other. After it was over, I went back downstairs. Everyone was still there. The party hadn't skipped a beat.

I didn't remember anything until my early twenties. All the painful memories flooded in on me on an ordinary day. I was driving home . . . .nothing major . . . then all of a sudden, I remembered. I never told my family. I knew they'd believed me, but I didn't think they could handle it. So, like so many other things, I kept it to myself. I have not shared this story with anyone . . . until today.

> *The function of art is to do more than tell it like it is—it's to imagine what is possible.*
>
> —bell hooks

Two: Making the Road by Walking It

The question of accountability as a radical form of love makes me think about my childhood and the way many children of my generation were raised. To me, linking punishment, accountability, and love is not a new concept. Many of us were told we were being spanked out of love. And lots of people still believe in and enact various forms of punishment to keep children in line "out of love." So, for me, it's not about people's inability to make the leap between accountability and love. It's about whose well-being is valued in our society and whose is not. I can't talk about transforming societal understanding of accountability as a radical form of love until society begins addressing the impact of adult privilege effectively.

To me, accountability would look like no statute of limitations on child sexual abuse (CSA) anywhere in the United States. As a society, how can we say we care about children and not do everything in our power protect them, their childhood, and their right to move unmolested through the world? How we can say they're our future when many are not safe at home, in school, on the sports field, or in church?

Accountability is believing children when they share that they've been harmed. It looks like:

- Not re-traumatizing them by forcing them to sit at holiday tables with their abuser and act as though that is normal.
- Not simply giving girls tactics to "protect" themselves around the known abuser and then praying that the tactics work.
- Acknowledging that boys get raped too.
- Not protecting the abuser because he is a man of color.
- Having difficult conversations with family and friends. I've had to have conversations like, "I know he's your favorite singer, but he has a history of X, Y, and Z. Don't you think that's a problem? Why would you support him financially?"

Accountability looks like creating environments where children feel safe to disclose and providing training for parents on how to deal effectively with them when they do disclose. Accountability looks like communities of color addressing mental and emotional illness from multiple perspectives. When I think about the girl who says her mother's partner is abusing her and the mother essentially says, "I'm sorry for your loss. I'm staying"—that is a woman who may have been abused. How can we talk to her about holding her partner accountable if she's been dissociated for years? Will what we're asking her to do even register? She may even think, "Hell, I got over it. She can too." Families need mental, emotional, and energetic healing to heal patterns like these.

When people come to me for Reiki, they come with all the consequences of a society that prioritizes the needs of adults over children.[1] The trauma of parents who made a decision *not* to make a decision is lodged in the cells of the people I treat. There are more wounded children masquerading as adults than folks might think. Those "child adults" then go on to have children of their own, and the untreated and unacknowledged family trauma is transmitted right into that unborn child.

Holistic healing practices such as Reiki, acupuncture, cupping, yoga, and other traditional approaches are often more effective than mainstream healing methods and need to be more readily available in communities of color. These days I am often invited to "hold space" for large groups of people doing difficult work, and in spring 2016 I was called into the Black Women's Truth and Reconciliation Commission (BWTRC), held at the United Nations, where Black survivors shared their stories of abuse for an entire day. This is a step in the right direction and it needs to happen more.

Lastly, I believe that healers need to be more vocal and participatory when it comes to issues like domestic violence and CSA. I believe in "praying and watching," but I also think it's a good thing for healers

1. Reiki is a Japanese technique for stress reduction and relaxation that also promotes healing.

to demystify themselves. I think it helps when healers lay themselves bare and let folks know that they've dealt with some of the same issues in their own lives.

On the question of justice and whether we can get it without punitive means: I never intended to involve law enforcement and the courts in my life. However, my ex-partner's actions made it impossible not to involve them. They were not helpful in my case. In fact, they were the opposite of helpful. Luckily, my artistic voice and the trust I placed in its wisdom saved my emotional and spiritual life after my experiences with domestic and sexual violence. I gained personal power through books, poetry, and theater. I joined the domestic violence movement and funneled my anger, frustration, and hopes into that work. As a result, my spiritual nature revealed itself, and I followed that to a completely new life as a healing artist. So in some ways I got nontraditional justice.

That said, I recognize that many survivors want their day in court. And they should get that. I know the criminal justice system has major problems. And I'd have no problem seeing it overhauled or dismantled. But I don't see that happening for a very long time, and I do not believe we are in the energetic space where punitive justice is no longer an option. We will know that time has come when the needs of all members of our community are prioritized equitably. That's the reality I envision, and that's the world I am working toward.

[This essay was first published in the #LoveWITHAccountability online forum in *The Feminist Wire*, October 20, 2016.]

CHAPTER 29

Silent No More

The Unheard Echoes of Childhood Sexual Abuse in the African American Community

Indira M. Henard, MSW, Executive Director, DC Rape Crisis Center

When I think of my childhood, I think of growing up Black. My grandmother raised me. My father was not in the picture, and my mother was in the picture part-time. I spent long summers in the Deep South with my cousins and great-aunts and uncles that I saw a couple of times of year. I was in church multiple times a week. It was the village that raised me and the church that sustained me. I learned at the tender age of nine that when your innocence is lost, the world never looks the same again. As an adult woman I struggled to reconcile with the little-girl-self embodied in the adult woman that I am today. I want to re-parent the little girl within. I want my childhood back. I want my innocence back. I want to feel loved and be loved for the little girl I was, the woman I am, and the daughter I will always be. I stand broken but still usable. I had to fight not just to survive the trauma but also to survive life. However, I have learned that my greatest tragedy in life will not be my greatest highlight in life. I often wonder, when my soul is tired and my heart cries, what does compassion and healing look like for the little girl who was once lost and is now trying to be found?

These are the thoughts that come to me as I reflect on the countless number of childhood sexual abuse (CSA) survivors that I have journeyed with over the years. Further, they remind me of the many roles that I embody: healer, activist, social worker, professor, friend, daughter, and sister. However, while each of those roles have shaped and continue to shape who I am today in unique ways, the role that has allowed me to think about and continue to cultivate this work of ending sexual violence in a new way is my current role as the executive director of the DC Rape Crisis Center.

As the first rape crisis center in the country, the DC Rape Crisis Center is the oldest; it is also the only rape crisis center in Washington, DC, dedicated to creating a world free from sexual violence. It was started as a hotline by a group of women considered to be the "early founders of the center." Today the center's hotline operates twenty-four hours a day, seven days a week. It is one of the many crucial services that we offer. The first tagline of the center was "Stop Rape." Then it evolved to "Turning Anger into Change." The current tagline is "Powering a Culture of Consent." The center operates from a framework that shows that all forms of oppression are interconnected.

As the center celebrates its forty-sixth year of continual service, I am not only thinking about the state of sexual violence in our country today but also about the work that still needs to be done as it relates to ending sexual violence. There are still so many missing gaps and so many areas that can and should be focused on. What has become especially apparent to me in this #MeToo era is that there is critical work we must do before we are able to adequately talk about sexual violence. We must develop a vocabulary that strengthens our voice in order to name sexual violence, to define sexual violence, and, most importantly, to break the silence on sexual violence.

There is so much power in words, as they have the ability to influence the consciousness of a nation, bringing voice to the voiceless and serving as a moral compass for all who value the sacredness of human dignity. However, one community has struggled to find language and voice to break the silence on sexual violence, specifically CSA, and that has been the African American community.

Historically and culturally, talk about CSA within the African American community has been taboo. It has been the dirty little secret that, if named at all, is done in whispers. There is a multigenerational unspoken code within African American families that enforces the collective belief that "we" do not air our dirty laundry in public. The secret is not only kept in-house but also often unacknowledged and kept *in silence* in the house. The uncle whose hands are too "frisky," the brother who "plays too rough," and the father who comes to and for you in the middle of the night is brushed off with nothing more than "girls should not be left alone with boys and men." I often think of the phrase in Alice Walker's novel *The Color Purple* when Ms. Sofia says, "A girl child is not safe in a house full of men."

To fully examine the extent that CSA within the African American community needs to be examined, we must begin not only to build a container of safety to hold these complex conversations and emotions that will arise but also practice compassionate accountability. Compassionate accountability is going to look different for each individual and family. However, for the purposes of this discussion, compassionate accountability looks at the following:

- Building language around sexual violence to be able to name and define your experience.
- Fully examining how sexual violence and racial injustice are irrevocably linked and threaded into the moral fabric of this country.
- Calling in others instead of calling out others about the sexual harm that is being done in our communities and families. We have to hold each other accountable before we can hold outsiders accountable.
- Creating sacred relationships with each other that honor and acknowledge the harm that has been done, while also making room for healing.
- Looking at alternative forms of healing through the lens of restorative justice.

What I know for certain is that if you don't heal from what cut you, you will bleed on the people who did not hurt you. Through compassionate accountability, we can honor our wounds and stop the bleeding. If it takes a village to raise a child, it will take compassionate accountability to heal a family, and by extension a community. Healing is possible. We also must always remember there isn't a straight path to healing.

CHAPTER 30

The Vanguard of Love, Accountability, the Young Advocates Institute, and You and I

Tracy D. Wright and Monika Johnson-Hostler

When Tracy D. Wright and Monika Johnson-Hostler were invited to write about the origins of the Young Advocates Institute (YAI) for this anthology, they reflected upon their seventeen-year journey from mentor and mentee to collaborators, colleagues, and, most importantly, friends, in their long-term work in the anti-sexual violence movement.[1] *It is their shared journey that laid the foundation for the creation of YAI, and it continues to be a guiding force seven years later.*

This is a written call-and-response.

Tracy: By far the most liberating and healing work I have done is with the Young Advocates Institute. Originally created for North Carolina–based youth, the institute is a social justice summer camp that has empowered and trained over 1,400 youth, ages thirteen to seventeen, on prevention/intervention education, advocacy, and leadership. The purpose of the Young Advocates Institute is to give youth a voice, the opportunity to share their experiences regarding social justice issues, and help them become an integral part of the solutions. To date, the project has showcased genius-level thinkers, has been replicated in two states, was featured at the inaugural United State of Women Summit in 2016, and has inspired intergenerational thought leaders throughout the United States.

We celebrated our seventh anniversary in 2018. Seven is the number of completion. With our eighth year looming and ushering in new beginnings, it's time to share the true "love with accountability"

1. Launched in 2012 by the North Carolina Coalition Against Sexual Assault, the Youth Advocates Institute is a social justice summer camp that annually empowers and trains 200 youth ages thirteen to seventeen from across North Carolina during a weekend of prevention/intervention education, advocacy, and leadership development. http://www.nccasa.org/cms/projects/2016-young-advocates-institute.

story behind the creation of the Young Advocates Institute. It wasn't until I received this welcome opportunity to write and contribute to the anthology that I have been able to glean the real meaning of the Young Advocates Institute. The acronym and brand of the Young Advocates Institute is YAI. Monika, the institute is a testament and manifestation of "You AND I." The real YAI began seventeen years ago with your mentorship of me. Monika, you are still the most fascinating person I know. Every day I remain in awe of who you are. I could never repay you for all of the lessons and the truly unconditional love you have given me. I would be the first to admit that loving me is much like what I convey in my adaptation of Langston Hughes's "A Dream Deferred" poem: "Loving me ain't been no crystal stair. It's had tacks in it. And splinters. And boards torn up. And places with no carpet—Bare."

Yep, bare is what we have done. You are my person. You are the first person I called when my grandma died. You are the person who loved me just as she did. You were the first person I disclosed to. You asked me if I wanted to live or die and gave me permission to seek help for my mental health. When I first started working with you, you really should have fired me because I was a horrible and crappy employee. In every disagreement and its complicated season, we bared our souls, fell into vulnerability, and let love lead us. You gave me space to reconcile, carve out my niche, and create. The greatest gift you have given me is to teach me how to work. That gift has been rooted in understanding that two things can exist at the same time. And even when those two things are in conflict, you can't opt out of contributing. You must work despite how hard life is. Work despite your broken self-esteem. And work because you have God-given gifts. Essentially, this shared wisdom, your lived experiences, and how you give it your all every single day how the Young Advocates Institute was created and continues to flourish. There isn't anything about the Young Advocates Institute that is easy. However, it thrives because we never quit, which is a mirror reflection of our relationship, Monika, "you and I." Folks often ask how our relationship works. It works because we work at it.

Then we add some leadership, lots of vulnerability, and you have love with accountability. Thank you, Monika Johnson-Hostler, for all that you poured into me and believing in me when I didn't. May God continue to bless you!

My core is made up of the highest trinity. The Father, the Son, and the Holy Ghost. I lead with my heart. I am a poor kid from Bossier City, Louisiana. I am a survivor of childhood sexual abuse. I can't believe I wrote that. It's my truth. As a kid, I didn't have access to the resources or the tools to understand my victimization and its accompanying trauma. I yell the charge to be great, but often I feel like I will never live up to what comes across my plate. I miss my grandma. I cry when I need to. I am grateful and humbled for every opportunity. I believe accountability is the greatest form of love. My life changed when I became accountable for my actions, which made me a better steward of my gifts. Love with accountability has defined my journey. I am sure it will lead and continue to guide me. The practice will grant me success wherever the soles of my feet shall tread. I am at peace.

The Young Advocates Institute is a reflection of my journey. YAI, the "you and I" of the institute, creates the legacy. I am a better person because of you and I and the young people of the Young Advocates Institute. Each has added a deeper layer and fabric into my life. To create something from pain and produce goodness should be the focus in life. This is what we strive to do. At the end of the day, we try to give each young person at the Institute what has been given to us: space, unconditional love, leadership, knowledge, and accountability.

Monika: "You And I" is foundational to what I practice and preach daily to anyone who will listen. I believe and live for a higher purpose; my actions are governed by my Christian upbringing and the religious beliefs I hold true and continue to practice today. It is evident in my investment in you—the personal and the plural. It may sound cliché, but I strongly believe that it only takes one person to believe in you, to stand with you, and then the gates of blessings open for all. I believe that to stand in the gap for you is bigger than YAI, it's bigger than me. My purpose and your purpose were destined. We were obedient to hear the calling to invest in young people, more specifically young people of color. Being raised as a good southern girl taught me that compliance leads to success. While that was true for me, it was also the prayers and support from my village that I credit for our success. I vowed to teach every other Black and Brown young person that we are better and greater than compliance. YAI's "love with accountability" is the stage to embody your full self, knowing that your village is there to uplift you. YAI as an institute is about nurturing the gifts of each person, recognizing that the skin they were born into is no coincidence. We were born with enough, and our role is to provide both the opportunity and platform to showcase those gifts. The last seven years have been a lesson in love. It is okay to love someone or something, but loving them, or it, without accountability could be detrimental. As we open ourselves up for new beginnings, we will courageously demonstrate love with accountability.

You and I utilized the same practices, the ones we were familiar with and the ones we were raised with. However, we both knew the institute had to be different. It had to be more. It had to be rooted in the lessons and nurtured in the new practices. The roots are the beliefs that love is limitless, your intelligence is accepted, and your gifts have made room for you. The practice is about accepting your truth and others' truth. The old habits continue to show up as we transition from "for youth by youth," to "for youth by youth with accountability." While the institute is still the seed from Tracy, the nurturing of Monika, and the manifestation of young people, the new practice must include holding all partners accountable to each other and the young people who haven't seen themselves reflected in the end product.

The institute is ready to be shared with the masses, and it shall be reflective of its community of origin. Unlike many possessions, the institute doesn't have an owner, and the boundaries are limitless. So while it began with gender-based violence awareness and training on how to plan an event, it has evolved into bystander intervention, idea development, and music that embodies our beliefs. We can truly say that we have come a long way over the past seven years. However, as with our own evolution, the institute will continue to reflect our culture with good food, great music, and lots of laughter.

If someone drew a picture of YAI, it would be an array of beautiful images of Black and Brown folk, both young and old. The images of older folk not only represent "You and I," they also represent my family, the tribe that loves on all 1,400 young people. Healthy familial love is love with accountability, which reminds me of how I learned how to ride a bike: I knew my grandfather was there to hold the back of the bike and my mom was in front to watch me. When I fell because my grandfather had let go, one gently assured me all was well, and the other physically helped me back on the bike. Together in that moment they taught me that failure was an option, but quitting was not. That is the practice I strive to show you and share with our young people, Tracy.

* **

Tracy and Monika: Together we will liberate our young people and they will fully embrace all that they have to offer the world. It is better because of all of us, it is better because you and I remain committed to creating a safe and joyous pathway through our love with accountability. YAI is a shining example of love with accountability.

Breathe

CHAPTER 31

Sunset

Seeking True Accountability after All of These Years

Tonya Lovelace

But I can't remember your face
I can only remember watching the sunset
Behind your back as you tried to enter me
My va-china too small to allow

—Excerpt from the poem "My Innocence"[1]

Sunset. This is the bewitching hour that both mesmerizes and haunts me.

That was the time of day that my assailant liked the most. Sitting by him in my little body, I was forced to please him in ways that a tiny girl should never know, should never have to do. It is this very point, this need to have me meet his silent demands, guided by his hands and mouth and breath . . . it is this that bubbles up in all of my actions today. My relationships. My motherhood. My life.

I was too young. Too young to know and too young to understand. I was helpless yet powerful. He wanted something from me, and I gave. Until I stopped. Until I told him that I would tell if he didn't stop. I was my own savior. And he complied.

This is after grooming. After his insistence that his daughter and I bring in other girls. After hide-and-seek with naked pictures he took of us. After we complied.

I finally told my grandmother when she was giving me an innocent bath. Our ritual. I said, "When you wash me there, it reminds me of when he touched me." She gently asked me to share my story and promised not to tell.

1. TLove (Tonya Lovelace), "My Innocence," September 27, 2005.

She then told as she needed to . . . she brought the phone to me and told me it was okay. I could tell my mom. I was safe.

My mom said it was not my fault. That I had a choice. She had a way of making me laugh. She said, "Your dad can kill him. But then he may have to be away for a long time if he did. Or we could go to court. It is your choice." I chose court.

In the early seventies, this was revolutionary. A little Black girl in court, talking about how he touched me there. All that he did to me, his daughter, and other girls. I was breaking ground. My mother and father were breaking ground. And the court complied. He was sentenced and put on probation. Pushed out of the military.

But it didn't stop there for me. I reenacted the scenario over and over again, but this time I would be in charge. I would orchestrate the time, the place, the play. Boys, girls, teenagers. I was in power. We will do what I want to do. And it never filled the emptiness, the fear, the trauma.

I do not remember his name. I do not know where he lives or who he is. But I smell him. I feel his touch. And I remember the sunset.

I hope that as the sun sets across the country each day, little girls are vindicated. I hope that accountability is bestowed upon those in family roles, extended family, or family friends like my sexual predator was. I would like to see it in the form of restorative and transformative justice. He needs to know, they need to know, what they do to little girls who grow into adult women like me.

I am a CEO of a national nonprofit working to end violence against *all* women by centralizing the voices and leadership of women of color, and my little girl is present every day. She is wounded and hurt.

Court made me feel like I was my own superhero, but I had no real, therapeutic help. With young parents, and with a court that did not yet understand, I was not given counseling at the time. I was left to figure it out and to repeat the same patterns. I still repeat the same patterns. I am a child sexual abuse survivor, bullying survivor, teen-dating violence survivor, and domestic violence survivor. My early child sexual abuse (CSA) predator set me up for life.

I count the years . . .
1, 2, 3, 4 . . .
The years that she gets older than I was
When I was first touched
I count the tears . . .
The tears that flow from her eyes
That are not related
To being violated There

I count the lies . . .
7, 8, 9, 10 . . .
The innocent lies that she tells
That aren't intended to hide her shame
Shame from someone else's sin
Someone else's need to
Be in you and on you
While your tiny bones tremble under the pressure
No, she is Being,
Being 10
Being raised
Being protected
So much so
That I have to talk myself
Out of stopping her from
Living[2]

I would like for him to understand his role in impacting every facet of my life. And the life of my adult daughter. She was not ever sexually assaulted as I understand. But she carries the scars. She was kept in shackles by ME. By my vigilance. My fear. My trauma. She holds my worry and my loss of innocence and is seeking her own healing every day.

2. TLove, "My Innocence."

I want him to know. And I want the courts to make his knowing possible.

And I want to see all children who have experienced any form of child sexual abuse to receive counseling, meditation, and mindfulness training. I am just now getting this information in my late forties after recently leaving an abusive marriage. I am just finding myself, and attempting to leave a life of disassociation. I just attended my first CSA support group. And I am for the first time finding me.

I have some solace in knowing that my perpetrator was held accountable in court so long ago. Without a criminal justice response, I am not sure that an interruption in behavior will happen. While I hate the bars and chains within this Eurocentric, Black-hating system, it is presently the only way I know to halt the predatory behavior until other options come about. I would like to see the creation of national, state, and local platforms that allow for the visioning of systematic solutions, ones that develop and steer accountability practices that put child sexual abuse assailants on the hot seat and put CSA survivors in charge. CSA survivors need to steer this process, and the nation and our communities need to listen.

Because, as I cry writing this piece, and know that his touch will never go away, he needs to know. Systems need to know. The world needs to know.

At sunrise, and at sunset.

[A version of this essay was first published in the #LoveWITHAccountability online forum in *The Feminist Wire*, October 24, 2016.]

CHAPTER 32

#OnTurning50

Kalimah Johnson, LMSW

In October 2018, I turned fifty years old. In June of that year, I decided that I would engage in fifty activities that I have always wanted to do. They included some things new I had never done and reintroducing myself to some things I enjoyed as a kid. So I did many things, from getting my first Brazilian wax to playing jacks and coloring and wearing a midriff blouse outside, in the daytime. I was enjoying this excellent idea of ushering in my fifties immensely until I had a flashback of my childhood sexual abuse that was so powerful, I found myself in a puddle of urine the next morning from wetting my bed. I had not had an incident like this in years. I could have easily chalked it up to my coming of age, but as a clinician who works primarily with survivors of sexual assault abuse, I knew better. After cleaning up after myself, crying, and feeling like a complete failure, I knew I had to have a conversation with *her*. I pulled up a blank note on my cell phone and wrote a letter to my six-year-old self. I reminded her that, over time, her life gets better, through it all. I posted the letter on social media (leaving out the bed-wetting incident), and it moved many who read it. I also left out the many instances of child sexual abuse I had endured as a child. The memories were right there with me as they always are, but in this writing, I had placed it where it belonged—in my past and on the perpetrators.

While I ebb and flow between being well and not being well, overall I would say that those experiences have been fully integrated into my life. I recall my past traumatic childhood experiences as a source of strength to always remember what happened. I also use those experiences to understand myself fully as I work to help others who have been sexually abused and assaulted. Acknowledging my multiple rapes is my way of taking my power back and using it to make change for myself and others. The earliest and most unforgettable incidents of sexual abuse that I encountered were from the ages of five through nine years old, at the hands of my female cousin, for her between the ages of fifteen and nineteen. She had semi-consistent access to me because my mother suffered from mental illness and was hospitalized periodically. It was during those stretches that my aunt would have to care for my older sister and me. Later in life, I learned that my beloved cousin was also being sexually abused by her mother's (my aunt's) boyfriend during the same period that she was sexually abusing me. Yes, you read it right—I refer to my molester as "my beloved cousin." Outside of those harrowing moments, outside of the dynamics of power and control and mean-spirited tactics my cousin practiced to keep me silent and victimized, we shared some good times.

I lovingly invited her to co-write this chapter with me to share our dynamic story of struggle, love, reconciliation, justice, and forgiveness. I reminded her that this was my story. I went on to share with her that my selfish vision was to give her a chance to share her version of this tragic and, at times, triumphant story, while understanding that I was going to tell my story, regardless. I shared that without her voice, it would be one-sided. Lots of questions went through my head. Would family, outsiders, and readers of this anthology be triggered? I thought about both of us possibly being triggered writing together. And I thought about family and folks wanting to *pull* triggers, and the awkwardness of it all.

Timing is everything. She just was not ready at the time. The door is still open. I am hopeful that we will get an opportunity to write together about our past, but this will only happen if she and I are in the right place to approach this undertaking.

My cousin was and is not perfect. She too has been victimized. She is still surviving, praying, holding on, and dealing with all that life brings. Over the years I witnessed my cousin suffer both from what she endured and what she did to me (and perhaps others). She was addicted to crack cocaine. At times she was homeless. The hardest blow was when my cousin's eldest son was murdered by the mother of his child. Currently she has various health issues and complains continuously of aches and pains. I believe one of the main reasons I can express empathy in the context of everything is that I made a conscious decision to also remember that my cousin is a breathing human being, a Black woman, mother, sister, cousin, helper, lover, a collection of what I call "*and both*."

I committed to not allow child sexual abuse to control my life and fuel my anger. I used my creativity to fill my day and deliberately chose love for myself and others in spite of what I endured. This is my story. I am not saying or suggesting that what I did for myself and for my cousin is a good idea for anyone. I will say that I am in a much better place (I believe she is too). It took years of work, cursing and tears, wet beds and drama, counseling and creativity, poems and songs, candles and sage. Therefore, before I move on to share how my early life trauma of child sexual abuse has formed and structured my beautiful, complicated yet simple and loving life that taught me healing, justice, and reconciliation, I must thank my cousin. I thank her for the many times she cornrowed my hair in beautiful, intricate styles; beat that girl's ass on the block for trying to feed me a shit sandwich; and introduced me to good music, leotards, and homemade Halloween costumes. She birthed the best second cousins ever, whom I love like my own. Just recently, after I let folks know I had been hospitalized through a group text that included our entire family, she responded by telling people to stop group text messaging. When I saw that response, it made me smile a little. While I know this is complicated at best, I will say that I would rather be free and able to smile because of her than hold us both down in some dark gutter because of the numerous traumas we both faced and endured as children. In that text message to the whole family she said, and I quote, "My cousin said stop texting in this group message, she is busy healing right now," and to that, I say I hope she is healing too. *Amen*, *asè*, and *boom shakalaka*.

My healing has been directly and indirectly tied to my life's work and purpose. The trauma of child sexual abuse put me at risk, and I was raped again at the age of fifteen and then again at the age of nineteen. They were both committed by young men. One rape happened on a date, and the other was committed by a so-called boyfriend. The cops were called after my rape when I was fifteen years old. Their response was horrible. As the report was being filed, the words escaped me. After I had told my mother what had happened, I was unable to describe the sexual assault to the cops. The white cop told my mother, who was only trying to help me, to sit down and be quiet. My little sister, then four years old, spoke up, and with terror in her voice, began pleading with my mother to please stop talking. In response, my mother snapped. What I witnessed was not the familiar schizophrenic snap I had observed from this intelligent woman, but the kind of snap you expect from a hardworking, Black woman protector of her children.

That's when the Black officer took me outside to get the story from me, away from my mother. The white cop apologized and stayed with my mother to explain to her why she needed to be silent during the report. Before giving me the opportunity to gather myself, the Black cop inquired, "Stop, before you even start again, where is your father? You were raped because you don't have a daddy." I was done, silenced, debilitated, and no longer wanted, felt, or believed I needed their help. These horrific experiences set the stage for radical forgiveness and my commitment to addressing sexual assault, childhood sexual abuse, and trauma in the Black community.

At the risk of my writing sounding like a résumé, I want to share a few amazing, restorative things that I have accomplished in my life that I believe were a direct reflection of my childhood sexual trauma, the sexual assaults I suffered as a teenager, and the lack of voice, visibility, and justice that I experienced while trying to recover. After attempting a career as an emcee and rapper, I dropped out of high school. I earned a GED and attended Wayne State University in my hometown of Detroit. I earned a bachelor's and master's degree in social work during the 1990s. My first job was working for the Detroit Police Department as a victim advocate/counselor/therapist for domestic and sexual violence victims. I had to integrate my horrible experience that I had with the cops when I was a teenager so that I could perform my job.

While working as an advocate for victims of sexual assault and intimate partner violence, I realized that in Detroit there was a huge gap in service provision for African American women who were sexually assaulted. It was a standard for me to see various service providers interacting with Black women and treating them as if they were subhuman, unworthy, less valued, and inherently incapable of being raped. This included a general negative attitude toward survivors who were of African descent, long waits in the emergency room for survivors after having been raped, inadequate collection of the evidence, victim-blaming questions, and unhelpful comments that reinforced stereotypes and hindered Black women's healing. Despite this, I also found some genuine human beings learning lessons along the way. Some advocates and health professionals were amazing with survivors, and some were not.

My only goal was to treat survivors and *experiencers* of sexual trauma with dignity and respect. One activity that carried me through my work was reading, reciting, and writing poetry, after my career in rapping tanked. Hip-hop grew up, and I no longer found it enjoyable or validating; it no longer spoke my truths or poured into my spirit. In its place, I started writing poetry to process my trauma and to attempt to understand the stories of others who I had to support daily. Two white women who had interned at the job, Sue Coats and Karen Lang, introduced me to Take Back the Night (TBTN), a sexual assault awareness event that took place every April, which is sexual assault awareness month. They wanted me to read my poetry at the event, held in a suburb that was predominantly white. I attended for a few years and hardly saw any women of color. Despite this, I quickly learned the power of having your voice to break the silence. I longed to have an event like this in Detroit. I wanted an event in April that was designed for and led by women of color, with white women who knew how to support us in the background, not the foreground. Author Lori S. Robinson and I put out a call for all women of color to get involved. I led TBTN-Detroit from the spring of 2007, when I was thirty-nine years old, until the spring of 2018, the year I turned fifty.

In an act of radical love, I passed this sacred and healing event on to other sisters of color to lead. There is something profound about turning fifty. It is teaching me to trust the process of letting go and allowing other sisters to create, lead, and steer an event that resonates with them in the here and now. I am confident that I have left the leadership of TBTN-Detroit in excellent hands with other sisters.

I resigned from the Detroit Police Department in 2005 and took on consulting and leadership roles with the Michigan Coalition to End Domestic and Sexual Violence as a trainer and adviser to member agencies throughout Michigan. I had experienced racist comments, assumptions, actions, and attitudes, mostly from member agency leaders who were supposed to be serving *all* survivors of sexual assault. Something was missing. I decided to start my own nonprofit, the SASHA Center (Sexual Assault Services for Holistic Healing and Awareness). The SASHA Center concentrates on public awareness, provides resources, and conducts peer educational support group services to self-identified survivors of sexual assault and rape—in any context.

Our first actions included staging a protest of an R. Kelly concert at the Fox Theatre in 2009 (which became a blueprint of sorts for the more recent actions concerning this artist) and continuing to hold the women of color–led TBTN-Detroit rallies.[1] The first-ever woman of color–led Take Back the Night in Detroit (that I am aware of) included a wide range of diverse individuals seated at the organizing table. Muslims and Christians, trans and cis, vegans and meat eaters, gay and straight, Black and white, survivors and non-survivors came together. Everyone did not necessarily agree on a wide range of issues, but we agreed that all survivors of sexual violence needed voice and visibility. TBTN-Detroit was an event that would advance that priority in our communities. Serenity Services, a domestic violence agency based on the east side of Detroit, housed the very first

1. Jessica Hopper, "Read the 'Stomach-Churning' Sexual Assault Accusations against R. Kelly in Full," *Village Voice*, December 16, 2013, https://www.villagevoice.com/2013/12/16/read-the-stomach-churning-sexual-assault-accusations-against-r-kelly-in-full.

TBTN. Our event was different than most TBTN events because we presented it as a "party" for survivors. The music was loud and good. It represented many genres and didn't include misogynist songs. Sometimes, this meant that DJ InCreDuBle had to play the instrumentals without the lyrics because some of the beats were too good not to play. There was a march and rally, a healing tent, an art project, a beautiful collage of support for survivors. We served everything from vegan food to Church's Chicken.

I learned that if we were going to create healing spaces collectively, sometimes we had to bend a little, work across differences, forgive and embrace. While leading my tenth (and last) consecutive TBTN, I reflected upon all of the bodies we celebrated and voices we heard. We each paid homage to those who have healed through their work, art, activism, and creativity. I am proud of us, but more importantly these events helped me tremendously on my healing journey.

I want to now address a horrible discovery that was made in my beloved Detroit in 2009. Over eleven thousand rape kits that had never been tested or processed were found in an abandoned warehouse.[2] Almost every rape victim I had met or saw through a police report or emergency room visit while working in the Detroit Police Department (that had collected evidence) was in this abandoned warehouse, left to gather dust and usurp justice. Eighty-one percent of those kits had Black people's DNA in a box, belonging to Black victims and primarily Black perpetrators. Although the rape kit crisis in Detroit has been addressed by our amazing and brilliant expert prosecutor Kym L. Worthy, I thought it was equally important to work to address the needs of Black women who have been sexually assaulted.[3] This discovery was

2. Diana Pearl, "Inside the National Effort to Combat the Rape Kit Backlog – and How Detroit Is Leading the Fight," *People*, June 9, 2016, https://people.com/crime/rape-kit-backlog-testing-how-detroit-became-the-leader-of-the-movement; *I Am Evidence*, directed by Trish Adlesic and Geeta Ghandbir (New York: HBO Documentary Films, 2017), https://www.iamevidencethemovie.com.

3. Nancy Kaffer, "Kaffer: 8 Years into Tests of Abandoned Rape Kits, Worthy Works for Justice," *Detroit Free Press*, December 17, 2017, https://www.freep.com/story/opinion/columnists/nancy-kaffer/2017/12/17/rape-kit-detroit/953083001.

devastating, heart-breaking, earth-shattering, and atrocious. I was left feeling helpless, hopeless, weak, and deeply disturbed by this dismissive act of Black women's bodies. I was mad as fuck and more motivated than ever to create programming for survivors in Detroit. I was unapologetic. I only did what I knew how to do. I delved as deeply as I could into learning, reading, and researching every cultural nuance and state of being related to healing in the context of our culture. I watched the film, *NO! The Rape Documentary* probably a thousand times. I found other Black women survivors who wanted and needed healing.

Larmender Davis, director and founder of Serenity Services, and I sat down and devised a plan to address sexual assault in Detroit through the SASHA Center. Other colleagues involved in this process included Kim Trent, Kendra Ventour, Zenobia Kindle-Davis, Omari Barksdale, Cheryl Rogers, Mary Keefe, Paula Callen, Shirley Williams, Shelia Hankins, and Cheree Thomas.

The SASHA Center became a place for survivors to share and be believed, accepted, respected, honored, and revered. We thought that it would be impactful if we also created programming that directly and intentionally addressed the needs of marginalized women. These are the women who are racialized and systemically and continuously ignored, specifically in terms of the trauma of rape and its impact. Therefore, we have programming that includes a nuanced perspective on cultural aspects such as ancestor reverence, hair texture and cultivation, art, music, Afro-Cuban dance, skin tone and complexion, culturally specific food, urban gardening, mental health, and health care. We are consistently and deliberately allowing women to share their stories in a way that they will be welcomed, not judged.

We create safe space for *all* women and people who are cisgender, transgender, Black, Latinx, white, straight, queer, Muslim, Christian, and more. The SASHA Center also has workshops for well-intentioned men who need guidance about rape and Black women. We provide some technical assistance and create events to educate our community about rape and sexual assault. We also allow women to share their stories in ways that they want to share, without fear of judgment. This includes the use of satire, irony, and humor, as well as urban legend tropes. We also discuss and share the challenges we face with cultural identity and loyalty to our race while holding rapists accountable in our community. We unpack and address the impact of slavery and police brutality as it relates to justice and healing. Tragically, what we know for sure is that, historically, justice and healing are not synonymous. At the SASHA Center, when we have an opportunity to post about our events, sessions, and workshops on our website and also on social media, we use the hashtag #healingispossible. When our survivors who participate in our groups are ready, we invite them to challenge themselves to answer the question, "What is the good news?" We know that through all the pain, sorrow, memories, and triggers there is some good news. This may include anything from focusing solely on the breath in the body to being able to experience the sunrise, sunset, and everything in between.

I am invigorated by survivors and their tenacity to show up in the world "as is" and still manage to maintain their lives as best as they can after such trauma.

When I read the words "love with accountability," I see opportunity. I also know the capacity with which we can work together continuously and bring voice and visibility to African American women survivors of child sexual abuse and sexual assault. "Love with accountability" means we must see Black cis and trans women and girls as human, worthy, and valued members of society. We must change the narrative around Black women and girls, which includes how we view Black women and girls, how we speak about Black women and girls, and how movies, songs, and books portray Black women and girls. I have a profound sense of urgency to remind everyone to respect and protect Black women and girls.

The SASHA Center focuses on the collective well-being of Black cis and trans women, men, gender non-binary people, and the safety of all of our children. We support each other through being vulnerable, listening intently, creating collectively, sharing, integrating, truth-telling, and bearing witness.

We must have intergenerational dialogues about sexual assault, identities, and belief systems. We need to integrate the traumatic experience of childhood sexual abuse and its impact on us now. We need to embrace the parts of our culture that reinforce our greatness, beauty, and capacity for healing. We must take our healing into our hearts and hands. Radical love knows you do not have to do heal alone.

Measuring whether we are loving with accountability is simple. Did we create, hold, and maintain a safe and sacred space? Did we increase connections? Did we encourage healing? Did we learn something new, share a story, hold a hand, hug with consent, free a tortured soul, honor our history, and embrace our culture? Did we allow a survivor to be in the space without forcing a disclosure because we know that being present is enough? Were we able to identify action steps to collectively take in our lives? Were we intentional in removing the shame and guilt associated with being sexually assaulted as a child? Were we able to offer more than community policing as an option for safety? Have we had the chance to release our stories that have been killing us, slowly and ever so softly? Too often we have been taught and expected to take trauma to our graves. Loving with accountability occurs when we are all intentionally moving into our healing harmoniously, identifying the wrongs, celebrating the rights, peeling the layers back, and, in a safe space, challenging and even removing the stereotypes and stigmas. It's embracing our capacity to love again and ultimately to restore, rebuild, and rejoice.

I am a descendant of enslaved African people who survived the Middle Passage and slavery in the United States. I have my ancestors' assets in my cells and bones. I am a survivor of child sexual abuse and rape who is doing exactly what my ancestors, the universe, and God created me to do. I am thankful, humbled, and honored to serve survivors through my work at the SASHA Center.

CHAPTER 33

Poetic Justice

Nicole "Kqueen" Denson

Dedicated to Kaylee, Keyona, and Raquel, the loves of my life. I am honored to experience loving you. Continue to set this world on fire.

How did I get here? Is it destiny, love, faith, or God? I believe it is a combination of it all. When I was a young Black girl in Detroit, I didn't have any idea that my journey and my career would lead me toward finding my life's passion to end all forms of sexual violence. I struggled with what to write, which path of healing to publicly share. Like everything in life, I walk by faith and not by sight.

Memories

At times, I didn't know if my childhood felt like a dream or a nightmare. My parents were both from the South and came to the Motor City (Detroit) for better opportunities. I remember my family being compared to the Huxtables during my childhood.[1] If only people really knew what was occurring behind closed doors. For many African Americans, we know the phrase "What happens in this house, stays in this house." During my formative years, that phrase was my reality. Physical abuse was a daily occurrence in my household. My father abused me repeatedly when I was young. I do not ever recall seeing him hit my mother. However, from the time I was three years old, I never felt like I was good enough for him. All I ever wanted was for him to love me.

1. The Huxtables were a fictitious Brooklyn, New York, upper-middle-class African American family who were the protagonists in the hit NBC studio sitcom *The Cosby Show*.

When I was a toddler, my dad gave me baths at night while my mom worked at a local hospital. I loved riding with my dad when we picked my mom up from work in the early morning. I stared at the lights on Woodward Avenue in Detroit. I began to recognize certain landmarks that informed me that we were getting close to her. When I saw my mom, I would peek up and gaze at her. She was the most beautiful woman in the world to me. She wore all white at work and appeared almost angelic. When she would see me after work, she would give me the biggest smile and say, "Hi, Bunny, good morning." I felt so loved and felt safe.

Journey back in time with me as I recall the day that forever changed my life.

I was four years old and taking my usual nighttime bath in the tub at our family home in Detroit. I remember that my toys, especially my rubber ducky, a toy boat, and my favorite blue towel, were all with me while I splashed about in the tub. My father came into the bathroom, and I heard him unbuckling his pants. If I allow myself to go there, I can still hear the slow creepy sound of the zipper gliding down his pants. My four-year-old self watched as my father committed the monstrous act of removing his penis and began masturbating in front of me.

Despite what I had to endure both as a toddler and as an adolescent, I moved forward in life while holding onto this deep-seated trauma. At times I completely blocked it out. The physical abuse that I referenced earlier did not get better. It became worse. It was so bad that I remember my mother begging my father to stop hitting me with his belt. She would try to physically run interference, and he would throw her off him. Many times I would run to the bathroom because it was the only room in the house with a lock. I eventually got smarter and would bring toys into the bathroom before locking the door and waiting him out. He would pace back in forth in front of the door. The beatings were for many unfathomable reasons, including my room not being cleaned to his standards. People cope with trauma differently. I continued with my life and kept a close relationship with the trauma induced by my father.

By the time I was eight years old, I leaned more toward sports and being a "tomboy." By presenting myself as a boy, I was safe from his advances. It worked. We played basketball together, watched sports, and took drives around the city. My father would show me the dilapidated parts of Detroit as well as educate me with historical facts about the city. The drives were followed by brunch. We watched football and basketball every Sunday. This ritual continued up until I was fifteen years old. Then we were involved in a fatal car accident that ended his life. I will never forget that night. We were on our way from my cousin's house. Shortly after we left, we were hit on our way home by a school bus carrying children. The blessing is that all the children survived and so did I. My father was the only fatality. I watched my father die in that car. I was only fifteen years old, yet I watched his spirit leave his body. I could not describe it. Part of me died that day with him. Contemporarily, however, I realize that my father's death was actually the beginning of my slow but very steady rebirth.

Sweet Sixteen

After my father's sudden death, I dealt with complex post-traumatic stress disorder, guilt, and grief. I was angry. I had completely blocked out my memories of molestation. My mother enrolled me in a grief group as well as individual counseling, both of which helped. However, my family was never the same again with all that I had already experienced in my life. As a result of this trauma, I felt like there was a void that needed to be filled. During this time I thought having relationships with boys as well as men was the answer to fill my loneliness. My early molestation opened up a gateway for intimate partner violence, sexual assaults, and, tragically, human trafficking.

Less than one year after my father had passed, I celebrated my "sweet sixteen." My mother planned a surprise birthday party. She distracted me by sending me to the mall. This is the day I met my "boyfriend," who I knew by the moniker "Vo," aka my human trafficker, at Northland Mall. Many people do not realize that malls are trafficking hubs for men to recruit teens. "Vo" happened to be twenty-five years old. He was charismatic, funny, and a good listener. He even caused my mother to swoon.

Last year I became angry with her as well as myself. When I reflect upon that time, I unfortunately blame her for letting me go out with him. However, as a result of her extensive history with trauma, I was able to forgive her. This was part of my healing journey.

My mother displayed different personality traits. She would vacillate between being present and attentive, and distant and cold. In hindsight, my mother was doing her best with me, while coping with her own trauma of losing her mother when she was fifteen years old.

My "relationship" with Vo consisted of him trafficking me for sex in exchange for drugs and money for about a year. The trafficking culminated with Vo creating a "sex tape" of me being sexually assaulted by him and an unknown man. He memorialized it on camera. I felt disgusting! I still remember the tripod in the room of the almost-empty house, and being told I should be an actress. After the assault, they took me to McDonald's, and then, on the ride back to my house, they forced me to ride in the back of Vo's truck to take me back. In my subconscious, I thought, "I'm worth more than this."

One day Vo drove me to an unknown house with the intention, I believed, for me to perform sexual acts. But he didn't get out of the truck and instead began crying, saying, "I am so sorry I have done this to you." In response, I said, "Baby, do not cry." I watched as the tears fell down his eyes. I felt humility, sadness, and freedom. That was the last time I saw Vo.

Years later, one of my childhood best friends saw Vo homeless and possibly addicted to crack. He asked to wash her car windows for money. I heard this news while I was a student at Michigan State University. I must admit that I felt empathy for him.

Michigan State University

College was where I began to continue to craft the details of this beautiful, human mosaic of who I am today. My freshman year, I identified as a member of the LGBT community. I had experiences with women on campus that made me feel alive again. I was also dating a great man whom I met when I was seventeen. He was loving and supportive and eventually became my first fiancé. It felt great to experience love and the feeling of being cared for again. He was a local DJ who taught me about the importance of being in love with your talents and being driven to push through despite obstacles. We both experienced abuse in our families, and as a result we had each other to lean on. I also discovered feminism in college, which was foreign to me. In my home, the stories of slavery, Emmett Till, and the Civil Rights Movement were essential, but they weren't feminism. Feminism is the theory of political, economic, and social equality between genders. It was at that point that I learned that my race, gender, and sexual orientation were all an integral part of my full identity. I felt powerful. I began to participate in Take Back the Night marches and connect with local sexual assault organizations. I volunteered at a crisis hotline. I was also sexually victimized on campus, but, in spite of it, I was able to transform the victimization into empowerment through therapy, activism, and outreach.

In college I was in and out of therapy. I was in therapy again when I was twenty-five. I broke up with my fiancé and realized I needed support. Throughout this time, my female friends and family were supportive and instrumental to my survival. The women in my life served as a mirror of strength. I cannot begin to describe this mirror of strength because it was so powerful, especially during that time. In therapy I uncovered my molestation, and then anger overpowered me. It was too much. I discontinued therapy and instead began to use substances to block out the unbearable pain. During this time I met the man who would become the father of my child. We soon developed a toxic relationship. However, I was able to maintain hope because of my career. I was working as a court advocate/first responder at a local domestic violence agency.

I remember the day a few years later that I found out I was pregnant. I told my ex-fiancé at a Meijer gas station we had stopped at on the way back to our apartment. I remember him looking nervous. It didn't affect me because I was ecstatic. For the first time, I had control over my body and the ability to create life. Kaylee's father was supportive during the pregnancy and afterward until she was two years old. It became a toxic relationship, but then he walked out the door, and we came to an end. Ever since then we've co-parented Kaylee together.

Kaylee and the New Era of Detroit

The painful memories of my father recently came back with a vengeance. My daughter, Kaylee, turned four this year. She is the love of my life. Her big brown eyes and amazing smile are two of the many reasons I vowed to help protect her—and all the people in the city of Detroit and survivors of sexual assault everywhere—each day, with every breath I take. Kaylee's birth reminded me that my body is beautiful, from every stretch mark to every blemish. Instead of trauma occurring throughout my body, I was loving as well as present within my body when I experienced giving birth to a beautiful baby girl four years ago. One day this past January, something happened as I was bathing my daughter in her grandmother's tub and she was playing as I sang to her. I suddenly began to dissociate and have flashbacks. I immediately asked my mother—Kaylee's grandmother—to watch her. I ran out of the room and began praying. All of a sudden, I was the four-year-old girl again in that same tub who looked up while my father opened his pants and masturbated in front of me. I collected my thoughts, used grounding techniques that I learned through my work, and became present again. Unlike in previous flashback experiences, I now had a plan in place to support myself when flashbacks occurred.

Kaylee is a beacon of light in the darkness of this world. She is bright, hilarious, and a wonderful dancer. I admire her bravery and creativity. Ms. Kaylee will unapologetically wear both a cape and a tutu at the same time! As a result of my trauma history, I'm sure I parent differently than some, if not many. Kaylee knows the correct terminology for all of her body parts. She is empowered with body autonomy. I pray every night to completely interrupt my family's generational cycle of trauma. I want to be the last person in our line who has experienced child sexual abuse, trafficking, and intimate partner violence.

As a survivor of child sexual abuse, I've been dealing with sexual violence almost my entire life, and I have worked professionally to end sexual violence for the past fifteen years. I am the former director of advocacy services at the WC SAFE (Wayne County Sexual Assault Forensic Examiner's) Program. WC SAFE provides those affected by sexual assault with immediate and ongoing comprehensive services, at no cost, that encourage survivor healing and empowerment, promote public awareness, and lead social change. WC SAFE is a nonprofit, 501c3, comprehensive organization that provides compassionate and trauma-informed care to survivors of sexual assault throughout Wayne County. WC SAFE provides a safe, quiet, confidential environment with specially trained forensic examiners, who provide medical examinations and forensic evidence collection for rape victims.

I love our community, colleagues, volunteers, and, most important, the courageous survivors who break their silence. When I saw survivors walk out of those exam doors and counseling offices, I often saw warriors with armor and wings ready for battle. It's not easy being a survivor, especially for those who also must navigate the racism, sexism, homophobia, and transphobia that affect their daily lives.

WC SAFE annually assists almost one thousand survivors of sexual violence at its offices and clinic sites. In 2009, we learned that many of the stories of the survivors who are seen every day were completely buried. I am referring to the over eleven thousand untested rape kits that were found in an abandoned warehouse.[2] It was an unconscionable tragedy and has been painful for us in Detroit. Over 81 percent of the untested rape kits involved African American women survivors. Before this atrocity was exposed, many of us hadn't believed the criminal justice system took our stories and cases seriously. Now we had tangible proof of what our lived experiences had informed us about. Even apart from injustices like this one about the rape kits, it is hard as an advocate to cultivate a hope for justice for the rape survivors that we currently see through exams or counseling.

It took over eight years for the DNA evidence in the kits to be tested. An interdisciplinary team of us pushed Michigan's state legislature to implement mandatory requirements ensuring that every kit was tested. Since learning of the tragedy, WC SAFE has been involved with assisting the Wayne County Prosecutor's Office in working with the survivors connected to the previously untested 11,341 rape kits. My fear, however, is that because of a lack of resources and the high level of victimization, we will unfortunately witness similar problems in the future. In Detroit we lack adequate medical care, schools, housing, and even shelters for people who are homeless. So when we ask a woman who was sexually assaulted as a child fifteen or twenty years ago if she would like to testify, most people involved in the process do not consider whether she has a safe place for her and her children to stay. This is unacceptable for me. My main motivation for shouting from a megaphone, chanting, and marching is for my sister-survivors, for all of us and our children. We must remember that not everyone wants justice or will receive it, however it is defined. But all survivors deserve opportunities for stability and space to cultivate empowerment.

2. Nancy Kaffer, "We Should Be More Outraged about Rape in Detroit," *Detroit Free Press*, June 6, 2018, https://www.freep.com/story/opinion/columnists/nancy-kaffer/2018/01/06/crime-detroit-rape/1007490001; *I Am Evidence*, directed by Trish Adlesic and Geeta Ghandbir (New York: HBO Documentary Films, 2017), https://www.iamevidencethemovie.com.

Muting R. Kelly in Detroit

One night in November 2017, shortly after #MeToo went viral and forced the national mainstream media to acknowledge that sexual violence is a serious problem in this country and around the world, I was at work alone in my office. My candles were burning. I was listening to Jhené Aiko and was in a groove. I took a break and I checked Facebook.

As soon as I had logged on, I read that Robert Kelly (the artist commonly known as R. Kelly) was coming to Little Caesars Arena in Detroit. I also read that a very close family member of mine was interested in attending this "pro-human trafficking fundraiser," as I like to call R. Kelly concerts. "Oh, hell naw," I said out loud to myself in the office. For over twenty years, there have been consistent reports that R. Kelly has engaged in a pattern of controlling, coercive, and sexually abusive behavior toward girls and women of color. Examples of this include R. Kelly marrying Detroit's own Aaliyah in 1994 when she was only fifteen years old. Kelly was twenty-five years old. This illegal marriage was annulled, with the media reporting that Aaliyah severed all ties with Kelly after the annulment. In 1996, a woman accused him of having sex with her when she was a minor. By 2003, R. Kelly had been indicted for child pornography. His pattern of alleged predatory behavior continues to this day. This includes allegations of him holding women in homes in Chicago and Atlanta, where he controls their every move. In 2013, journalist Jim DeRogatis created a twenty-five-year timeline of R. Kelly's history with allegedly victimizing women and underage girls.[3] He has since written other articles on R. Kelly, most notably "Why Has R. Kelly's Career Thrived despite Sexual Misconduct Allegations," in the *New Yorker* in late November 2017.

3. Jim DeRogatis, "The Life and Career of R. Kelly," WBEZ Chicago, July 11, 2013, https://www.wbez.org/shows/jim-derogatis/timeline-the-life-and-career-of-r-kelly/f6aed43d-d7a4-418c-b707-385640a43dfb; Jim DeRogatis, "Why Has R. Kelly's Career Thrived despite Sexual Misconduct Allegations?," *New Yorker*, November 30, 2017, https://www.newyorker.com/culture/cultural-comment/why-has-r-kellys-career-thrived-despite-sexual-misconduct-allegations.

Additionally, and most importantly, R. Kelly was finally indicted on ten counts of sexual abuse in Chicago on February 22, 2019.

Typing as fast as I could, I immediately composed and sent out an urgent call to action on Facebook. Kalimah Johnson, SASHA (Sexual Assault Services for Holistic Healing and Awareness) founding director, my mentor and sister in triumph, answered my call immediately. A trailblazer in this movement, Kalimah organized a protest against R. Kelly performing in Detroit in 2009. She immediately tagged other sisters in the struggle, including Kim Trent, Lawmenda Davis, and Piper Carter. Sisterhood is truly the only thing that has been my safety net and developed my leadership skills. My village is my lifeline. We began organizing to do everything possible to stop his concert. Kalimah was also in touch with Kenyette Barnes, from whom we learned about the #MuteRKelly national movement that she cofounded with Oronike Odeleye.

While our focus was on Detroit, we were connected with sisters and allies who were taking R. Kelly protests across the country. Kalimah was essential to describing the origins and implementation of her impromptu efforts in protesting R. Kelly in 2009. She, along with other community leaders and I, co-created a specific protest before the Detroit City Council to voice our disdain that a sexual assault predator was going to perform at a new arena, one funded by taxpayers. This concert was, in essence, financially supporting R. Kelly's misconduct against girls and women. After days of testimony from many of us, the Detroit City Council signed a resolution in support of us and our opposition to R. Kelly performing in Detroit.

Conveniently, WC SAFE is less than a ten-minute walk from the Little Caesars Arena. On February 21, 2018, we didn't just walk, we *marched* to the arena. Black women survivors and advocates led the demonstration, proclaimed our disdain, and held our banners for the whole world to see. Many media outlets were there covering the protest including HBO, the *Washington Post*, Fox 2, Local 4 News, and dream hampton, a Detroit native, writer, and executive producer of the six-part documentary series *Surviving R. Kelly*.

We Black women survivors and advocates in Detroit, Michigan, let the nation know that we are still here. Despite the gentrification that is displacing too many of us, the people in Detroit matter. "Black Girls Lives Matter." As taxpayers, let alone as human beings, we deserve better. We certainly don't need an entertainer who has allegedly committed multiple unspeakable sexual acts on underage Black girls performing in our city.

Many individuals didn't realize that this was a well-planned and strategic demonstration that was in the works for over two months. The core organizers faithfully fulfilled our vision to organize a wide and diverse range of individuals, including artists and musicians, feminists, activists, and LGBTQ, Black, and Latinx people and their allies, in the same space, planning and organizing. We drew connections between multiple issues while keeping the safety of Black girls at the center. No one was forced to choose between their multiple identities in order to participate in our #MuteRKelly protest, as I often have to do as a queer, Black, and Indigenous woman survivor. We succeeded in showing that diverse individuals care about the rights of all sexual assault survivors, especially little Black girls. However, make no mistake, the struggle continues.

My Personal Is Political

There is still a lot of work that must be done in our communities. Despite all of the documented allegations, there are many women, including survivors of sexual violence, who unapologetically support R. Kelly.

All of this underscores that if we truly want to end child sexual abuse, rape, and other forms of sexual violence, we must have more education, accountability, healing, and action.

I recently began to structure a survivors' speakers bureau called Poetic Justice. I am an artist who has embraced my voice through drawing, painting, sculpting, and spoken word. I have witnessed the transformational impact art has on my healing. My goals are to encompass poetry, rap, song, dance, and all forms of art to showcase healing and thriving. I believe seeking this blend of approaches and talents is a perfect way for the wonderful survivors who I meet through Muting R. Kelly to use our voices on our terms!

I don't do this work solely for the healing, though healing does occur whenever I witness a victim transform into a survivor. I don't do this work because it "feels good." In fact, there are times when the work doesn't feel good at all, but, regardless, I am certain that this work is necessary, life-affirming, and life-saving. I am committed to this work because I never want a little girl, little boy, or gender non-binary child to be haunted by secrets they are forced to hide away. When I was a little Black girl, my father selfishly chose to open a traumatic door, which left a permanent imprint on my life. I am blessed that I've been able to turn my trauma into healing and action together with a steadfast commitment to support all victims and survivors, while working to end all forms of violence against children and adults. There is hope.

CHAPTER 34

The Truth as I Know It

Jey'nce Mizrahi Poindexter

Testimony

For a long time, I did not carry identification because it would expose my identity. I feared retaliation from the police officer who had sexually assaulted me many years ago when I was a teenager and who I had reported. Presently, I don't feel as much like a victim as I do a survivor. Today I can use my voice to speak out against this type of victimization that most people don't survive at all, much less thrive in the aftermath of.

The abuse I endured is so etched in my memory that I can recall in precise detail what happened to me as if it were yesterday. The painful reality is that it didn't happen yesterday. It happened almost two decades ago. This is the lingering impact of sexual assault at any age, but especially when you're not an adult.

I remember, before I was assaulted, repeatedly telling the police that I was not the person that they wanted to arrest. I have a crystal clear memory of the police not believing me. I can still hear the chuckles in the background as I, a teenager, tried to inform them that they had the wrong person. I was deeply hurt because no one in the position of authority believed what I was saying. They didn't even appear to try to investigate whether what I was saying was true.

I can still feel the pit in my stomach when I, a teenager, was moved in the middle of the night to a condemned area of the police station that for reasons unknown to me was not being used regularly. I was terrified and bewildered about the police moving me in the middle of the night.

I can still smell his cologne. The smell was all over his uniform.

The Black police officer entered the cell and approached me without my consent. He forced himself on me. I tried to push him away, but I was frightened of the power he held as a police officer.

After the sexual assault, I tried to tell anyone who would listen what happened. None of the police during that shift believed me. They walked out of the area where I was locked up. I can still hear the slamming of the cell door. I tried to tell another officer on a different shift about the sexual assault, and he, like his colleagues, also did not believe me. I suffered silently alone for what seemed like an eternity.

Hours later, it was Sergeant Ali, another Black police officer, who ultimately believed me. He saved me from suffering indefinitely. Sergeant Ali called my family. Afterward, he called Internal Affairs, which started the investigation into my sexual assault.

Tragically, I was re-victimized throughout the investigation. I was repeatedly made to feel like I was on trial. Somehow, it was my fault for being the victim of mistaken identity, which resulted in my being jailed. I was wrong for living my authentic self—a teenage girl who was assigned male at birth. Their advice reminded me that the power of determining my gender identity and physical expression did not belong to me. Throughout the Internal Affairs investigation, they told me that I needed to be "careful" about how I dressed for court. They shared that I should consider deepening my voice. If I didn't, I would come across as too feminine, and that would not support my case. They told me that my feminine appearance in court would make it hard for the jury to believe that I did not want the abuse (sexual assault) that the police officer committed against me.

The painful irony of that trans-misogynist advice I received in the wake of my sexual assault by a police officer still lingers to this day. I was incarcerated for a crime I did not commit. I was sexually assaulted by a police officer in the cell where they held me. I was a terrified teenager who did not consent to anything. My femininity shouldn't have ever come into question in any trial, especially a sexual assault trial. Yet this is the case for feminine boys, trans girls, femmes, and transwomen. Our femininity is on trial. I never wanted the abuse.

I still do not want the abuse! I will never own that what happened to me was my fault. It was not my fault.

At the end of the criminal trial, the police officer who sexually assaulted me was found guilty, sentenced, and placed on the registry for sex offenders for the rest of his life.

While sharing my story, Aishah Shahidah Simmons asked my thoughts about the sentencing of the police officer who sexually assaulted me. I believe people can redeem themselves, and I also believe in second chances. I'm aware, however, that being placed on the registry for sex offenders for the rest of his life doesn't leave a lot of room for second chances because he will always be marked. I have mixed feelings because I do not believe I was the first teenager that police officer sexually assaulted. I believe he was a serial rapist, and I wouldn't be surprised if there were others he victimized. He had to be forced to stop abusing his power. If he weren't on the sex offender's registry, I believe he would have gone elsewhere, where no one knew his record, and very probably repeated the behavior.

Simultaneously, my faith tells me that I have to forgive. I work every day at forgiving and extending the grace to others that God has given me. This is a very complex situation for me.

It's not often that a survivor of sexual violence, especially a Black trans girl or a trans woman survivor, can have one's day in court and witness one's perpetrator be held accountable for his crime. I recognize that I am one of the fortunate ones who received justice in the criminal court of law. After the success of the criminal case, my mother sued the city of Detroit for negligence. The civil trial lasted longer than the criminal trial, and she won the case.

Healing and the Work Ahead

My healing and recovery process didn't happen until many years after the assault and the trials. There were very few people in my life who knew what happened. Aside from the testimony I gave in the court cases, I wasn't able to fully talk about any of it until 2016. During that time, I went through in-depth training facilitated by Nicole Denson, former associate director of the WC SAFE (Wayne County Sexual Assault Forensic Examiner's) Program, which taught participants how victims process their sexual trauma neurologically and psychologically. We learned about the impact of secondary trauma and the reality of fight-or-flight. We saw films, including *NO! The Rape Documentary*, that taught us about the lived experiences of women of color survivors—most of them cisgender.

I took the training so that I could learn how to be a strong victim advocate for transgender women of color. I support victim-survivors who've been sexually assaulted. Nicole's training not only strengthened the skills I already had, it taught me new skills. Something was both awakened and ignited at that training. It created the internal space for me to break my silence beyond courtrooms and beyond my family.

My "victim evolving into survivor" coming-out process led me to Nicole and Kalimah Johnson, founding executive director of SASHA (Sexual Assault Services for Holistic Health and Awareness), who invited me to speak at Take Back the Night (TBTN) in Detroit. TBTN was one of the first times that I spoke about what happened to me in a public forum beyond the courtroom. It was an affirming and empowering experience. My full healing journey as a survivor began in Nicole's training and kept stretching exponentially further ahead afterward. I committed to no longer hiding in my own victim-shadow and simultaneously I supported my trans sisters whose experiences mirrored my own but were also completely different.

I'm still on the healing journey, which is ongoing. I am no longer a victim but instead a survivor who endured the unspeakable, lived to tell my story, and now works hard to do all that I'm able to stop sexual, physical, and lethal violence against Black trans girls and women. This is a huge task that requires a greater burden than trans women should have to carry by ourselves. It is work that anyone who is committed to racial and gender justice must do.

When I reflect upon what love with accountability looks like to me, I believe it's important that we see the full humanity of Black trans girls and women. We must recognize that trans and genderqueer children are among the most vulnerable individuals and are more likely to be sexually assaulted by family members, clergy, police, and anyone in a position of power than any other demographic. Society must move beyond the vicious stereotypes of our being deviant perverts who are solely focused on sucking penises and getting fucked by men. I am not calling for "respectability politics."[1] I am not anti–consensual sex. But this is a non-negotiable reminder that we, trans girls and trans women, are not solely sexual beings who "get what we deserve." We are not "he-shes." We are not pretending to be something that we aren't. It is society's fault that our gender assignment at birth doesn't reflect who we truly are.

I believe in a communal effort that includes all sectors of society (familial, religious, educational, civic, legal, and political) working toward eradicating violence, especially child sexual abuse. I am not opposed to working with police and using the criminal justice system in response to violence. I'm fully aware that there is a ton of work that must be done to ensure that those who are the most marginalized receive the most support. Specifically, the members of my demographic, trans girls and women of color, experience extreme forms of discrimination, violence, and institutionalized oppression from the police. However, it's not only the police who commit harm against us.

I'm not romanticizing the work ahead. I am acknowledging that whether we like each other or not, we all share space in our counties, cities, states, and nation. I am suggesting that we remain steadfast in a commitment to work across all our differences in Black communities and undoubtedly beyond. We must hold each other accountable for the harm caused. I shared what happened and worked for me when

1. Shannon Rodgers, "How Respectability Politics Stifle Black Expression," *Medium*, June 19, 2017, https://medium.com/@sheneversleeps/how-respectability-politics-stifle-black-self-expression-c162d9418ff. Dr. Evelyn Brooks Higginbotham is credited with first articulating "respectability politics," in *Righteous Discontent*.

I was a teenager, but I do not believe that is the only way to seek and receive accountability and justice.

I am adamant in my belief about the need for an informed communal effort that requires anti-oppression, sensitivity, and competency training for everyone, from toddlers to the elderly, in all areas of society. No one should be able to opt out. These types of training need to happen everywhere to counteract the "school-to-prison pipeline" and the rampant racism, trans-misogyny, sexism, transphobia, and other forms of oppression that plague Black people regardless of our gender identity and our sexual orientation. All Black lives, regardless of age, gender, gender identity, sexual orientation, religion, and physical ability, are valuable. Black Transwomen's Lives Matter!

CHAPTER 35

Sometimes, the Wolves Wear Lipstick and We Call Them Auntie

Kenyette Tisha Barnes, Cofounder of #MuteRKelly Campaign

Sometimes the wolves wear lipstick.

And we call them Auntie. Or Mama. Or Grandma. Or sister. Or Ms. Annie.

I realized very early in my life, that my girlness was coveted by those who wished to exploit, corrupt, break, and fuck it, with impunity. I also learned many of us lived in a consistent constant dissonance, knowing that men and boys only wanted one thing from you and that your worth was also based on the ability to keep a man.

I also learned that girls are not protected and that often the enablers of sexual pathology in the Black community were other, usually older, Black women.

I've found that during my activism work I tended to encounter one of two narratives surrounding Black women and girls who've experienced sexual violence: they are either the product of bad parenting, or they simply are sexually precocious. Neither placed responsibility on the perpetuator; and both often centered toxic, patriarchal, misogynoir, shaming and blaming messages about how fucked up these girls and women were for allowing themselves to be raped and abused.[1]

I accepted that, generally speaking, white people and white women in particular marginalized our race, and Black men marginalized our gender. Yet what made me most heartsick was the degree

1. Coined by queer Black feminist Moya Bailey, "misogynoir" is a word used to describe how racism and anti-Blackness alter the experience of misogyny for Black women specifically. See Trudy, "Explanation of Misogynoir," *Gradient Lair*, April 28, 2014, http://www.gradientlair.com/post/84107309247/define-misogynoir-anti-black-misogyny-moya-bailey-coined.

to which Black women, who were themselves often victims of sexual abuse, were also the enablers.

Black women, who were supposed to protect, empathize with, and support prepubescent girls, instead more often than not blamed them for not having the social-cognitive ability to navigate the pathological misogyny that they, as fully grown-ass women, could not even extricate themselves from.

Older women in numerous cultures in countries across the African continent held girls down while their clitorises were ripped from their bodies, in the name of "being acceptable to men"—the same men who would rape, malign, and abuse these torn baby-pussies with impunity.

The church ladies who told the girls to wear longer skirts yet closed the office door while the pastor was slipping under elongated hemlines. The same ones who sent pregnant girls away and snatched their babies from their arms as punishment for shaming the family, while they told the boys to sow they oats, and if one woman won't, another will.

Yes, older Black women cosigned this shit.

Because they are fucking wolves.

For years, this was a conundrum that I struggled with. For me, this was the most difficult to deconstruct and analyze. I, like many Black girls, had my psyche mutilated, was force-fed a poisoned stew of stupid shit, in the name of being a "good woman." We were told to learn how to please a man sexually but to not be sexual. We were taught that sex is a "duty," and enjoying it makes you a ho. You know, stupid shit.

Always with the end goal of being some man's wife or boo'd up with some nigga who more than likely learned how to be a man from street pimps and hustlers.

Black girls and young women were always at the bottom of the pile. Grateful that someone would acknowledge us, despite the toxic sludge we had to shovel just to paint on a fake-ass facade of happy.

But, "You's married now! And you better watch out, cuz if you ain't pleasing yo man, some other bitch will!" Meanwhile, he's grooming your twelve-year-old daughter to be his next meal.

"And if that hot-ass little bitch fuck with my man . . ."

I remembered learning that "it's better to have a bad man than no man at all!"

I remembered the assorted stories of those "fass ass girls" who only wanted to seduce the "good men" away from the "good women," by the same women who understood that "men will be men."

The stories of young girls who sat in the pews, shamed by the church mothers, forced to inhale a tainted salvation, laced with innuendo and contradictions, spewed from the same pulpit that left a lump in her pubescent womb.

I remembered the girls who got pregnant, usually by a man who shouldn't have his dick near anything teen, yet instead of being protected and supported were told to "get outta my motherfucking house!"—by the same mother who is now "Nana" to the babies left by her brother.

I remembered the young woman who trusted the boy she'd been friends with since kindergarten, only to be called "a stupid ass ho" by the auntie she trusted, when she was tricked into having a train run on her.

Why do older Black women throw sexually abused Black girls under the bus?

Jealousy, mostly. Evolutionary psych? And the cis-heteropatriarchal narrative that we are always in competition, for men, with younger women. Somewhere between playing with Barbie dolls, training bras, and eighty, women have been socialized to believe that our "stock" is highest when we are younger and that it dramatically decreases as we age. I have unfortunately come to the conclusion that for many Black women, all others are simply viewed as competition for the scarcity of "good Black men." And what do you do with the competition? You destroy it. Or allow it to be destroyed.

This misguided dogma has created a space in which Black girls and women have no allies. We are pitted against each other by a toxic patriarchy, which seeks to feast on the young. And our own mothers, our supposedly "sistren," many of whom were themselves harmed by this very same shit, sat, pious, self-righteous, in judgment, served us up, to be slaughtered and feasted upon by ain't-shit niggas who these same women called "husband."

Over nine short months, from the first tweet of #MuteRKelly, by Dr. Stephanie Evans, to the subsequent launch of the #MuteRKelly campaign by Oronike Odeleye and me, the movement had expanded to seven cities and eight protests to include Charlotte, Chicago, Dallas, Detroit, New York, and St. Louis.[2] To date, the momentum of the campaign has resulted in thirteen cancelled concerts and twelve global chapters including Rkellystummschalten, and MUTE R Kelly, Amsterdam. In January 2018, #MeToo Movement founder Tarana Burke publically expressed her support of the campaign. In May 2018, #TimesUp Women of Color publicly supported the #MuteRKelly Campaign.[3] For all intents and purposes, the #MuteRKelly Campaign was a success. Since the broadcast premiere of the documentary series *Surviving R. Kelly* in January 2019, the momentum to censure R. Kelly has grown exponentially, and even RCA Records and its parent company Sony Music have dissolved their working relationship with him.[4] Additionally, and most importantly, R. Kelly was charged with eleven new counts of sexual assault and abuse on May 30, 2019.[5]

Throughout this campaign, we've also been met with an onslaught of opposition, purportedly demanding that we are

2. Ann-Derick Gaillot, "The Story Behind #MuteRKelly," *Outline*, May 1, 2018, https://theoutline.com/post/4379/a-conversation-with-mute-r-kelly-cofounder-kenyette-barnes.

3. Joe Coscarelli, "R. Kelly Faces a #MeToo Reckoning as Times Up Backs a Protest," *New York Times*, May 1, 2018, https://www.nytimes.com/2018/05/01/arts/music/r-kelly-timesup-metoo-muterkelly.html.

4. *Surviving R. Kelly*, produced by dream hampton, Tamara Simmons, Joel Karlsberg, and Jesse Daniels (Van Nuys, CA: Bunim-Murray Productions, 2017), https://www.mylifetime.com/shows/surviving-r-kelly/about; Jem Aswad and Shirley Halperin, "R. Kelly Dropped by Sony Records," *Variety*, January 18, 2019, https://variety.com/2019/biz/news/r-kelly-dropped-sony-music-1203106180.

5. ElizabethA.Harris and Robert Chiarito, "New Sexual Assault Charges Filed Against R. Kelly," *New York Times*, May 30, 2019, https://www.nytimes.com/2019/05/30/arts/music/r-kelly-new-charges.html. See also Maeve McDermott, "Timeline: R. Kelly's History of Sex Abuse Arrests, Indictments and Lawsuits over the Years," *USA Today*, February 26, 2019, https://www.usatoday.com/story/life/music/2019/02/26/r-kelly-history-sex-abuse-child-pornography-arrests-indictments-and-lawsuits-over-years/2978781002.

vindictively attempting to destroy R. Kelly's career—despite that fact that he's had a history for more than thirty years of sexually abusing underage Black girls. "Naw, but them hos are lying!"

Most of those who are angry at us are Black women.

The conundrum.

I have no answers. I only offer anecdotes and a burning need to unfuck this dogma.

All I can do is speak on what I observe. And use this platform to be a beacon of light for those young Black women and girls who are left with only the choice to swallow this shit, like a street trick, and accept it right.

And to say that, yes, sometimes our aunties wear lipstick, and sometimes these heffas are wolves.

And so I'm here.

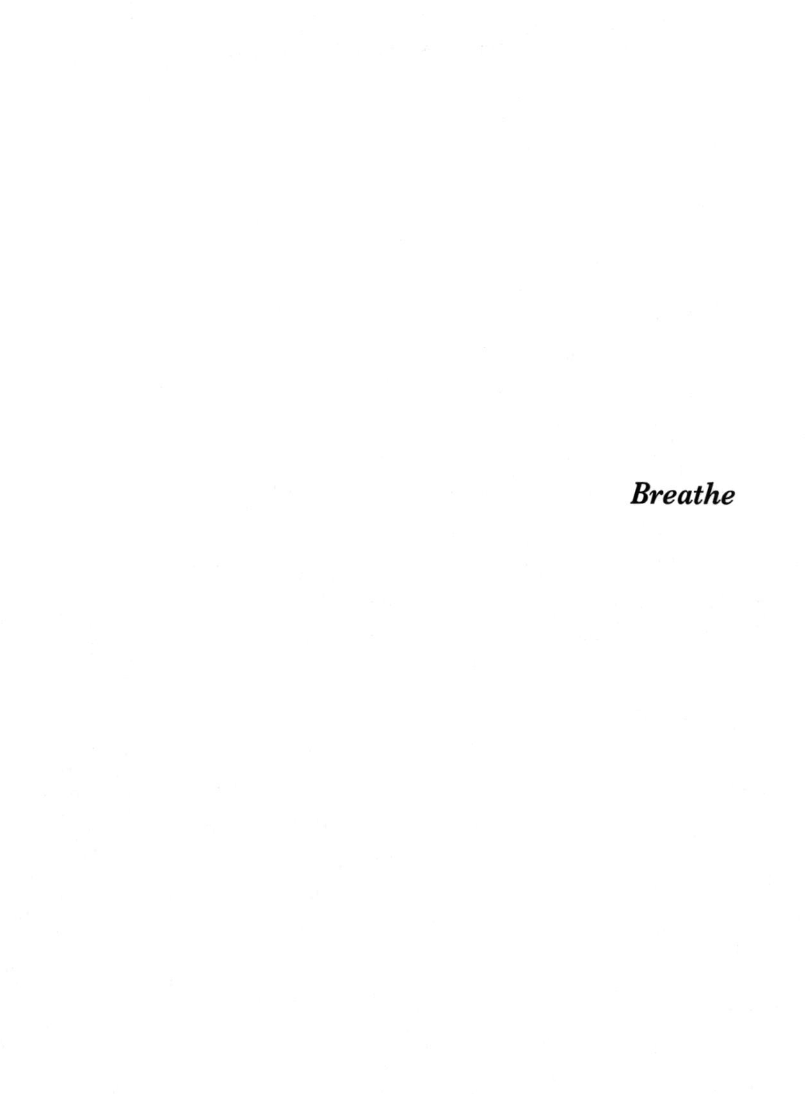

Breathe

CHAPTER 36

The Compassion Imperative

From Hurt to Healing: A New North

Mel Anthony Phillips

Introduction

Held at Louisiana State Penitentiary (more commonly known as Angola State Prison), the 2017 Day of Compassion summit was conceived by Lara Naughton, a graduate of the Compassion Training Institute at the University of Stanford in Palo Alto, California.[1] Lara allied with prison officials to bring her unique training into the facility via a twelve-week inmate-centered program. It was this cadre of graduates, in collaboration with Lara and Angola administrators, who organized this original summit, the first of its kind in any US correctional facility. The event took place at one of the facility's onsite chapels. I had already known Lara Naughton in Portland, Oregon, where she was the guest lecturer for OAASIS (Oregon Abuse Advocates and Survivors in Service).

I have family with a long history in Louisiana and surrounding areas. When the event had been slated, I was honored to be part of it. I was grateful not just because I was going to be part of a rare and historic moment for humanity, but also this was the moment when I made a sharp pivot in a new direction.

As a survivor of child sex abuse, I have been an activist and advocate going as far back as I can remember. Recently I had to acknowledge a major shift in my personal and professional outlook. I admit that for many years I was fiercely fighting for the ones on

1. Laura Naughton, "Compassion in Corrections," *Compassion Institute* (blog), September 7, 2017, https://www.compassioninstitute.com/single-post/2017/09/07/Compassion-in-Corrections; See also *Voice of the Experienced*, https://www.vote-nola.org/blog/how-is-your-heart-today-vote-attends-day-of-compassion-at-angola.

"my side." No one else mattered. This attitude, however, overlooked the ample lineage of abuses, violence, rape, and neglect of my family and kin. Not to mention the horrid impact of racism, unemployment, poverty, drug addiction, and incarceration—all of which are systemic ills through no fault of our own. In essence, in order for me to help a family member, I had to deny the other. I needed a better way forward.

Contemporarily, I try my best to offer compassion to all, if not personally, at least in my perspective. When I show compassion, I feel that I create more positive change by reaching across that aisle. Compassion, let me be clear, is not #LoveWITHAccountability. Compassion does not mean forgiveness, nor does it necessarily require the accountability of those involved. Compassion is my avenue to healing that, for many, leads to Aishah Shahidah Simmons's expanded freeway of #LoveWITHAccountability. Without the intersection of compassion, the road leading to "love *with* accountability" can be that much more difficult to discover and navigate.

In December 2017, I gave a keynote address at the first Day of Compassion summit at the Louisiana State Penitentiary. The prison is located on land that was originally a plantation named Angola, after the homeland of its former slaves. It traced its origins as a prison back to 1880, when inmates were housed in the old slave quarters. By 2008, Angola State Prison had grown to eighty thousand acres—the size of Manhattan. It is the largest maximum-security prison in the United States, and a 2010 report found that its inmate population that year was almost completely African American while the officers who oversaw them were entirely white.[2]

Making my way to the podium to give my keynote, I considered the cruel history of this place with its centuries-old stories of pain, suffering, and trauma. I imagined all those eyes upon me, and I saw myself looking back at them. In their faces I saw the eyes of my father

2. Laura Sullivan and Steven Drummond, "Angola State Prison: A Short History," *Voices behind Bars: National Public Radio and Angola State Prison*, http://ccnmtl.columbia.edu/projects/caseconsortium/casestudies/54/casestudy/www/layout/case_id_54_id_547.html.

and uncles and brothers and cousins. I saw their eyes, deep brown like mine. I know my message is as much for me as it is for them: compassion heals.

The Keynote Address

As a victims' advocate and as one who stands for the rights of the disenfranchised, I am the one you want at your side in a crisis—and I am not boasting. In fact, I'm quite proud of it. I say this because I go about my work carrying the personal experience of someone who has been harmed, violated, and trespassed upon in unthinkable ways by people who went largely unaccountable for their crimes, which left a stain inside me like shit on a bright silk sheet.

Yes, I am intimate with shame; I was once its most loyal concubine, holding it tight like a bleeding wound while slowly, over time, becoming numb to its cold grimy hand, constantly stroking the soft tissue beneath my skin. I know shame, deep and crystal clear as any ocean on this earth. I have felt red-hot embarrassment scald my face and neck like a grease fire. I know that self-hatred feels like a sharp icicle stuck in the middle of your heart, going through your back, and you can't pull it out. I know some things up close and personal.

No, man, don't try and tell me what the weather is. I know many degrees of suffering. I have been a blizzard of furious contempt and distrust for people I judged and misjudged. I have erupted in volcanic rage at matters beyond my control and have quaked in fear of someone knowing my secret. I understand better than some, the conflicting and shifting emotional patterns produced by trauma. I know the unbalanced climate of criminal justice, and the cumulus stigma of our society and culture where violence—particularly sexual violence—is concerned. No, man! Don't tell me the weather. I've been through it.

Now, today, all these years later, I can say that most of the old hurt is gone. I am humbled to walk in witness with many individuals, each at a different phase of trauma and healing and each with their own unique needs, but the first one—that first survivor—is almost always the toughest. The first was me. Today I strive to do in my advocacy what I wish had been done for me. I have committed a solid chunk of my life working with anti-violence allies, wanting to help people who are hurting get to the other side of that pain. I ask two questions: "What do you need, and how can I help?" Say no more. Trust me: I see you; I feel you.

I got you. You are not alone.

The greatest thing I find about working for a good cause is being surrounded by really good people. Fortunately, I often get to collaborate with and watch these really good people doing really good things in clever, bold new ways—and in real time. Over the years, as I've gathered and honed a lot of useful social justice tools, along the way I've also discovered a few things about me, the world, and my place in it. I am grateful for the gifts of wisdom, each a rare asset from kin, friends, colleagues, and strangers. I do my best to personify and share this collection of visions, voices, values, and virtues. With this arsenal, I am your armor, the shield and the helmet. I am the 140-pound battering ram. I am the Eveready flashlight of hope. I am the hammer of truth and the nails of purpose. I am the measure of sense and reason. I am the iron shoulder: lay down your heaviest burden, and know my full strength. I am a rock, both a steady, grounded presence, and the cool smooth stone that laid Goliath low. When the time comes, I am the peaceful watchman or the loud, squeaky wheel. You need it, I got it. For fighting the good fight, I have at my disposal all this and more. Even so, with all this, the dullest tool in my bag, the most unused and least appreciated has been, in fact, the single most important of them all: real, true, simple compassion. Today I want to talk about this, our compassion imperative. It is necessary for me, for you, for all of us. I believe compassion for self and others is the remedy for the pandemic inhumanity infecting the world at large.

Family, friends, colleagues, and acquaintances would probably say I am a decent, free-spirited, thoughtful, open-minded kind of person. They would be partially correct. Truth is that, in the past, my spirit was anchored to a hard-hearted place, allowed to move only a few links from that spot. That wide door of perceived mindfulness opened only for some, and only so far. I was a good person but not my best. I was trapped in a dim inner lockup of my own design. For years I was chained to those flawed ideals of paternity that often are so closely bound to antiquated stereotypes of machismo masculinity. In ways I did not notice, this anchor kept me from reaching outside that rigid construct of what I imagined as equality and justice.

But one day it all changed. It was when I engaged compassion that I learned to use this untapped inner-guidance system. Until then I had been misdirected on my life path, my bearings slightly off-center. Looking back, I see how I sometimes totally missed the point of my aim. Presently, as I reset myself on a more restorative track, the slender needle of compassionate awareness guides me in steering the vessel of my values. It drives me, directs me, buoys and steadies me when crises arise. My hope for humanity is lifted by the life raft that compassion offers to all of us in need.

When I talk about compassion, I like the analogies of setting sail, a ship on the open sea, life rafts, lifebuoys, and voyages. The compass is to mass transportation what compassion is to mass transformation. The words "compass" and "compassion" originate from the same root. "Com" is a prefix meaning "with," or "as one" or "together." It also implies that this with-ness, this oneness, this togetherness has intensity and force. And the word "pass" means to go beyond what has been done. In essence, "compassion" means coming together and, with intensity and force, going beyond or rising above whatever boundaries stand before us to fulfill our highest callings. A compass in our hands gives us longitude and latitude as well as the four directions: north, east, south, and west, and all the space in between, in order to go to those difficult and challenging places in the far reaches of the globe. Compassion in our hands gives us integrity, intention, an attitude of gratitude, and all the space in between, in order to go to those difficult and challenging places in the far reaches of ourselves. Like a compass and its four directions, compassion has four directives:

1. See/witness/acknowledge
2. Feel/sympathize
3. Wish to relieve the suffering
4. Act/do something

When carried out with intention, these basic principles generate a reaction of true healing. Moreover, the practice of compassion, though complex and difficult, is a win-win option, working both ways, to bring relief and healing to both givers and receivers.

Applying it personally, I know the power of self-compassion, but it was a long time coming. In the 1970s and '80s people did not speak of the things happening to me at age seven, eight, or eleven. There were no words for it. I grew up, and, in silence, it followed like a growing shadow that never touched the ground. For years it was fistfights and foul language. I excelled at running and combat sports. For two years in the military, I did my damnedest to knock the block off any fool stupid enough to enter my ring of fire. No "pussy willow" here. Step right in, Mr. Meatloaf, and allow me to hand you your ass on a canvas platter. A boxing bell, school bell, dinner bell, church bell, or taco bell—if it's ringing, I'm swinging a fat sack of homemade whoop-ass! A couple years down the line, though, after a bruising loss, my head clanging like runaway mission bells, I took stock and asked myself why. Why all the fighting? It was simple, of course: I was fighting my childhood. I was pummeling myself to pieces on the inside, fighting a secret and trying to keep the past in a corner. I was jabbing myself with fits of loathing and guilt. I was in a constant battle with shame. It was important to prove to myself, you, him, and anyone else who met me in that square that I was nobody's "babycake."

I understood as well that after all the years of pounding, I had managed only to extend and amplify my inner struggle. This was not my first loss by a long shot, and boxing, tough as it was, had served me well, but the thrill was gone, and I was done with the fight game. At length, I sat with the thing from way back when, recalling what occurred and my role in it. What had I done that my childhood had to be relegated to a back closet in my mind? I was just a little boy. What *they* did was not my doing. So why did I feel such awful shame? Why did I hate myself so fiercely? With these questions I traveled back, going deep, all the way back to him, that first precious one. I had to strain for the near-forgotten image of him, my memory as pale as his powder blue . . . T-shirt. But I clearly remember the flutter in my stomach and chest as my image began to breathe and move. Slowly, he scratched his way out of my swollen flesh, breaking through the fabric of my consciousness like a baby bird. He was cute as a chickpea and his skin shone rose-gold against my own. He was good, innocent, curious, shining, and perfect. Perfect! That's what he was—perfect, with his white sneakers laced with a lopsided bow he tied all by himself, like how Momma did it. We were silent a long time before he spoke to me. His voice was barely a chirp when he looked up and said, "I'm sorry." He said he was sorry. He said it again and again and again. He was sorry for not running away.

Just then I noticed his legs, the two thin brown sticks of soft marrow and pinkish bone. He said he was sorry he didn't punch that man and kick his ugly friends, sorry for not biting them hard—really, *really* hard. He gnashed his small milk teeth and described tiny white talons with his rice-paper fingernails. He was sorry for not saying anything to anyone; he was afraid the police would take him from Momma. He was so scared. Everywhere around him I saw overlapping ripples of fear and could feel his monsters circling beneath him, waiting. He finished by saying "I should have been bigger."

For a long time, I sat right there with him and my tears and thoughts, trying to take this in. Finally, I faced him and said he had nothing to be sorry for. I told that little man that apologies were not for him, not his responsibility, nor burden or worry. He was eight years old, eight and innocent; what happened was not his fault. And then I apologized for being the way I was, for denying his existence and stashing him away like a filthy magazine. I said to him then a version of what I still say now . . . *I see you. I feel you. I love you. You are not alone.*

I picked him up and held him close, sniffing the pomade in his curls. He is a Bayou boy who smells of moss and swamp greens and river musk. For many days afterward, I held him firmly in mind and close to heart, all the time reflecting on his experiences—*our* experiences—letting the past and present soften and melt in the warmth of our new shared truth. I held him there for some time before I ate him, heart and soul, first bringing him up to my lips and kissing him like the cherry on top before gently pushing him down my throat. He tasted like a Twinkie, a light, soft, sweet, lingering comfort. I swallowed him down, took him back into myself, put him back into every pore of my being, and every strand of my DNA. Then I went about the task to find a new space for him. He needed a room with a little more light and a lot more love. It's what he deserves. It's what he needs. It's what I need. Maybe, right here and right now, you need it too.

It was in that moment of clarity that the light bulb in my head switched on. It was in that moment of truth—in a space of deep self-compassion—that I had a seminal moment of transformative growth. Compassion, the very thing I denied others and myself, was, in itself, the antidote for my very own hurts. It was a potent pill resting in the palm of my hand the whole time. It was a tiny caplet of humanity, unused and still secure in its original silver lining. Compassion for others and myself is what redirected my work, shifted my mind-set, moved my heart, and calibrated my moral GPS.

Following a brighter guide star, I am now on a more fulfilling course, finding another way, a new north. Compassion is power you can hold. What an affirmation for someone you love or care for to hear you say, *I see you. I feel you. I love you. I got you. You are not alone.* To be able to hear those words re-gifted and wrapped in the voices of the someone(s) who love you most. These words have substance. These words hold weight. These are words you can stand on even if they come from a complete and total stranger. If you see me now, if you feel me and also feel the truth in my message, then, friend, we are halfway there to a place of grace, understanding, and healing.

Perhaps some of you are here today because you abused, misused, or lost control of your freedom. Now your power is modified, limited, restricted, repealed, and suspended. Does this make you so powerless that you are unable to relieve your own suffering? Not if you turn to each other with compassion. The truth is: in here, all you have is each other, that's it. You. Just yourselves—that is all—and that is enough. Compassion starts with you, right here, right now. The healing ointment you need rests just beneath the palms of your hands, just beneath your feet, at the tips of your toes, at the tips of your fingers, and on the tips of your tongues. Compassion is an intense, forceful act of resistance against inhumanity. It is an act of courage and faith, and it is only degrees away from us. Our sun is ninety-three million miles away, but with the right perspective I can hold it between my finger and thumb. Sometimes we feel as if we are ninety-three million miles away from any kind of salvation, honor or redemption, atonement, comfort, or forgiveness. But with compassion, the space between hurting and healing closes exponentially. Instead of being light years from hope, the possibility is only one degree away. Step out. Reach out. Speak out. Compassion is a cure for the suffering human condition, and it is almost always within our grasp. I stand before you right now as a person in the midst of change, with a changed mind and redirected goals. Today the glowing quasar of compassion is what guides my personal path and lifework. Today I perceive my worldview through a clearer and much more focused humanitarian lens. Lack of compassion is a prison cell of its own, and I will not live there anymore. I will work to make room for a dramatic change. There is space for a new reality, and in this expanded realm there is room for us all.

Let me close by saying in the spirit of advocacy and compassion, and the fighting spirit of this day, and that boxing ring tonight—I will dig deep into my arsenal of justice to offer you this for the good fight in all of us: Let us be the gauze and tape and the salve to fortify and soothe. Together we are the bucket, the towel, and cool drink of water. We are the mouthpiece of our convictions and the gloves of defense and protection. We are the sharp needle, the unbreakable thread, and the stitch sewn in the nick of time. *We* are the sound of the bell! I will be a champion for you and with you. Together, with compassion and grace, we will triumph over the forces of violence, injustice, and oppression wherever they may be. Right now I am stepping out, into the bright light of this new day, to say to every glowing one of you, "I see you." I speak out today in this harsh and humble place, to say to all incarcerated persons here today, "I see you. I feel you. I hear you. And I thank you. I got you. You are not invisible. You are not disposable. You are not unredeemable. You do have value. Your life has worth. You are not without power. You are not debris. Your life is significant. You can make a difference. You are enough, and you are not alone.

Peace.

[This essay includes the full text of Phillips's keynote address for the first Day of Compassion summit at the Louisiana State Penitentiary in December 2017.]

CHAPTER 37

Thoughts on Discipline, Justice, Love, and Accountability

Redefining Words to Reimagine Our Realities

Qui Dorian Alexander

I have always felt that "discipline" is such a loaded word. As an adult, I think of discipline as consistency, a deliberate and intentional regimen—coming back to something even when I don't always have the desire to do so. I often thought that if I couldn't commit myself to writing every single day, then I couldn't be a writer. This idea often prevented me from showing up to the practices that keep me well, because I internalized the idea that I couldn't really be committed to something if I didn't have discipline. If I wasn't the most disciplined, then I wasn't a master and therefore my ideas were not valid. To get beyond this propensity for self-sabotage, I had to confront my own ideas and relationship to discipline.

As a child, I thought of discipline as punishment and often rejected it because of that notion. We live in a world that teaches us that the only way to create discipline is through punishment. Discipline becomes laced with shame, fear, guilt, and failure. It serves as a method of control for those in power, often when their sense of control is being questioned. It is through a system based on the use of fear to maintain that power that we come to equate power with domination and authority. This fear-based ideology teaches us that power can only reside in the hands of the few. One must maintain that power at all cost, and someone else's access to power becomes a threat to their own. This ideology becomes particularly pertinent in regard to teaching children how to engage with the adults in their lives. There are so many ways we deny a child their autonomy over their bodies, from forcing them to hug and kiss their relatives, to scolding them for questioning adult behavior, to teaching them that any physical discipline they receive is administered out of love.

We all have an aversion to punishment. We learn these patterns of punishment as children; they show up in our homes, schools, and larger communities. The conflation of discipline/punishment, power/abuse, and structure/fear becomes normalized. So much "order" in our society is maintained not by people's desire to genuinely to do the right thing, but rather by people's desire to not get caught for doing the wrong thing. So what happens when young people experience harm from the people who are supposed to protect them? These conflated ideas and patterns teach young people that any harm they experience is brought on by themselves. They too must "maintain" order in their families, and if they challenge any behavior that has become normalized, they become a disruption to the family.

Negative reinforcement doesn't help people change their behavior, whether they have caused or received the harm. People do not learn through shame. But our (in)justice system is set up in such a way that it isolates both the people who have caused harm and the survivors. It is set up to scare people into changing, through the negative consequences of their actions, rather than to confront the issues that set the conditions for abuse.

Sitting with the word "discipline," I realized that I similarly struggled with the word "justice." What does justice look like in the context of child sexual abuse (CSA)? Our society tells us that when justice is served, holding someone responsible means punishing them. They are thus thrown into a system that promotes more fear, shame, and isolation. There are a multitude of reasons why survivors of CSA don't speak about their abuse, often because they experience those same conditions of fear, shame, and isolation. These are conditions that don't actually help people heal, change, or grow. Is it really justice if someone suffers from abuse as I did? Is justice served if someone is robbed of the community and the care it takes to become a better person? Is it justice if someone gets locked up in a box and is not given the opportunity to heal, just to harm others again?

What might the world look like if we approached justice from a place of love rather than fear? We are taught that leading from a place of love will only get us taken advantage of and lead to more pain and hurt. No one wants to talk about love, especially within the context of child sexual abuse and other forms of sexual violence. Violation of any form of intimacy is devastating, particularly in the familial context for children and young adults. It can affect our lives into adulthood. This can become difficult for folks to unpack as love is often used as a way to manipulate young people. We don't want to talk about love when it has been taken from us or used against us, so why would we offer love to someone who has done that to us?

This led me to sit with another word: "love." What do we mean when we say that word? Do we mean an experience, or do we mean a tangible item of value? We often teach children to accept problematic behavior under the guise of love. That it is something to give and take, and if it is taken from you, you did something to deserve it being taken. This skews a young person's ideas about the difference between love and abuse. As we get older, we are taught a romanticized version of love, not understanding that love requires work. Instead, love is presented as effortless, and we aren't encouraged to take the time to think about the discipline love requires from us. In actuality, love is a verb, love is an action, and it doesn't always feel good. Black feminist theorist bell hooks describes love as a "the will to extend one's self for the purpose of nurturing one's own or another's spiritual growth."[1] This is a process that requires intention.

If we understand that love asks for more presence and practice from us, the real question becomes, Do we think everyone is deserving of love? Who gets to decide who is worthy of it? Using the systems and structures that are currently in place as our standard, the answer is no, not everyone is worthy of love. Our systems teach us that both survivors and people who cause harm do not deserve love. We often ignore the conditions that lead to abuse and that perpetuate an acceptance of rape culture. Rape culture is built on the assumption that not everyone is worthy of love and that those in power get to decide who is worthy of being dominating and who is worthy of

1. bell hooks, *All about Love: New Visions* (New York: Perennial, 2018).

being dominated.[2] A result of the continued conflation of power with abuse, and punishment with justice, rape culture continues to manifest itself in our social, cultural, and political lives. It is built on the backs of vulnerable bodies, particularly children and young people, women and femmes, trans and gender non-conforming folks, people of color, poor and working-class people, and disabled people. Rape culture teaches us that some people are entitled to power while others must "earn it." It teaches us that vulnerable bodies bring this injustice upon themselves.

Rape culture operates like an institution, a systematic structure of power to which all other structures of dominance contribute. A structure that determines where and how we place value. This capitalist-based framework teaches us to commodify our world. We even base our relationships on what we can gain from the exchange. Capitalism is the system in which we have been taught to exchange value. But whose bodies do we value? Who gets to determine that value? And who gets to decide if and when that value can change?

Rape culture reinforces an underlying ethic of fear. Child sexual abuse and rape culture are inextricably connected as rape culture enables child sexual abuse to go unspoken. It rationalizes problematic behavior according to unequal power dynamics. These ideas just become accepted as truth and don't leave space for people to challenge or complicate the narrative around them.

There have been many contexts and frameworks to envision these words—"discipline," "justice," "love," "value"—in new ways. I think that sci-fi and speculative fiction, as artistic forms, help provide one of those frameworks. Prison abolitionist Walidah Imarisha says:

> When we talk about a world without prisons; a world without police violence; a world where everyone has food, clothing, shelter, quality education; a world free of white supremacy, patriarchy, capitalism, heterosexism—we are talking about a world that

2. Shannon Ridgely, "25 Everyday Examples of Rape Culture," *Everyday Feminism*, May 10, 2014, https://everydayfeminism.com/2014/03/examples-of-rape-culture.

doesn't currently exist. But being able to envision these worlds equips us with tools to begin making these dreams reality.[3]

That type of imagining, visioning, and building is the core pursuit of speculative fiction. What would our world look like without child sexual abuse? What are the ways we are learning to love differently? How do the relationships we have with our own bodies manifest themselves in our relationships with others? All these questions allow us to dig deeper in order to find a different way of responding to child sexual violence.

When I tell people that I believe in prison abolition, their first reaction is usually fear or puzzlement. Common reactions include: "I know it's not perfect, but it's all we have" and "Some people should just be locked up." People hold these sentiments to be true, all while recognizing that police brutality and mass incarceration are very real issues within our communities. Our reliance on the state to define words like "discipline," "justice" and "value" has impeded our ability to envision new ways of dealing with harm, change, and fear. Transformative justice (TJ) offers a new vision. TJ is way of practicing alternative justice that acknowledges individual experiences and identities and works to actively resist the state's criminal injustice system. It's a method of responding to violence outside of the state's involvement. Because I'm a queer Black trans person, the state is contributing to the erasure of my existence. The state doesn't want me to exist in the first place. I can't rely on the state to solve the issues my community is facing. So what happens when the abuse I've experienced comes at the hands of my family members? How do we handle the dilemma of wanting accountability but knowing that the state can't actually provide that?

It brings me back to examining what I think justice really is. What are we actually asking for when we say we want justice? Our fear-based approaches to justice tell us to denounce the harm one does

3. Walidah Imarisha, "Imagine a World without Prisons: Science Fiction, Fantasy, Superheroes, and Prison Abolition" *The Abolitionist*, 21 (2013): 4–5.

in society but also to accept those same actions as a consequence for one's behavior.

We need to hold people accountable for the things they do. However, accountability and punishment are not the same thing. Punishment never looks at the root cause of conflict. It only addresses the value of the conflict—you have to "pay for" what you have done. Accountability acknowledges the conditions that caused a person to act in the ways they have. It recognizes the context in which one understands one's own actions and creates a framework for someone to understand and be responsible for the impact of those actions.

To believe in TJ, you have to believe in change. You have to believe that people have the capacity to change, while understanding that not everyone will. You have to believe that if we help people heal from their own hurts, they can recognize how they have taken those hurts out on others. They can start to change their behaviors. Prison locks you in a cell, takes away your humanity, isolates you, and takes away your worth. That fear-based model doesn't make space for people to change. The model takes away your humanity so it can profit off your body. This is a practice that applies to survivors of child sexual abuse as well.

So what can accountability look like for a survivor of CSA? What does a support system look like? Can survivors' healing be prioritized regardless of whether the harm-doer is being held accountable? These questions provide us with the foundation to think of accountability as something more than checking off "accountability to-do lists." It requires doing the hard work of sitting with what it is that we believe and what words we let define our experiences. It is difficult to acknowledge harm you have caused or harm that has been done to you. TJ provides a framework for us to accept that we are still worthy of love and belonging when we do or receive harm. No one is disposable. Oppressive structures cause folks to make harmful decisions and teach us that any harm we've received is our fault.

Accountability also cannot be done in a vacuum. It requires connection, trust, and vulnerability. We have to be willing to be seen in our mess. "Vulnerability" is another word to sit and struggle with.

Our fear-based world teaches us to conflate vulnerability with weakness. But vulnerability is the basis of human connection. When we see and hear our own experiences reflected in others, we know we are not alone. The connection allows us to feel held in the process of change, reassures us that we have support, that there is something worth changing for. The vulnerability of asking for what one needs to heal is essential for both survivors and those who cause harm.

Research professor and author Brené Brown said, "Feeling vulnerable, imperfect and afraid is human. It's when we lose our capacity to hold space for these struggles that we become dangerous."[4] Our reactions to being seen in our vulnerability are based on fear. If we can only deal with interpersonal conflict by reflecting the values of the prison-industrial complex (isolation, commodification, taking away humanity), we are just perpetuating the same systems that kill us. Learning to deal with interpersonal conflict in new ways allows us to unlearn harmful behaviors and envision new ways to push up against larger systems of oppression.

As we continue to reflect on the words and ideas that we hold to be true, are we giving ourselves the time and space to complicate those narratives? Are we asking more questions to dig deeper? Are we giving ourselves permission to be honest with how we react to those questions? I invite us all to think about words that we've grown to accept, the words that don't sit right with us, and the words that prevent us from showing up for ourselves from a place of love. As we heal the wounds and the trauma that certain words hold for us, we can begin to re-create and reimagine our existences. We can begin to create new visions for our realities.

[A version of this essay was first published in the #LoveWITHAccountability online forum in *The Feminist Wire*, October 26, 2016.]

4. Brené Brown, "The Courage to Be Vulnerable," November 22, 2012, *On Being with Krista Tippett*, podcast, https://onbeing.org/programs/brene-brown-the-courage-to-be-vulnerable-jan2015.

CHAPTER 38

Casting Aspersions

Tashmica Torok

I don't know where my father's urn is. At the age of twenty, I moved and left his box in the top of my closet. It wasn't an accident. I made a conscious decision to not carry that man any further into my future. I wish that symbolic gesture of physically leaving him behind had transferred easily to a mental reality, but there is no leaving traumatic memories of severe childhood sexual abuse completely behind. Those memories are folded into the deepest corners of my brain, where they will remain until I die.

I don't remember when the sexual abuse started. I only remember that it ended with his unexpected death. My father was training to become a Green Beret in the army, and, while paratrooping, a blood clot burst in his brain, and he died. The abuse had come to an end, but I was now left with a secret that loomed overhead as my family grieved and attempted to move on.

My father had threatened that if I told, I would destroy the family. If I told, my mother would hate my father and it would be all my fault. I was also told that he was preparing me to be a wife. I still remember him explaining that it was like the nudity in *National Geographic*. This was my early education.

A year after his death, I told a trusted teacher and, with her help, my mother. I was believed and supported immediately. When people ask me about what made the biggest difference in my healing, I tell them that I was believed and tremendously loved. I never felt blamed or shamed into silence.

When I am working with families who have been impacted by child sexual abuse, I have to admit that the idea of seeking accountability is unfamiliar to me. Even though my father's early death turned out to be my salvation at the age of nine, I also knew that my father would never be held accountable for his actions. I would have to be the one who bore the consequences for defiantly sharing my personal story. I would be the one held responsible for ruining his reputation. I knew that my father would always get off easy. I thought of his death as a clandestine escape route. Even though he didn't die by his own hand, I still blamed him for leaving me holding his secret in my two little hands.

As an adult, I watch our communities wrestle with the idea of accountability. I watch our conversations as they circle around what should be done with perpetrators. We discuss treatment, transformative justice, incarceration, and often, in internet forum threads, violence against perpetrators. We struggle to pull together the pieces of what we think should happen and then watch much of it fall away as our current system is not capable of fully addressing the complexity of child sexual abuse.

I will not tell you that I have an idea of what I would have wanted had my father survived. I cannot be sure that I would have ever disclosed what was happening. I often joke that my only form of accountability was to cast aspersions on an urn in my closet. "Damn you, dead dad." I don't know that I would have wanted him to go to jail or if transformative justice would have been something that would have helped my family. I am almost certain my father had his own story of abuse to tell, and for that I have found within myself a space for understanding and compassion. I often find myself wondering what my childhood would have looked like had my father been given what he needed to heal.

Here's the thing, though. The children who experience sexual abuse in our communities are often completely disconnected from the process of accountability. Much of what happens after disclosure is controlled by laws, requirements, and processes that have little flexibility in allowing a survivor-led approach to addressing child sexual abuse within a family structure.

If you read that and it scared you a little, know that you are not alone. I recognize that moving toward treatment, transformative justice, and survivor-led accountability places the faith of the community in a new form of justice. It is not our country's norm to ponder healing measures over punitive ones. I struggle with the idea of being able to ever trust perpetrators to participate in what feels like a lenient system. Before falling into fear and rejecting these ideas outright, I challenge us all to recognize that there are many options between incarcerating a perpetrator of child sexual abuse and allowing them to hurt children without accountability. If we are willing to listen to survivors and think creatively, I believe we can cultivate a safer environment for all of us.

Still, we have to recognize that the systems that we have put into place are not decreasing incidences of child sexual abuse. If anything, as we challenge dangerous stigmas and become more vocal about child sexual abuse, we are likely to see an increase in reports. We are not fully approaching prevention if we are not addressing the trauma and violence that have historically impacted communities of color. Considering that our ancestors were raised to emulate overseers and taught that rape was a common form of abuse to clean up and to later pray away in church pews, we have to recognize that child sexual abuse is deeply intertwined with an inability to heal from our past. We have to acknowledge that what's missing is not punishment; it's the survivor's voice and guidance.

To move in this direction, we must all agree that survivors are to be trusted (or believed) when they tell us they've been harmed. We must decide, as a community, that their healing and well-being is our first priority. We must reevaluate our justice system to ensure that the policies and procedures related to addressing child sexual abuse deal with long-term cultural shifts in addition to short-term public safety. There is a laundry list of things we must do if we decide to move toward a survivor-led focus on accountability, but I'm not sure we'll get past that first one.

When given the opportunity, our community at large will allow perpetrators to make excuses for their behavior, whereas accountability requires a full and truthful admission of guilt. If we advocate for the truth, we have to let go of the idea that our religion, respectability, morality, and discipline will keep us safe. When a child's report of abuse disrupts the notion of safety that adults cling to, they push the child to view the world in a way that consoles themselves rather than protecting and validating the child.

We know that we cannot incarcerate, ostracize, or shame our way toward ending child sexual abuse. Violent responses do not prevent child rape or the trafficking of our Black and Brown children. Focusing our prevention efforts on the behaviors of the survivor, rather than the rape culture our children exist within, will not get us the results we desperately need.

It is time to consider where interventions might take place for those who might harm children. Teens who do not have an understanding of bodily autonomy and consent will not respect the bodies of others. There is no national movement to make services available for people who have caused harm or who are contemplating sexual violence toward children. There are not enough publicly accessible accountability support groups or cognitive behavioral therapy programs in service of changing the behavior of perpetrators of sexual violence.

Why do we always lay the burden of ending sexual violence at the feet of those who have survived it?

A cursory review of news stories about sexual abuse in the year 2016 alone reveals that one victim of sexual trauma was asked by their faith community to apologize to their perpetrator, another was punished by her school for lewd behavior "regardless of consent," and, in the case of the USA Gymnastics scandal, team members had their sexual assaults by Dr. Larry Nassar publicly justified as "treatments" for injuries sustained during gymnastics.[1] (If you're guessing that

1. Michael Stone, "Pastor Rapes Teen, Church Asks Victim to Apologize to Pastor's Wife," *Faith on the Couch*, September 09, 2016, http://www.patheos.com/blogs/progressivesecularhumanist/2016/09/pastor-rapes-teen-church-asks-victim-to-apologize-to-pastors-wife; Tyler Kingkade, "Girl Suspended after Being Sexually Assaulted in School Stairwell," *BuzzFeed News*, September 22, 2016, https://www.buzzfeednews.com/article/tylerkingkade/girl-suspended-after-being-sexually-assaulted-in-school-stai; Marisa Kwiatkowski, Tim Evans, and Mark

gymnastics injuries are not typically treated with intravaginal procedures, you would be correct.)

These are not all instances of child sexual abuse as seen within the family structure, but they do indicate that culturally we prefer to protect the reputations, titles, and honor of individuals or systems above and beyond the child survivor. We choose to ostracize and ignore the serial nature of these crimes rather than create non-carceral mechanisms to change our culture in ways that prevent them from occurring in the first place. These examples cannot occur on a macro scale without a rape-supportive culture operating on a micro scale in our homes.

Instead of believing children and allowing them to lead us toward the truth, we gaslight them until they no longer recognize the truth in themselves, others, or the world around them. If we do not allow for survivor-led accountability when a child has been victimized, then we cannot claim to love that child. All we can claim is loyalty to a system that often excludes them. All we can say is that we are willing to make a living sacrifice of that child in exchange for what makes us comfortable.

If our focus were on healing, what might our response look like? Where might we start?

[A version of this essay was first published in the #LoveWITHAccountability online forum in *The Feminist Wire*, October 21, 2016.]

Alesia, "16 More Women Accuse Former USA Gymnastics Doctor of Sexual Abuse," *Indianapolis Star*, October 27, 2016, https://www.indystar.com/story/news/investigations/2016/09/25/16-more-women-accuse-doctor-sexual-abuse/90410436.

CHAPTER 39

Accountability to Ourselves and Our Children

Ignacio G. Hutiá Xeiti Rivera

Love is overwhelming. Not the act or ability to love but the very idea of loving. Love has many meanings and interpretations, but the feeling of love, however subjective, should be good, right? In that good incarnation of love, how does accountability show up? What does love with accountability look like? Specifically, what does love look like in the context of survivorship?

The practice of accountability has gained more attention in the last few years. We revel in the philosophy of accountability, yet the practice of accountable loving is not as simple. Perhaps that's because accountability, like love, is subjective. There are guidelines that aid us in our interpretation of what love and accountability mean separately and together. Aishah Shahidah Simmons, a long-time comrade and a fellow recipient of the Just Beginnings Collaborative Fellowship for adult child sexual abuse survivors of color, asked me to contribute to her project and reflect on this quandary.

As I ponder, I am reminded how our projects—the HEAL (Hidden Encounters Altered Lives) Project and #LoveWITHAccountability—although different in approach, circle back into one another. They connect as pieces of a puzzle that ultimately form a broader framework for addressing and ending child sexual abuse (CSA). In explaining the #LoveWITHAccountability approach, Aishah speaks of love as a verb— an action that often gets derailed or eliminated and lacks accountability when it comes to confronting CSA within the family unit. In the HEAL Project, we are exploring a preventative approach to accountability in which it becomes a collective effort to equip our children with information and support against CSA.

The majority of us are taught from birth that regardless of any transgression we may experience at the hands of a family member, we must protect the family at all cost. Love is all too often used as a weapon against survivors of abuse. "If you love me, if you love this family, you wouldn't tell," is a familiar sentiment I've repeatedly come across in the anti-violence movement within LGBTQ communities. These "protections" have been encouraged in the face of incidents of intimate partner violence, to avoid any potential negative impact that disclosure would have on the struggle to win basic rights and gain legitimacy for our queer relationships. "Uncovering the violence would harm our fight for rights"—or so some have thought.

The focus of #LoveWITHAccountability is on families of color, specifically those of African descent. The silencing of sexual, physical, psychological, and economic violence within these family structures is anchored to our experiences of oppression. Normalcy, fitting in, not ruffling any feathers while trying to survive a law enforcement system that is homophobic, transphobic, racist, and sexist comes at a cost. This is where the cultural, historical, and community-driven measures of addressing CSA become a necessity. Survivors who need and want restorative justice and a resolution should have access to more widely accepted options.

Restorative justice and transformative justice are distinct frameworks that allow alternatives to prison time through rehabilitation. They each incorporate reactive and proactive accountability—reactive because they immediately and compassionately respond when harm has been caused, and proactive because they have the potential to instill a long-term accountability action plan. They also facilitate the shifting of power and allow for healing on survivors' own terms. In revisiting the concept of family "protections," especially from state-sanctioned violence, restorative and transformative justice are viable frameworks that integrate collective accountability.

Accountability, more often than not, has been experienced as a form of punishment in response to wrong-doings. Accountability has been reduced to the aftermath: the reactionary process of blame and shame, often through call-outs—and more recently, "call-ins"—to address the misstep. This process is underutilizing the potential of accountability. Accountability should be a part of the very foundation of how we interact with one another. It should be how we come to expect respect as part of our culture, communication, and problem-solving. Love cannot be maintained without accountability. Accountability, in essence, should be experienced as proactive and reactive, never reactive alone.

In search of a definition for accountability, I found that most stop at taking responsibility for one's actions, admitting to one's mistakes, and being answerable to someone. However, accountability should be understood as a broader framework of trustworthiness in addition to showing responsibility for one's actions. Accountability does not have to be structured to only be punitive (in response to the act) but should also function in a motivational manner (to prevent the act, if possible).

Love is accountability, and accountability is love.

Love, as a verb, requires the intention to be proactive. When we navigate accountability only in reactive ways, it contradicts the intention of accountable love as both proactive and reactive. When love, as a verb, manifests in the form of active movement and constant intentional action, then we are processing through accountability. I believe that we have the capacity to love with accountability in proactive ways: to take responsibility before there is an issue, a misstep, or, in the case of CSA, a violation.

Accountability has multiple levels: internal, interpersonal, and community-wide. How am I engaging in and understanding the power of accountability? What boundaries am I putting in place for myself? How am I questioning myself? Since accountability cannot function with me alone, how am I making myself vulnerable and available to cooperation? What am I sharing with and asking of my peers? How am I listening to their input and critique? And, most importantly, how am I engaging with the wider community?

Accountability can function as punitive on all three levels. On a personal level, self-reflection is critical: "What did I do? Do I understand the ramifications of my actions?" On an interpersonal and community level, we are required to engage in the practice of telling on ourselves. We must engage with our peers, chosen family, family of origin, and others, and make space for critique, advice, and action steps. The process of accountability goes beyond accepting responsibility and includes doing work—hard work. Saying you accept responsibility, are taking steps to maintain that responsibility, and are rectifying mistakes are each pieces of the larger framework of accountability. The practice of accountability is not fulfilled by doing any one of these things; rather, it requires a holistic approach that goes beyond punitive action.

Child sexual abuse is an epidemic. It is traumatic. Surviving it increases the chances that you will be sexually assaulted as an adult and/or experience intimate partner and domestic violence—as I have. We know that the most vulnerable children—those at the margins of oppression—suffer at an increased rate. Children are targeted because they are vulnerable and are seen as easily manipulated. The effects of CSA are long-lasting, especially in regard to sex, sexuality, and relationships. How would loving all our children—sons and daughters, nieces and nephews, grandchildren, and godchildren—with accountability transform this abusive reality?

***
***

I grew up thinking that child sexual abuse and what seemed like the widespread occurrences of child abductions were synonymous with stranger danger. What little I did know about these scary topics was always in the context of somewhere far away from home and our family. But in fact 90 percent of child sexual abuse and a large percentage of child abduction cases take place close to home and by people familiar to children. Whether a parent, uncle, grandparent, babysitter, or teacher, we need not go far. We know the harm-doers. If we acknowledge that reality, we have work to do to interact more intentionally with those around us; if we do not acknowledge it, we are left only to rely on reactive measures based mainly on delivering repercussions.

As a survivor of CSA, parent, and grandparent who is working to prevent and end child sexual abuse, I've found that #LoveWITHAccountability is the very framework needed to move CSA prevention forward. When I was a small child, my older sister psychologically and sexually abused me for years. She was only five years older than me. My first memories of abuse started around the age of eight, and the abuse continued until I was fifteen. It wasn't until young adulthood that I began to realize all the ways in which her abuse permeated throughout my childhood, which it still does. My mother told me all there was to know about the dangerous strangers, but she didn't know to teach me about the harm-doer with whom I was sharing a bedroom. More specifically, to her there was nothing else to know about abuse besides not trusting strangers.

My mother was a fierce protector. She was very careful as to who she let in our home and whose houses we could go to, and she kept tabs on who was in my friendship circle. As many parents do, she constantly reminded her children that family was everything: "Trust only those you know." In the context of our impending puberty and her fear of teen pregnancy and sexually transmitted infections, the focal point of the warnings she gave were strange men acting as sex monsters. There was no accountability process in place for others. Boys, men, and strangers were "othered," and my mother worked hard to protect me from them all.

I've been contemplating my past abuse for over two decades, trying to figure out what went wrong, how to heal, and how to stop this from happening again. I've felt that I owe it to myself, to my daughter, and to my newborn grandson to understand this process and proactively address it. While the traditional battle against child sexual abuse has been to focus on strangers—to question them, suspect them, fear them, and run from them—how does the work need to shift? This is where #LoveWITHAccountability replaces avoidance and fear with engagement and courage.

When I became a parent, the first few years of my daughter's life were full of terror for me. I had insomnia. I repeatedly battled the urge to commit suicide. I handled the task of protecting my daughter with rage and fear: "No one will touch my baby!" At the same time, I was struggling to understand my sexuality and its connection to my abuse. I was a mess. I was in agony on a daily basis—at bath time, diaper-changing time, and even when I received her innocent hugs. I thought for sure I would abuse my own child. But one day when my anxiety was so intense that I thought it would destroy me, I reached out for help. That help led me to begin my lifelong journey of healing. It also led me to rethink how we discuss sexual trauma and how insufficient our attempts are to prevent and heal from it.

***

My work in the HEAL Project is about giving our children the information and tools they need to understand their bodies in the context of our society and providing this information while refraining from teaching fear. This information goes beyond the lessons of good touch, bad touch and stranger-danger. The HEAL Project picks up where CSA prevention has left off. It pushes parents to engage with their children around sex and sexuality and helps create well-informed young people. The HEAL Project aids children in finding their voice and agency, and it opens up the lines of communication in a more significant way. Our work eliminates shame and uncovers secrecy—the very places where abuse breeds. This accountable love is radical because it is intentional, proactive, and goes beyond individual wants and needs.

Accountability is collective work. How are we accountable to our children? Who will hold us accountable in that work? How do we expect our children to be accountable? I have been accountable to my daughter by giving her information about her body and about sex, sexuality, gender, power, agency, oppression, and so much more. I listen to her. I don't respond with a top-down perspective. I teach her using many perspectives and resources. I help her form her own opinions, and I allow her the space to talk to me about *anything*. She has been accountable to me with her honesty and her vulnerability and by respecting me. I am accountable to my chosen family and my tribe as we have intentionally set a similar process in place. They keep me true to my beliefs, and they have my daughter's best interest at heart. I have needed this system to survive. When I was working through my trauma, this process allowed my daughter and me to feel supported and not do it alone. I unearthed the secret. I asked for help. I set a plan in motion. This is the very same process advocated for by #LoveWITHAccountability.

When we teach our children to swim, we don't engage them with fear. The lesson goes beyond fearing the deep end and the possibility of drowning. We talk about our relationship to water, what it feels like to walk, run, and dive into the water. We talk about the joys of swimming, and we inform our children of the potential dangers. Most importantly, we engage them in a discussion about safety and steps to take in case of an emergency.

In comparison, consider the way we teach sexuality to our children and young people. Most of us leave it to the school system to handle, or we have one talk with them at a designated age, or don't speak about sex at all. Why are we holding back vital life information that can help our children, families, and community address CSA?

If we begin to think about sexuality education as an imperative tool for life, we could minimize the likelihood of sex talks that are fear-based or incomplete—or don't exist at all—and engage in lessons in accountability for parents and guardians as well as children and young people. This approach to sex and sexuality education is an evolving life lesson with opportunities for growth and learning on all accounts. It covers body image, reproduction, sexual desire, masturbation, sexually transmitted diseases, pornography, sex and love, sex without love, sexism, homophobia, consent, boundary setting, relationship building, negotiating what we want, and much more.

Staying informed about holistic sexuality is a lifelong process that sharpens our ability to function as connected humans. Even a lifeguard has to recertify every two years. Likewise, accountability with love is important enough to require a routine "refresher" course regularly. The same way a lifeguard is responsible for swimmers, I am responsible for keeping my child and myself informed. I understand the role that power plays here: I am the lifeguard. I have the skills to protect and save the swimmers. I am a parent, guardian, grandparent, aunt—I am the adult. I must keep myself informed, teach all that I can, speak with my child beyond "the talk," and show her that she can trust me and talk to me about anything. This is a commitment. It is a process. It is the action of love. This is love *with* accountability.

[A version of this essay was first published in the #LoveWITHAccountability online forum in *The Feminist Wire*, October 20, 2016.]

CHAPTER 40

Confronting Harm Past and Present for Tomorrow

Edxie Betts

A Summer 1996 Perspective

As I watch my father gather himself, grab his beeper, and stick his ballpoint pens into the pocket of his beige pseudo-military jumpsuit for work, he seems a bit unnerved, as he should be. He's had a long and unrelenting night trying to convince a man, a stranger, my sister's music manager, that he hasn't hurt his own family. My father wanted to assure this man that he hadn't done the worst possible things he could do to his own girls. After all, he's been an okay dad who has done all he could to protect us and instill within us and his entire family all the love he can.

Convincing myself that I can wash these damn dishes before my sisters or dad tell me to do them, I begin to stack plates in the kitchen. I know the fact that I'm doing this will cheer him up a bit, 'cause I hate washing them. I fill the sink with dish-cleaning soap while he stomps around the house doing whatever it is that fathers do before they leave for work.

I pour some old Kool-Aid into the sink and begin cleaning a glass, and I think to myself: *My father wouldn't do these things, right? This is just some sort of joke my sisters must be playing on the family. Or maybe he just pissed them off enough for them to spread stories to hurt him somehow.* Though there's still that hot feeling in the back of my head—"What if?"

Scrubbing off the dried ramen noodle on an oversized soup bowl, I ponder about what my father and I discussed several hours earlier, at about 1:00 a.m., just after he got off the phone with that prying stranger, my father sitting alone in a dark room.

"Ed, you don't believe what this man and your sisters are saying about me, do you?" asked my father.

"No," I say without hesitation.

"Why?"

". . . 'Cause you're . . . a Christian . . . and . . . that's not what Christians do?"

"Good boy," he had said to me as though I were a pet, without noticing that my reply was actually a question.

Now, in a huff and a puff, my father comes into the kitchen with a stressed, furrowed brow and unforgettable, confused look on his face.

"You're washin' dishes all by yourself?" he asks me in that proud tone he gets.

"Yeah," I say, smiling, with my tail wagging.

"Gosh, that's great, Ed," He shuffles through his pockets to pull out a misleading crumble of money to give to me. Blast! It's just a ten-dollar bill.

"I'll be back soon," he says, as he gives me a kiss on my forehead, along with the biggest, longest hug I think I've ever gotten from him, and he begins to cry.

Throughout the rather long and strict eleven years I've known my father, I've never seen him cry once. My mom has known him for decades longer and hasn't seen him cry either. Not even at his father's funeral. I can tell that the tone behind his crying isn't tears of frustration or even sadness for the situation he's in. No, these are tears of great regret. But the crying turns into sobbing as he slowly, sadly, drags himself down the stairs to leave for work. As I see this sad man exit our house and my life drastically change, I realize . . . he did it. He's not coming back.

He did these horrible things to my sisters. He is indeed a bad man and always has been. The religion he strictly forced upon us was just a facade for his own evils.

I feel relieved. All these years I've never loved him anyway. I honestly tried. There's just always been something about him I resented—in fact, maybe even hated. I could tell the difference long ago—that it wasn't love that I've ever felt, it was fear. It's been intuition all this time.

I have so many reasons not to like him and to fear him instead. For example, the strictness, the emotional abuse of my family, the forcing of strict religious doctrine on us, the punishment with a belt when he's been angry, and the countless, tortuous chores he's created for us over the years. But those things weren't quite it. I instinctively knew there was something more to why I didn't like him—something very secretive, off, and too terrible to guess about him. I guess he wasn't the only one guilty of pretense. Because, up until this point, every hug, every "I love you" had been a performance on my part. I'll never have to pretend for him again. What's more significant is I'll never have to see him under his terms again. I was never his son. Never a boy. Let's move from his lies to recognize my own.

A Summer 2018 Perspective

Society and its institutions designated me a boy at birth without my consent. So it's safe to say that I was pretending to be a boy up until I finally had the knowledge and language to understand that I didn't fit so neatly into such rigid gender roles and constructs. Although I was living this lie for so long, it didn't protect me entirely from people seeing the glimmers of femininity that I just could not hide. I felt many folx pick up on this energy of mine. Although I was very terrified of anyone seeing my femininity, I still yearned to be seen as anything but the kind of man my father was.

Growing up, the people who most picked up on this were cisgender/non-trans boys and men. They clocked my T before I even knew the T.[1] I'm not sure if what I endured and witnessed counts as microaggressions or assault—the boys slapping my ass as I walked by them in class, me being coerced into wrestling with a thirty-year old cis male math teacher after school, me being bear-hugged from behind

1. "T" is for "tea," which in Black femme slang also stands for "truth."

by a fellow student until I yelped, "Stop! Let me go!" The paradox of growing up trans or gender non-conforming is that I was always visible to these men. They could see that innermost truth within me that I wanted to hide, and their gaze punished my unruly femininity with violence. There are definitely experiences too painful and unresolved to revisit or even mention or expand upon in this writing. I'm still learning and can only hope others from my past are committed to collective self-reflection. But accountability is not achieved through hope alone.

When I was younger—before Black feminism, bell hooks, Audre Lorde, anti-carceral feminist gatherings, or *The Color of Violence: The INCITE! Anthology*—I came up with what I thought was a great revelation and rhetorical question that I shared with my mom.[2]

I told her, "Mom, every single traumatic experience we've felt has a man behind it, huh?"

I wish there was easier access to fuel the beginning stages of critical thinking and questions like these as a child. What my own past experiences have taught me is that many people, most of them men, have been socialized in the ways of sexual violence to such a degree that they place their own individual sexual gratification before anyone else's. This isn't an individual issue. It's a systemic issue tied to power and our familial relationships, and it is entangled by our relationship to the state and its institutions. Perhaps the men in my life behind these traumatic experiences would have had a better way of dealing with violence if what they were exposed to wasn't so normalized. Maybe they have punished the feminine qualities out of themselves in different, more outward ways than I have.

I've only been intentionally organizing in social movements since 2011. I have seen how cis-normative heteropatriarchy plagues our communities in and outside of movement spaces; it's a perspective that has been compounded by my life experiences. In 2014, I participated in, and bore witness to, testimonies given at the Afrikan People's Liberation Tribunal, which was facilitated by a committee of elders in

2. INCITE! Women of Color Against Violence, *The Color of Violence: The INCITE! Anthology* (Durham, NC: Duke University Press, 2016). See also https://incite-national.org.

the Los Angeles Black community in response to the abuse and harm caused by General T.A.C.O. aka Mischa Culton and his leadership of the Los Angeles chapter of the Black Riders Liberation Party.[3] He and his organization have since been sanctioned by the committee because he failed to address his abuse. The tribunal set the standard for how people within Black movement communities and others can take on community accountability and transformative justice without the state's involvement—all while creating guidelines to help cultivate respect, confront abuse, and shape revolutionary discipline for the greater good of liberation struggles. Community practices like these, even years after the harm has been done, are as inspiring as they are necessary.

As much as individuals often seem to bear the blame for abuse or sexual assault, cultures of apologism are often the reason why this harm has gone on unchecked for so long. Whether within movements—such as in Black Power, Indigenous resistance, and UndocuQueer communities—or within our own families, it's the reputation of the hardworking patriarch or even the nurturing mother that often absolves these communities of accountability. And it leaves many to drown in silence and heartache from past situations that should have been confronted.

When it comes to the people or persn[4] who perpetuates harm, we have to look at the issue in a way that ensures that this harm doesn't occur again. We have to have a critical examination of the social hierarchies that may compel some to remain silent. In my accounts of mediating abuse, I have often encountered obstacles when someone who has committed harm (the "abuser") does not acknowledge their harmful behavior. This creates a fundamental problem with restorative accountability itself. The process shouldn't wholly be left up to the conscience of the persn doing harm, because we're often seeing that persn not heed their conscience or feel remorse at all. So when

3. Committee, Afrikan People's Liberation Tribunal, collection of public documents, March 13, 2014 to January 8, 2016, Los Angeles.

4. The intentional misspelling or removal of male-centric words within the English language aims to disrupt and decenter the masculinity in colonizers' written hegemony and language.

the behavior goes unchecked or unaccounted for, sanctions might have to occur and/or boundaries must be created to prevent future harm. This does not have to be punitive or even restorative for a relationship between someone who has experienced harm and someone who has committed harm. Nor should this be relegated to a carceral solution.

Child sexual abuse (CSA) is likely occurring even when children are unaware. This is why conversations about consent and political education are so important to address in a communal setting with children, teenagers, adults, and, yes, even elders. Children especially need to be taught that they have the ability to give permission to whoever touches their bodies and when.

In the summer of 2018, I participated in an initiative co-organized by Community Partners and the Mirror Memoirs project to train homeless shelter workers on how to intake trans and gender non-conforming peoples in trauma-informed ways. During the initiative, I learned the following:

> According to the U.S. Centers for Disease Control 1 out of 4 girls and 1 out of 6 boys will experience sexual abuse by the age of 18. According to the Harvard School of Public Health, for gender non-conforming children, the rates are even higher. Gender non-conforming children who are designated male at birth are especially vulnerable, up to six times likelier to be sexually abused. Studies suggest that this is due to a lack of family support for transgender and gender non-conforming children. That means many transgender and gender non-conforming clients experience childhood trauma and especially child sexual abuse.[5]

This trauma is compounded when factoring in the experiences of growing up impoverished on Indigenous reservations or in the hood. These conditions, in combination with the conditions of white

5. Sabel Samone-Loreca and Amita Swadhin, "Supporting Trans and Gender Non-Conforming Clients: An L.A. County Shelter Training," Community Partners, Fall 2018–Spring 2019.

supremacy, constructed poverty, and police state–sanctioned violence, make post-traumatic stress disorder a normal occurrence. This compounded trauma makes many of us targets for further sexual abuse when we are alienated by gender policing. Additionally, we don't talk about consent when it comes to our gender identity. Consenting to whom we wish to be has never been the topic of discussion.

It isn't a surprise that even wealthy celebrities have shared similar experiences of sexual and gender violence that extend beyond class and cultural lines. I hope the #MeToo Movement, like other movements against sexual assault, can center more messages and testimonies on the absolute importance of getting consent. This includes explaining what consent is, what it means, and how to properly acquire it. More importantly, however, we must acknowledge the relationship between consent and the root causes of sexual assault that stem from the state—its violent and coercive strategies, its colonization of communities—and corporate control of the media.

I want to expand these communal conversations about reclaiming our consent and accountability beyond the parameters that the state has provided and confined us in. We must include, and simultaneously move beyond, our interpersnal sexual encounters. While it's especially important to this conversation, we shouldn't always need to sexualize the notion of "getting consent."

We need to teach children that they should receive consent before they touch someone. We need to teach children that they have the right to say "no" when someone wants to touch their bodies without explicit consent. We also must remember that asexual people exist. They, too, should not be thrust into unwanted sexual encounters and have to practice consent in their everyday lives.

Consent does not have to be sexy. Consent is not an ideology so much as it is a cultural mode of expression that can help us counter the dominant, white supremacist, patriarchal culture and economies of violence.

We're all being socialized by a state that was conceived of and maintained by coercion, rape culture, propriety, and domination.

How can we have real conversations with children or each other about consent when we aren't simultaneously expanding our understanding and analysis of the relationship between consent and coercion and how we are governed?

We shouldn't continue to allow the state to be the mediator of these interpersnal harms that occur in our communities. Especially within colonized communities. As long as we collectively ignore the original harm that the state imposed and still imposes on Indigenous peoples from the so-called Amerikkkas, we will always be under a colonial rapist regime.

To be clear, this requires tremendous emotional, psychological, spiritual, and physical labor to dismantle, delegitimize, disband, divest from, and abolish an entire system of governmental apparatuses coordinating with other interlocking systems of domination. But we must. This requires mass withdrawal from the carceral state and mass implementation of shared, autonomous conflict-resolution models.

One such model is community accountability, which encompasses transformative justice work. Entire communities or other configurations of large groups of people could be organized and taught to rely upon one another to resolve conflicts in ways that highlight and center the survivors of harm and abuse. Tragically, transformative justice work and care work have been mostly relegated to feminized labor. Men and those who benefit from their masculinity must do more to assume the responsibility of using the required emotional labor and communication skills to resolve conflict.

I'm still developing my thoughts on how we can live within a punishment culture and also how people who claim to be using an "abolitionist lens" today aren't using the same abolitionist practices that former enslaved Black people took up to free themselves from being owned property. In my view, this strategy of co-opting abolitionist rhetoric, without adopting abolitionist practices, is entrenched with liberal Western binary logic that fails to see different levels of power. It has established a false dichotomy that dismisses any force or violence as a "bad" or "depraved" practice that only proliferates more violence. The state shouldn't have a monopoly on force or even the violence necessary to defend oneself from its harm. How can many liberal career abolitionists today continue to demonize past slave revolts, current militant counter-violence, and direct actions? There is undoubtedly violence that has been deployed strategically by and for the love of survivors or oppressed peoples who've experienced intergenerational systemic harm. To want and will for the state's sanctioned violence to no longer exist is to want and will for the state to no longer exist. Our collective demand to "end violence" must not make invisible how the state fortifies itself through organized violence, conceived and sustained through its own hegemonic power by way of historical ableism, anti-Blackness, anti-Indigeneity, capitalism, and white supremacist heteropatriarchy.

Consider the following relevant questions and concerns: What about current and past Indigenous warrior societies who have *ourstorically* used force and violence to protect the land and people from the great threat of colonization? What about other autonomous communities, before colonization, who have dealt with the issues of rape and molestation among themselves with death or beating?

I recently had a conversation with a comrade and scholar about the positionality of "the slave" and their global relationship to commodification and gratuitous violence. During the transatlantic slave trade, enslaved Africans on ships would often suffocate their newborns to death and/or literally jump ship because they knew their foreseeable future as property wasn't a life worth living for themselves or their children. Who has the right to make any moral judgments or objections about life, love, death, or hate within the context of a persn being owned or commodified?

I don't want to romanticize ancient societies as tokens, or as the best and only ways to organize our lives, especially since they've had their fair share of patriarchy and oppressive social hierarchies. However, I do want to acknowledge that perpetual reconciliation is integral to a constantly changing political climate. But we needn't be the neo-colonialism the state wants us to be or internalize the strict authority, rigidity, uniformity and moral appeal of westernized ways of societal organization and civil society.

Reflecting upon what my father and the men in my family have done to their children angers me greatly. It angers me that there is a culture of child sexual abuse, other abuse, apologism, rape, and other forms of violence that have been silenced and unseen in my family, and in so many others. It angers me that people who have or haven't experienced this kind of pain continue to victim-blame and weaponize these experiences against many of us as if we had a choice. As though this abusive way of relating to one another wasn't taught by the dominant culture as a whole. We are currently living in a culture born from the dynamics of slavery, the genocide of Indigenous people, the theft of Indigenous land, and the violence of our government, its laws, and its order. The damage that grown-ass men have done to our families has had a ripple effect on our psyches. But who taught them, and their father's, father's, father's, father's father harm, in a culture of legalized violent pedophilia and rape? How strong and powerful would we be if we understood that this harm and abuse stops with us? How can we learn from their mistakes even if they still haven't acknowledged them?

Again, I don't believe we can truly restore or transform our social relationships while living in a violent nation-state such as ours. We'll always be trapped, coerced, and compelled to live under these oppressive logics as long as the state institutions exist and have such a strong hold and control over our imagination. However, we can organize to begin to have these hard conversations about harm, oppression, and interpersnal and systemic violence within our families and among those of us who share the same goals and recognize the same root causes of institutionalized violence.

Any community that has taken on the issue of sexual assault should rely on the convictions and will of the abused with nuance and compassion. Subsequently, people who have been abused, and who may have committed harm themselves, can then acknowledge that this abuse doesn't need to propagate with them as a form of persnal accountability. Socialized accountability could look like ongoing therapy and counseling that centers the survivors and their wishes to undo the victim-and-abuser binaries. The US "criminal justice" system's solutions do not have the interest of survivors in mind. This is evident because it cannot establish what consent means to a colonial institution that did not receive consent even to exist. Many, including me, have received some sense of safety and justice from such a system. However, that shouldn't outweigh how much systemic injustice this system in the form of a nation now known as Amerikkka has imposed, from the time of its conception, at the expense of peoples it was never made to support. Most importantly, the system doesn't prevent cultures of *coercion conformity*, harm, and abuse.

Accountability to me is a gift that simultaneously acknowledges and halts harm done to restore love and lost trust. However, I am not searching for any accountability from anyone or anything that I do not have love for and doesn't in turn have love for me. Similarly, I am not searching for accountability from a state or its system that terrorizes its people and that teaches us and socializes us into these terrible ways of relating to one another. We should all know from the history of colonization that the raping, pillaging, and commodifying of our Black and Indigenous bodies and land for centuries has directly influenced how we are to relate to one another. This must be confronted in real ways as would happen with any abusive parent, partner, family friend, or family member—but on a broader scale that creates boundaries if and when they are needed. It is significant to me that the initial trauma imposed on us by the state and its oppressive institutions is an intergenerational violence being passed on to us again and again. Because power relates to the disempowered in systemic ways, individualizing the blame doesn't completely cut out recurring problems at their root. Love for oppressed people and the self is something I believe can transform an individual persn in ways that are just and accountable. The abolition of the state is something I believe can transform our social relationships now and in the future.

It Takes a Village: Acknowledgments

The #LoveWITHAccountability (LWA) project and this anthology would not exist without the support of many. As much as I would like for it to be exhaustive, the following is, without question, a *non-exhaustive* list of the many whose impact was felt and greatly appreciated.

The depth of my heartfelt gratitude and respect for the courageous and generous contributors to this anthology is boundless. Thank you, thank you, thank you for trusting me enough to take this public journey with me. I know it wasn't easy for many of you. Most of your plates were overflowing with work, activism, and family. Despite this, you accepted my "time-sensitive" and "urgent" email invitations to revisit excruciatingly painful experiences and envision what accountability for child sexual abuse can look like without solely depending upon a government that has brutalized our communities. With very little time to reflect, remember, process, write, and publicly share, you each pushed through many obstacles to participate. This is a profound testament of your shared unanimity to break silence and address child sexual violence in our diasporic communities. A full-body bow, filled with deep affection in honor of your courageous and liberatory contributions to this anthology and your transformative work in the world.

The LWA project has been fully supported by the NoVo Foundation–funded Just Beginnings Collaborative (JBC). I am one among their inaugural cohorts of eight fellows and ten grantee organizations that focus on ending child sexual abuse. I am indebted to the JBC advisory board, especially my dear colleagues and comrades Pamela Shiffman, Jesenia Santana, and Maura Bairley, for their enthusiastic and unwavering support for the continuation of the LWA project, including the publication of this anthology. The JBC Fellowship afforded me the gift of paid time to wade in the very murky waters of child sexual abuse. It was years in the making and a hard-earned sacred gift for which I am profoundly grateful. I lift up Emanuel (EB) H. Brown, JBC interim program coordinator and comrade, for all of his support. I also lift up former JBC staff and comrades Adriana Rocha, Esther Hyunhee Shin, and Marci McLendon for their immense courage and integrity. I am indebted to the 2016 collective-defined "survivor union," sujatha baliga, Amita Swadhin, Mia Mingus, Luz Marquez-Benbow, Ahmad Greene-Hayes, Ignacio G. Hutiá Xeiti Rivera, Sonya Shah, and Tashmica Torok. Several of us didn't know each other before being funded by JBC. Despite this, we swiftly organized, united, and worked across multiple differences in response to an institutional crisis. They are each doing incredible, groundbreaking work to dig up the roots of child sexual abuse in marginalized communities. I will always profoundly cherish our collegiality and steadfast sibling-survivor connection in response to injustice and also our difficult struggles, which were powerful growth opportunities for me.

I'm a huge fan of AK Press and have been for many years. I believe in its principles as a worker-run collective. I've taught and used some of its radical titles in my classes. I also had the privilege of writing the foreword to one of its anthologized titles, *Dear Sister: Letters from Survivors of Sexual Violence*, edited by my sister-friend Lisa Factora-Borchers. I am happy that AK Press is the publishing home for the *Love WITH Accountability* anthology. I want to thank my dear friend and comrade Dan Berger for graciously introducing me to Charles Weigl at AK Press. Immense, heartfelt appreciation for Andrew Zonneveld, Zach Blue, Charles, and the entire AK Press collective for partnering with me to *humanifest* this anthology.

This anthology is a continuation of the ten-day online LWA Forum that I conceived, curated, and published in the *The Feminist Wire* (*TFW*) in 2016. I've been a member of its editorial collective since February 2012 and an associate editor since 2014. I cannot think of any other online publication in which I would've been able for ten days to publish twenty-nine essays, reflections, and poems on child sexual abuse, healing, and justice in diasporic Black communities. There are very few, if any, online publications that provide the in-depth, left-of-center, radical, multiracial, pro–reproductive justice, pro-LGBTQ, anti-imperialist, anti–white supremacist feminist writings that *TFW* has consistently provided *for free* since its cofounding by Tamura A. Lomax in 2010 and the subsequent editorial leadership by co-managing editors Tamura, Monica J. Casper, and Darnell L. Moore. They, along with co-associate editors Heidi R. Lewis, Heather Laine Talley, Heather Turcotte, TC Tolbert, and Joe Osmundson, provided invaluable support with the publication of the forum.

When I shared my vision with the co-managing editors to transform the online forum into a print anthology, they were enthusiastic and unwavering with their support. Additionally, Darnell enthusiastically said yes to writing the beautiful foreword to this anthology. My love and gratitude are overflowing for all of *The Feminist Wire*'s managing and associate editors who are also my comrades *and* friends.

I had the opportunity to develop and work on the LWA project at two academic institutions—Williams College and the University of Pennsylvania (Penn). My professor friends and colleagues, Rhon S. and James Manigault-Bryant invited me to Williams College, on behalf of the Africana Studies Program, to be the 2015–2016 Sterling Brown Visiting Professor of Africana Studies. It is because of Rhon and James that I was very fortunate to teach, work with, and also learn from my former stellar student and research assistant Aunrika Tucker-Shabazz. While at Williams, in addition to Rhon and James, I was able to share my work-in-process and also a lot of much-needed laughter with faculty and staff colleagues VaNatta S. Ford, Rob White, Sophie Saint-Just, Daniel Goudrouffe, Meg Bossong, Will Rawls, Ferentz Lafargue, Merída Rúa, Rashida Braggs, and Anicia Timberlake, who quickly became friends while I was in residence.

When I returned home to Philadelphia from Williams College, John L. Jackson Jr., my friend and colleague and the dean of Penn's School for Social Policy & Practice, invited me to be a visiting scholar at the school. Later, when John became the Walter H. Annenberg Dean of the Annenberg School for Communication at Penn, he invited me to be a visiting scholar there. Additionally, my colleague and friend

Susan B. Sorenson, who is a professor and the executive director of Penn's Ortner Center on Violence & Abuse in Relationships, invited me to be an affiliate scholar at the Center. My residence at Penn continues to create important opportunities for me to have meaningful connections with faculty and staff colleagues, including John L. Jackson, Jr., Susan Sorenson, Deborah A. Thomas, Grace L. Sanders Johnson, Margo Natalie Crawford, Dagmawi Woubshet, Aimee Meredith Cox, Amelia Michelle Carter, Jessica A. Mertz, and Malik Washington, and students whose research, scholarship, work, and activism are focused on issues that are of a kindred spirit with my work. My gratitude for my colleagues *and* friends at both Williams College and Penn is unending.

Heartfelt appreciation for artist-designer Kathryn Bowser's beautiful graphic design work, poet Jaden Fields's wonderful administrative support, and scholar-activist Gavriel Cutipa-Zorn for reminding me of Toni Cade Bambara's prophetic words from *The Black Woman*, which open this anthology.

***
***

> *"Are you sure, sweetheart, that you want to be well? . . . Just so's you're sure, sweetheart, and ready to be healed, 'cause wholeness is no trifling matter. A lot of weight when you're well."*
>
> Toni Cade Bambara, *The Salt Eaters*[1]

What I know for certain is that my personal work on the incest and child sexual abuse I suffered brought me to my knees in January 2015. This was over two decades *after* I started working on sexual violence. If it were not for the following, I honestly do not know if I would have made it.

Unwavering and eternal gratitude for my Black feminist, licensed

1. Toni Cade Bambara, *The Salt Eaters* (1980; repr., New York: Vintage Contemporaries, 1992).

clinical psychologist Dr. Clara Whaley Perkins, who has been a steadfast anchor and guiding light on my journey for twenty-seven years and counting. During my period of very financially lean years, which was the overwhelming majority of my adult life, Dr. Whaley Perkins *never* allowed the balance of my checking account to determine whether she would provide her expert services to me.

My practice of Vipassanā meditation as taught by S. N. Goenka ("Goenka-ji") is a priceless technique that has been an integral part of my daily life for seventeen years. Full-body bow in honor of ancestors Goenka-ji and Elaichi Devi Goenka and also in honor of the 2,600-year continuum of all of the teachers and dedicated practitioners in this lineage.

Deeply heartfelt gratitude for some of my dear friends, mentors, and comrades who have been confidantes and anchors in the storm, provided solicited advice, and/or offered other forms of invaluable support especially for this specific work: Glenda Gracia, Theresa Lewis-King, Heba A. Nimr, Evelyne Laurent-Perrault, Pat Clark, Inelle Cox Bagwell, Enid Lee, Lisa Diane White, Sonja Ebron, amina wadud, Tracy Fisher, Heidi R. Lewis, Tamura A. Lomax, C. Nicole Mason, Luz Marquez-Benbow, Ignacio G. Hutía Xeiti Rivera, Erin Esposito, Jennifer Patterson, Amita Swadhin, Tashmica Torok, sujatha baliga, Thadious M. Davis, Joyce A. Joyce, Cara Page, Alexis Pauline Gumbs, Rachel E. Harding, Lynn Roberts, Jonathan Crowley, Carolyn Crowley, Bernadine Mellis, Andrea Lawlor, Sonali Gulati, Tiona Nekkia McClodden, Cornelius Moore, e nina jay, Josslyn Jeanine Luckett, Dan Berger, Darnell L. Moore, Denise C. Jones, Liz S. Alexander, Salamishah Tillet, Scheherazade Tillet, Linda Janet Holmes, Tyrone Smith, Ejeris Dixon, alicia sanchez gill, Cae Joseph-Massena, Chevara Orrin, Lyndon K. Gill, Kai M. Green, Ahmad Greene-Hayes, Savannah Shange, Lisa Factora-Borchers, Leah Lakshmi Piepzna-Samarasinha, VaNatta S. Ford, Meg Stone, Melissa Bennett, Kay Whitlock, Rythea Lee, and Donna Jensen.

My beloved "turtle twin" brother, Tyree Cinque Simmons, is precisely nine years my junior, which means he was one year old when my child sexual abuse began. For most of our shared lives, I expressed a lot of misplaced anger, sadness, and pain on him. This is one of my many painful legacies from both enduring and surviving child sexual abuse. My love and gratitude are everlasting for Tyree and his willingness to be engaged in a shared healing and accountability journey with me. Healing is intergenerational. Our work impacts the lives of his daughters, Zari, Avye, and Kylin. May the cycle of trauma be forever broken in their lifetimes.

My journey with my beloved mother, Gwendolyn Zoharah Simmons, is one where we each evolved and transformed our relationship. We are healing individually and together. Her contribution to this anthology is a profound testament to her unwavering love, immeasurable courage, a deep commitment to being accountable for the wrongs, and her affirmation to soar forward. There will *never* be enough words to express my eternal love, immense respect, and infinite gratitude for my mother and our continuous healing journey.

My beloved partner, confidante, and friend Sheila Alexander-Reid has been an abiding source of love, accountability, encouragement, and support in so many ways. Her anchoring presence in my life is an invaluable gift that I wholeheartedly cherish. I love, value, and appreciate her more than words will ever convey.

Finally, I lift up ancestral spirits who directly influenced and/or supported me and this work: Dr. Aaronette M. White, Kagendo Murungi, Jackie Anderson, Dr. Frances Tzivia Portnoy, Dr. Linda Spooner, M.D., Esq, Rev. Dr. Katie Geneva Cannon, Ntozake Shange, Audre Lorde, and my teacher, Toni Cade Bambara.

May their spirits be fully liberated in the ancestral realm. Asé-O.

Contributors

Liz S. Alexander, MA, MSW, is the founder of She Dreams of Freedom Consulting Group (SDFCG), a national consulting firm that is committed to improving the outcomes of young women and girls in the criminal justice system. Liz writes on themes of trauma, justice, spirituality, and healing.

Qui Dorian Alexander is a queer, trans, Black Latinx educator, organizer, consultant, and current doctoral student in education, curriculum, and instruction at the University of Minnesota. His work centers healing justice, transformative justice anti-violence work, and the intersections of gender, sexuality, and racial justice. Find Alexander on Instagram @ queerbrujx.

Esther A. Armah is an award-winning Ghanaian global journalist; playwright, lecturer, columnist, and radio host who has worked in New York, Washington DC, Chicago, London, Ghana, Nigeria, Kenya, and South Africa. Esther is creator of Emotional Justice, a framework exploring a legacy of untreated trauma due to our global history. Armah is on Twitter @estherarmah.

Kenyette Tisha Barnes is a legislative strategist, registered lobbyist, political consultant/commentator, social justice activist, survivor, and an unapologetically Black womynist. She is the owner of Nia Vizyon, LLC, a political strategy and lobbying firm focused on voters' rights, social justice, and reproductive justice; and the national cofounder and organizer of #MuteRKelly. Find Barnes on Twitter @LegisEmpress.

Edxie Betts is a Black, Blackfeet Indigenous, Pilipinx, Trans, autonomous organizer and insurrectionary cultural producer. Their work brings direct support to oppressed communities in need. Betts's work also involves political education, supporting political prisoners, art for the sake of propagating resistance culture, counter-narrative and, collective liberation through direct action. Find Betts on Twitter @bettsurevolt.

Sevonna M. Brown is the co-executive director at Black Women's Blueprint. Her work has been published in *Ebony*, *Time* magazine, and *For Harriet*. She serves on the board of Children of Combahee, mobilizing against child sexual abuse in Black churches. She is a birthworker, dedicating her work to Black maternal health. Brown is on Twitter @whereisvonna.

Dr. Thema Bryant-Davis is a licensed psychologist, ordained minister, and sacred artist who has worked nationally and globally to provide relief and empowerment to marginalized persons. Dr. Thema, a professor at Pepperdine University, is a past president of the Society for the Psychology of Women. Find Bryant-Davis on Twitter @drthema.

Rosa Cabrera is a Harlem native, born to Dominican parents, and a single mami residing in Oakland, California. Her essays explore motherhood, sexuality, Black feminism, and survivorship. She teaches English at Chabot College and Diablo Valley College. In 2017, she founded Reclaiming Our Own Transcendence to increase communities' healing capacity. Find Cabrera on Instagram @LaTigraC.

Mother, daughter, Detroit native, and social justice maven. **Nicole "Kqueen" Denson** is a national activist who has provided assistance to marginalized communities, with a focus on sexual violence and other traumas, for over sixteen years. Kqueen is unapologetically a Black, queer womyn. Kqueen believes that everyone deserves, respect, dignity, and safety. Find Denson on Instagram @kqueenkb.

Dr. Worokya Duncan has twenty years of experience and maintaining a commitment to students focused on social justice. She holds degrees in public policy, theology, and education. Through professional development sessions and workshops, Dr. Duncan facilitates conversations on equity, diversity, and inclusion. Find her on Twitter @drduncanhistory.

CeCelia Falls, MSEd., she/her(s), resides in Oakland. She is a writer, poet, and educational consultant working to end sexual violence, particularly childhood sexual abuse, in the African Diaspora. Find Falls on Twitter @CeCeF.

Zoë Flowers is a creator and author whose poetry and essays can be found in several anthologies and online journals. Her ChoreoDrama *ASHES* is a ritual performance piece that uses monologues, poems, and vignettes to explore domestic, sexual violence, and the journey to self-love. Her web series *RODE* is in post-production. Flowers is on Instagram @ IAMZOEFLOWERS.

Kimberly Gaubault (McCrae) is a womanist who focuses primarily on the holistic well-being of Black women and the normalizing of self-care as a proactive measure. Kim has enjoyed writing this chapter of her life in a way that honors her deep belief in community and loving with intention. Find Gaubault on Instagram @redefining_freedom.

alicia sanchez gill is a survivor with many years of experience engaging in intersectional anti-violence work. She's done crisis intervention with survivors of domestic violence and sexual assault, sex worker organizing, and HIV housing advocacy. alicia holds a master of social work degree, but other survivors have been her best teachers. Find gill on Twitter @aliciasanchez.

Dr. Kai M. Green is a shape-shifting Black queer feminist nerd; an Afro-Future, freedom-dreaming, rhyme-slinging dragon slayer in search of a new world; a scholar, poet, facilitator, and filmmaker; and an assistant professor of women's, gender, and sexuality studies at Williams College. Green explores questions of Black sexual and gender agency, health, creativity, and resilience in the context of state and social violence. Find Green on Twitter @Kai_MG.

Ahmad Greene-Hayes is the founder of Children of Combahee, a faith-based organization that works to end child sexual abuse in Black church communities. He is also a PhD candidate in religion and African American studies at Princeton University. Find Green-Hayes on Twitter and Instagram @_BrothaG.

Adenike A. Harris and Peter J. Harris (**Pops'nAde**) provide practical and loving lessons drawn from years of courageous "call and response" dialogue that helped them heal in the years after her predator stepfather was convicted and jailed. Their 2018 TEDx Pasadena Talk is called "Healing vs. Retaliation: Surviving Trauma and Sexual Abuse." Find the Harris's on Instagram @popsnade.

Indira M. Henard is the executive director of the DC Rape Crisis Center. Indira's direct service experience in many gender-based violence programs has helped to inform her policy analysis that has led to coordinating public policy initiatives and organizing and planning spaces for survivor-led advocacy. Henard is on Twitter @IndyDCRCC.

Sikivu Hutchinson, PhD, is an educator and author. Some of her books include *Moral Combat: Black Atheists, Gender Politics, and the Values Wars* (2011) and *White Nights, Black Paradise* (2015). She is the founder of the Women's Leadership Project, a Black feminist mentoring program for girls in South LA. Find Hutchinson on Twitter @sikivuhutch.

Tracy Ivy, a Black deaf leader, educator, and activist with a bachelor's and master's from the National Technical Institute for the Deaf (NTID) at Rochester Institute of Technology, was the first Black female president of the NTID Student Congress. Tracy is a certified teacher of American Sign

Language and currently teaches at Minnetonka High School in Minnesota. She is presently pursuing her EdD in education and social justice. Find Ivy on Instagram @TracyIvy.

Tanisha Esperanza Jarvis is a healer, scholar, and advocate. She received her MA in psychology from CUA, and her BA in anthropology & sociology from Spelman College. Tanisha aspires to obtain her PhD and continue her life work as a trauma psychotherapist. You can reach her on Twitter @SurviveHeal.

e nina jay is a Black, lesbian, womon writer who is surviving incest and rape. She uses poetry to break silence around violence against gurls and womyn. In 2018, she released a film based on her book of the same name, *Body of Rooms*, published in September 2016. Find Jay on Instagram @eninajaywords.

Cyrée Jarelle Johnson is a poet and essayist from Piscataway, New Jersey. *SLINGSHOT*, his first book of poetry, is published by Nightboat Books. Find him on the internet at @cyreejarelle or cyreejarellejohnson.com.

Kalimah Johnson, LMSW, is the founder and executive director of the SASHA Center in Detroit, Michigan. Johnson has twenty years of advocacy experience and created a comprehensive model for women of color seeking sexual assault services and advocacy, titled the SASHA Model: Black Women's Triangulation of Rape. Find Johnson on Facebook at / sashacenter.

Najma Johnson is a Black, deafdisabled community organizer and survivor of child sexual abuse. They are currently the executive director of DAWN in Washington, DC. Prior to leading DAWN, they cofounded Together All in Solidarity (TAS), a deafdisabled, deafblind, deaf and hard of hearing Black, Indigenous, and People of Color umbrella—operated social-justice community collaborative in Austin, Texas. Find Johnson on various platforms at DeafDAWNinDC.

Monika Johnson-Hostler is the director of the NC Coalition Against Sexual Assault. Boasting a rich career of twenty years, she is the president of the National Alliance To End Sexual Violence, managing partner of RALIANCE, and chair of the Wake County School Board. She has a master's degree in public administration. Find Johnson-Hostler on Twitter @mjh1908.

Ferentz Lafargue, Ph.D, is the author of *Songs in the Key of My Life*. His writings have appeared in such venues as *215mag*, *Americas Quarterly*, the *Huffington Post*, *Next American City*, *Social Science Research Council*, and *Social Text: Periscope*. Find Lafargue on Twitter @ferentzlafargue.

Tonya Lovelace is the CEO for the Women of Color Network, Inc., a women of color–led national nonprofit, and a survivor of child sexual assault, bullying, teen-dating violence, and domestic violence. Tonya holds a bachelor's degree in interdisciplinary studies and master's degrees in Black studies and women's studies. Lovelace can be found on Twitter @TonyaLovelace.

Luz Marquez-Benbow is a survivor of child sexual abuse (CSA), incest, and rape, and founder of the International Alianza de Mujeres Negrx (IamNegrx), a survivor-led network of Afrolatinx mobilizing to end CSA across the diaspora. From 2003 to 2012, Luz led the policy efforts for communities of color in the reauthorization of the Violence Against Women Act. Find Marquez-Benbow on Instagram @afroboricua3.

Thea Matthews is a poet based in San Francisco. She is a scholar and activist who writes on the complexities of humanity, resiliency, and ultimately the triumph over trauma. Matthews is on Instagram @theamatthews_.

Darnell L. Moore is head of strategy and programs at Breakthrough and the author of *No Ashes in the Fire: Coming of Age Black and Free in America*. Find Moore on Twitter @moore_darnell.

Dr. Danielle R. Moss is CEO of Oliver Scholars, a thirty-five-year-old education nonprofit, and cofounder of the Ebony Vanguard, an intergenerational collective for women and girls of the African diaspora. Dr. Moss currently serves on the New York Women's Foundation board and the New York City Commission for Gender Equity. Moss can be found on Twitter @DrDanielleMoss.

Chevara Orrin is an award-winning diversity and inclusion strategist, social entrepreneur, speaker, and survivor. She is founder of two nationally recognized campaigns, We Are Straight Allies and #WhiteAndWoke. Chevara aspires to build a more equitable world through awareness, accountability, and intentional action. Find Orrin on LinkedIn at / chevaraorrin.

Mel Anthony Phillips is a folk/street artist, writer, and natural-born storyteller whose appetite for creativity and fierce love for humanity shape and color the unique perspectives he brings to the work. As a victim's advocate, Mel often speaks to community groups about equity, interpersonal violence, and social justice. Find Phillips on Facebook at /oaasisoregon.

Jey'nce Mizrahi Poindexter is an award-winning advocate who became the first transgender victim's advocate employed by Equality Michigan.

She is a founding board member of the Trans Sistas of Color Project, member of the National LGBTQ Taskforce, and the legendary House Mother of the House of Mizrahi. Find Poindexter on Facebook at /jeynce .mizrahi.75.

Ignacio G. Hutía Xeiti Rivera, MA, who prefers the gender-neutral pronoun "they," is a Queer, Two-Spirit, Black Boricua Taíno. Ignacio is the founder of the HEAL Project. The project's platform is based on the blief that holistic sexuality information is a major tool in preventing, interrupting, and healing from child sexual abuse. Rivera can be found on Instagram @Blkbrownred.

Dr. Lynn Roberts is an assistant professor and interim assistant dean of student affairs and alumni relations at the City University of New York School of Public Health. Her activism and scholarship examine the impact of race, class, gender, and models of collaborative inquiry and action on the human condition. Roberts can be found on Twitter and Instagram @Womanist61.

Loretta J. Ross is a cofounder of the SisterSong Women of Color Reproductive Justice Collective and the co-creator, in 1994, of the theory of reproductive justice. She has addressed women's issues, hate groups, and human rights on CNN, and in the *New York Times, Time* magazine, *Los Angeles Times*, and *USA Today*. Ross is on Twitter @LorettaJRoss.

Aishah Shahidah Simmons is an award-winning Black feminist lesbian documentary filmmaker, activist, cultural worker, writer, and international lecturer whose work examines the intersections of race, gender, sexuality, and sexual violence. An incest and rape survivor, Aishah is the creator of *NO! The Rape Documentary* and the #LoveWITHAccountability Project. Simmons can be found on Twitter and Instagram @AfroLez.

Dr. Gwendolyn Zoharah Simmons is a veteran of the Student Nonviolent Coordinating Committee (SNCC), a feminist Islamic scholar, and professor emeritus of African American studies and religion at the University of Florida. She received her MA and PhD in religious studies and a graduate certificate in women's studies from Temple University. Simmons can be found on Twitter @gzoharah.

Farah Tanis cofounded Black Women's Blueprint and has been on founding boards of transnational feminist, human rights, and girls' gender equity organizations. She chaired the US Truth and Reconciliation Commission on Black Women and Sexual Assault and launched the Museum of Women's Resistance, Mother Tongue Monologues, and the March for Black Women. Tanis is on Twitter @FarahTanis1.

Tashmica Torok is a survivor-activist working to end child sexual abuse. As the executive director of the Firecracker Foundation, she incites riots of generosity and advocates for the healing of children and families. Tashmica is a storyteller, kitchen witch, mother of three, and wife to a talented tile installer. Torok is on Instagram @Tashmica.

Tracy D. Wright is a connoisseur of hip-hop and pop culture rooted in social justice, heir to a genius level of creativity, and ally to the leaders of tomorrow. Wright can be found on Instagram @the_po_oprah.

AK Press is small, in terms of staff and resources, but we also manage to be one of the world's most productive anarchist publishing houses. We publish close to twenty books every year, and distribute thousands of other titles published by like-minded independent presses and projects from around the globe. We're entirely worker-run and democratically managed. We operate without a corporate structure—no boss, no managers, no bullshit.

The Friends of AK program is a way you can directly contribute to the continued existence of AK Press, and ensure that we're able to keep publishing books like this one! Friends pay $25 a month directly into our publishing account ($30 for Canada, $35 for international), and receive a copy of every book AK Press publishes for the duration of their membership! Friends also receive a discount on anything they order from our website or buy at a table: 50% on AK titles, and 20% on everything else. We have a Friends of AK ebook program as well: $15 a month gets you an electronic copy of every book we publish for the duration of your membership. You can even sponsor a very discounted membership for someone in prison.

Email friendsofak@akpress.org for more info, or visit the Friends of AK Press website: https://www.akpress.org/friends.html.

There are always great book projects in the works—so sign up now to become a Friend of AK Press, and let the presses roll!